Courage to Survive

Courage to Survive

by

Aron Abrahamsen

Order this book online at www.trafford.com/07-1336
or email orders@trafford.com

Cover photo Copyright © by Aron Abrahamsen
Sunrise over Anastasia Island, Florida

Most Trafford titles are also available at major online book retailers.

© Copyright 2007 Aron Abrahamsen.

All rights reserved. No part of this publication may be reproduced, stored in a retrieval system, or transmitted, in any form or by any means, electronic, mechanical, photocopying, recording, or otherwise, without the written prior permission of the author.

Note for Librarians: A cataloguing record for this book is available from Library and Archives Canada at www.collectionscanada.ca/amicus/index-e.html

Printed in Victoria, BC, Canada.

ISBN: 978-1-4251-3403-7

We at Trafford believe that it is the responsibility of us all, as both individuals and corporations, to make choices that are environmentally and socially sound. You, in turn, are supporting this responsible conduct each time you purchase a Trafford book, or make use of our publishing services. To find out how you are helping, please visit www.trafford.com/responsiblepublishing.html

Our mission is to efficiently provide the world's finest, most comprehensive book publishing service, enabling every author to experience success. To find out how to publish your book, your way, and have it available worldwide, visit us online at www.trafford.com/10510

 www.trafford.com

North America & international
toll-free: 1 888 232 4444 (USA & Canada)
phone: 250 383 6864 ♦ fax: 250 383 6804 ♦ email: info@trafford.com

The United Kingdom & Europe
phone: +44 (0)1865 722 113 ♦ local rate: 0845 230 9601
facsimile: +44 (0)1865 722 868 ♦ email: info.uk@trafford.com

10 9 8 7 6 5 4 3 2

"Courage to Survive" by Aron Abrahamsen

A biographical narrative of a Jewish family life and its ordeal during the Nazi invasion of Norway in World War II
1. Jewish family life   2. Jewish traditions
3. World War II, 4. Escape
5. Life in a Concentration Camp.
I. Abrahamsen, Aron, 1921   II. Title

Dedicated
To
Those Who Survived
The Holocaust of World War II
And In Remembrance
Of Those Who Perished

Acknowledgments

I wish to thank those who took their valuable time to read the manuscript and give their suggestions – Paul and Kathleen McFann, who poured over the manuscript meticulously providing words and phrases that would help the work flow more smoothly; Al and Joy Perry, who advised that maps placed at the beginning of selected chapters would be helpful; Christy Perry, Warren and Elisa Grim, Michael and Motria Benson, Joel and Nancy Brender; Gordon-Michael Scallion and Cynthia Keyes after reading the first draft declared that the whole world should read this; Linda and Bill Wilson for their encouragement and support. Also thanks to Tano Publishing, Oslo, Norway, for permission to use text from Dr. David Abrahamsen's book "Jeg er Jode" (I am a Jew), and to Schroder Photo, Trondheim, Norway, for permission to use some photographs. I wish to thank Bjarte Bruland for his courage to write the research paper on "Forsoket paa aa tilintetgjore de norske jodene" (The attempt to liquidate the Norwegian Jews), his Master Thesis at the University of Bergen, Norway 1995, and for permission to use his information; also thanks to Kristian Ottosen for permission to use information from his writings.

I also want to thank my brothers David, Heiman, Julius, Leopold, Jacob, Oskar and Samuel, for the information about their escape. I'm especially grateful for the account of my brother Abel's experience during his escape, which was recorded when he visited me in Everett, Washington; as well as the account by our sister Beile, regarding what she and her family experienced during the war, recorded by Abel when he visited her in Amsterdam.

A special thanks to my beloved wife Doris, who so painstakingly edited and proof read the manuscript. Without her help and encouragement it would have been impossible to produce this work.

Aron Abrahamsen,
Lecanto, Florida 2007

Table of Contents

Chapter 1	Miracle in Norway	1
Chapter 2	Life with Mama and Papa	21
Chapter 3	Happy Days	56
Chapter 4	Tragedy Strikes	78
Chapter 5	Before the Storm	84
Chapter 6	September 1939–World War II	103
Chapter 7	Just in Time	115
Chapter 8	Invasion	136
Chapter 9	David's Escape	165
Chapter 10	The Trap	185
Chapter 11	Flight to Safety	199
Chapter 12	Crossing the Border	223
Chapter 13	Scattered Abroad	243
Chapter 14	Life in Jeopardy	254
Chapter 15	Worlds Apart	274
References		281

Foreword

This is the true story about my Norwegian family. There were 11 children, plus Mama and Papa. After Papa died in 1938, the series of events leading up to World War II impacted all of us. We had our own battle with fright, doubt, and defeat, but realized that we had to reach for the courage to survive, even though it resulted in our being separated from our homeland and spread to many parts of the world.

World War II brought to the conscience of millions of people that this was:

A time of unprecedented and unbelievable terror and brutality.

A time that no one should ever forget, and

A time however, that is too painful for some to want to remember.

This narrative tells of the plight of my family, caught in Hitler's web of violent anti-Semitism, involving the confiscation of our properties and the bank accounts, the escape of the family members from Norway, how they survived, and the beginning of their new life at the end of the war.

The developments leading to Hitler re-arming Germany, the vacillations of the Western leaders and the outbreak of World War II, are brought out as a point of historic perspective behind the events affecting my family.

I have combined information from my own memories and the experiences that were reported to me by other members of the family, to make this narrative as complete as possible. All of the events are true; I have added the dialogue.

Many Jewish families experienced similar trauma as ours and many others even worse. In all cases everything in all our lives was changed.

This story takes place prior to, during, and shortly after World War II. To my knowledge, I believe that my family was the only Jewish family in my hometown in Norway, with a brother imprisoned by the Nazis and a sister in Thereseinstadt concentration camp, near Prague, who escaped the horrors of the holocaust intact.

Even today, many people find themselves in severe difficulties. It is my hope that reading this book will help them draw on their inner courage to survive.

Aron Abrahamsen
Lecanto, Florida 2007

Members
of the
Abrahamsen Family

Salomon Abrahamsen	1877 - 1938 (Papa)
Miriam Abrahamsen	1878-- 1974 (Mama)
David Abrahamsen	1903 - 2002
Heiman Abrahamsen	1904 - 1994
Julius Abrahamsen	1906 - 1999
Leopold Abrahamsen	1908 - 1964
Beile Hess	1910 - 2005
Jacob Ilevik Abrahamsen	1911 - 1982
Oskar Abrahamsen	1913 - 1991
Asne Levin	1915 - 1958
Samuel Abrahamsen	1917 - 2001
Aron Abrahamsen	1921 -
Abel Abrahamsen	1923 -

Notes from the Author

The Conscience
of
Norway

Courage may come in different forms or for various causes. In the case of Norway's situation it was a matter of having the courage to right what had been wrong for five years during World War II. It was a matter of settling a criminal case, and also a moral issue.

This moral issue had been in hiding since the end of the war, and for more than 50 years it was still unresolved. Until the conscience of Norway began to stir nothing had been done.

As you know, the story you are about to read is true. I hope that you will find this family narrative helpful in understanding the cultural and traditional inner workings of my family, and will receive some insight into the mental anguish and emotional trauma experienced by them, as well as many other Jewish families during the Nazi holocaust.

We can look back on all the anti-Semitic events that culminated in the holocaust and learn from them. But will we? The Nazis hatred of Jews has risen again today and is not being squelched. Where will this lead?

History shows that we have not grown out of the pattern of prejudice and hatred. It has been said over and over again that if we will not learn from the past we are doomed to go through the same tragedies until we do learn.

During the war, atrocities against the Jews were at a high point. With the law conveniently on their side, the Nazis carried out their barbaric treatment against the Jews. Justice was a long way off. Norway had much to account for in regards to the treatment of the Norwegians Jews by the Norwegian Nazis. Several tragic events, which severely impacted the Jews, took place during the Nazi's occupation of Norway. Among those were these:

1 During the occupation several Jewish businessmen were executed on trumped-up charges by the Nazis.

2. All radios belonging to the Jews were confiscated.

3. All properties belonging to the Jews, such as bank accounts, insurance policies, business inventories, homes and personal belongings were confiscated by the Nazis.

4. About fifty percent of the Norwegian Jewish citizens were deported and perished in the gas chambers.

In August of 1945 the King of Norway returned to take up his duties as the Monarch of the country. In his party were the crown prince and the legal government of Norway. The King, Haakon VII, and his government had been in exile during the war in England. The Norwegian Underground had already rounded up and caught several Norwegian traitors and had them arrested, among them was Vidkun Quisling. They were tried before a criminal court and [1]"...convicted of high treason by a Norwegian court. Quisling, 58 years old, was found guilty of aiding the German invasion of Norway, of deserting from the Norwegian Army, of causing the death of thousands of Norwegians, including 1000 Jews who were deported to Germany, and of accepting money from the Nazis." At the end of their trial the judicial system and the

---

[1] Chronicle of the 20th Century, Page 601

military court convicted Quisling and 25 other Norwegians of treason. In October 1945 they were subsequently executed by hanging. Since 1876, Norway had no provision for capital punishment. This ban was set aside for these traitors because of the viciousness of their crimes.

At the outbreak of World War II, about 2200 Jews lived in Norway whose total population was three million. Of the 2200 Jews, 600 were not Norwegian citizens because they were refuges from countries occupied by the Nazis. During the Nazi siege of Norway, 767 Jewish men, women and children, (about one half of the Norwegian Jews) were sent to extermination camps. After the War only 29 of them returned to tell their story. Vidkun Quisling cooperated with the Nazis to bring about this deportation

But there was a another important element to be dealt with --- the moral issue in regards to the treatment of the Norwegian Jews during occupation by the Nazis. It took more than fifty years to awaken the Norwegian government to the reality of this unsolved issue. Finally they found the courage to do the right thing.

This is how it happened. On May 27, 1995 the Norwegian Journalist Bjorn Westline published an article in the daily newspaper "Dagens Naeringsliv" (Daily Financial News) on the confiscation of Jewish property in Norway during World War II. Westline's article awakened the Norwegian public to what had taken place against the Jewish population. The international press and The World Jewish Congress became involved in this moral issue. Westline was shocked to realize that the facts regarding the arrest of the Norwegian Jews and the confiscation of their property had been totally and systematically suppressed. In his investigation he discovered that many Norwegians, not all of them Nazis, had lined their pockets at the expense of the Jews. The inventories were auctioned off and the price was set by the Nazis – ten cents on the dollar. Many Norwegian merchants bought quality goods from the confiscated Jewish stores. After the War the Norwegian authorities made little effort to help the Norwegian Jews to recover their properties, and the Norwegian Government gave very little compensation to them.

In the same year Historian Bjarte Bruland, a graduate student at the University of Bergen, Bergen, Norway, presented his Master's Thesis "Forsoket paa aa tilintetgjore de Norske Joder" (The Attempt to Liquidate the Norwegian Jews). He presented detailed evidence of how the Nazis planned the liquidation of the Norwegian Jews, the confiscation of their properties and personal belongings, and their arrests and deportation to the death camp in Auschwitz, Poland.

In March 1996, responding to pressure from the political parties, the Norwegian Minister of Justice Grete Faremo, appointed a committee to investigate the case. The seven-committee members included the Psychologist Berit Reisel and the Historian Bjarte Bruland, both appointed by the Jewish Community in Oslo.

After 14 months of research and deliberation, the committee split into two factions, five members against two (Reisel and Bruland). The majority believed that their mandate was only to determine the assets of the confiscated Jewish properties. The other two committee members emphasized that it was a moral issue, that the absence of economic restitution was a symbol of the infamous injustice towards the Norwegian Jews. In June of 1997, the committee presented two separate reports to the Parliament.

The Norwegian Government courageously agreed with the minority report that restitution would be the honorable thing to do. As a result, in June 1998, 53 years after World War II, the Parliament recommended a $58 million package of economic restitution. Therefore, $25.8 million has been distributed to individuals who suffered the trauma of financial loss of having their properties confiscated by the Nazis during the war, with a maximum of $25,000 for each eligible Jewish person who was born before 1943. (There were 230 families who were completely exterminated and thus had no heirs). $19.4 million was to be administered by the two Jewish communities in Oslo and Trondheim. The rest was used to support Jewish institutions, and to establish a center for education of the Holocaust in Norway.

Norway is the first European country to extend restitution to their Jewish people. For this I applaud the Norwegian Government for its courage to take this honorable position. I also salute Journalist Bjorn Westline and Historian Bjarte Bruland for their gallantry in taking up this cause.

Aron Abrahamsen
Lecanto, FL

Chapter 1

Miracle in Norway

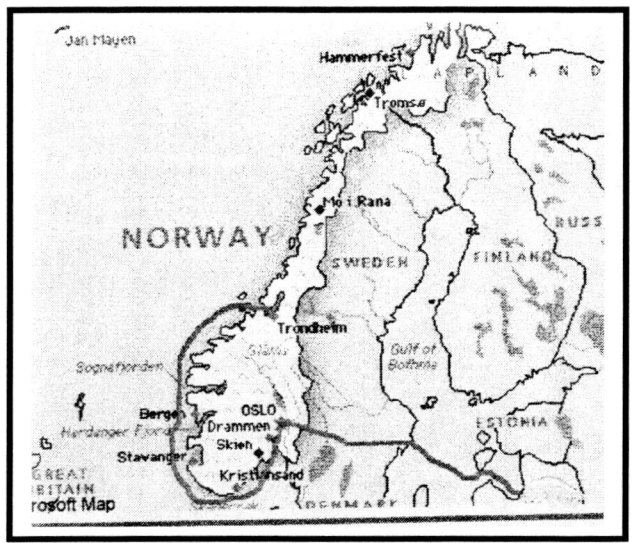

Route my parents took to go from
Lithuania to Trondheim, Norway

Even now, after so many years have passed, frustrating questions still burn in my heart. I struggle for answers that might help me, and maybe others, in similar situations. When I was a teenager in New York, in 1940, I asked myself, "Why doesn't my family, back home in Norway, realize that they need to flee from the Nazis before it is too late?"

I have often been perplexed why some people are able to recognize when to escape from danger while others aren't. Why do some fail to make the decisions necessary to assure their survival? My Norwegian relatives believed that the Nazis were not really a threat. Although the country was occupied, the Nazis had not done anything to them; so why flee? Many Jews believed it was not necessary; others knew it was crucial to escape. Some of those who tried to escape were caught and executed.

Most of us have no occasion to assess such a situation until long after it happens, but looking back, my family survived. Let me share that story with you.

Mama and Papa came from Lithuania to Norway. They met in Trondheim, got married, and started a business and a family. The business expanded in steps with the family. Over the years it grew to 11 children and I was next to the youngest. There were 20 years between the birth of the first child, David, and the last one, Abel. In between there were two girls and seven boys. I was born in August at the summer villa by the fjord.

Mama and Papa had a dry-goods store where all sorts of fabrics were available, like silk, cotton, woolens, brocade, and buttons and bows. The store became very prosperous by our hard work and long hours behind the counters waiting on customers. As soon as I finished my schoolwork I was in the store delivering packages to customers, sweeping the floor, and in the winter I shoveled snow from the front of the store. I did whatever else it took to keep me busy in case I should ever get bored. All of us were expected to work in the store. Of course David, who became a physician, and Julius and Jacob, who became dentists, also worked in the store before they began their professional careers.

The last store we had was on the first two floors in a five storied building. We had an apartment on the third floor and half of the next floor. Very often in the evenings the family gathered in the living room for conversation and entertainment. Samuel, the student of higher learning, usually started the discussion by bringing up the current world events. For local events we always had the latest gossip and the most reliable and true rumors. These were delightful and secure times and we felt safe from the turbulence of world events.

By 1933 everything had changed. Hitler rose to power in Germany, and started to re-arm the whole country. The Jews were declared enemies of the state, and were stripped of their citizenship, leaving them no protection from the police or in the courts. Great apprehension had grown that if the Nazis should invade Norway the same fate would befall the Norwegian Jews. As the Nazis marched into other countries and territories fear set in replacing the comfort and security we had known.

In 1938 Papa died. He was lucky to be spared the trauma that came upon our family a few years later.

The following year my sister Beile married a merchant from Amsterdam, and moved there.

That fall the USSR (Russia) invaded Finland, and Mama feared that the Russians, or Hitler's Nazi Army, might overrun Norway. She packed all her valuables to send to America for safekeeping. After much agony Mama decided that I would be the one to take the valuables to America. I left Norway in January 1940. My brother Samuel would follow on the next ship.

Mama was right! Within two months Norway was invaded by Nazi Germany. Within 18 months all of our properties were confiscated and the family had to escape to Sweden to save their lives. They had to leave everything behind. With Beile and her little family in a concentration camp, and one brother imprisoned by the Nazis, their lives were saved only by a miracle.

At the end of the war four of my brothers and Mama returned to Norway and picked up their lives again. The rest of the family, including me, decided to remain where the events of World War II had taken us.

I could easily say that it was a miracle that brought my parents to Norway.

For as long as anybody could remember the Norwegian Government had never been friendly to the Jews. But soon a change was to come to this nation. . (See note 1, page 18).

The year was 1851.

The change took place in the Norwegian Parliament. There had been a long and heated debate. The opposition was stiff. The Constitution had a clause that excluded all Jews from entering and/or living in the Kingdom of Norway. Finally, the members of Parliament voted to allow the Jews to settle in the country. It was both historical and unbelievable because this exclusion had been on the books for many years.

The daily newspapers made of a lot of it, for it was an impressive and dramatic decision by Parliament. In the foreseeable future it would have a far-reaching imprint on many countries and places, and would enable many Jews to build better lives for themselves.

For countless years the Jews in Poland, Russia and countries like Lithuania, had longed for religious freedom and protection from persecution. But nobody paid heed to the cry for equality. The Jews had been driven from country to country, always hoping that they could feel secure enough to establish a home some place. History is filled with tragedies about Jewish people, how they wandered from place to place, always seeking escape from the oppression of many countries.

When Norway finally opened the door of liberty to Jews, the window of opportunity for my parents, and many oppressed Eastern European Jews, had swung wide open. Freedom in Norway greeted the new arrivals making their future and aspirations as bright and hopeful as the coming of spring.

On the surface, Norway appeared very inviting, with opportunities for making a living, enjoying peace and religious freedom. However, with foreign immigrants trickling into their land, both Norwegians and the newcomers needed to exercise caution and adjustments in their thinking and behavior. Included in that mural of new life for the Jews were many obstacles and disappointments all of which were overcome by hard and persistent work that eventually led to success and acceptance.

As soon as Norway had opened its doors to the Jewish people it didn't take long before they began to arrive---fleeing from countries where persecution of the Jews was sanctioned by the government.

Later, in April of 1900, a small group of Jews arrived in the little town of Trondheim, Norway. They had been traveling for many weeks looking for the "right" place to settle. Though they had seen many small towns along the way, none of them was judged to be suitable. The Norwegian coastline is dotted with countless hamlets, placed like fields of flowers, among the towering mountains. Picturesque as it was, none of the travelers thought it was the "right" place. Even places like Stavanger or Bergen didn't meet with their approval. They continued north to Trondheim, where some of them had relatives, and decided to settle there. They had found the "right" place. (See note 2, Page 20).

Among the new settlers was my father Salomon Davidowitz Aronson. (Some members in my family had told me that this was his name. But I'm not sure what my father's real last name actually was. Shortly after his arrival in Trondheim, Papa changed his name to Abrahamsen. Could it be that the reason for changing his name to Abrahamsen was because he might have been afraid that the Tsar's people would hunt him down, with other Jews, and drag them back to Lithuania to serve in the Army? Or could fear of the Tsar have become so imbedded in their psyche that they wanted to take cover under different names?) Some other Jews also changed their names. Among them was my father's brother, Josef, who adopted the name Kahn. My mother's brother took the name Mendelshon. Her maiden name was Fischer.

All of them had fled their native country of Lithuania to escape the harsh prejudice and anti-semitic propaganda coming from the Russian Tsar, who, during that period, ruled Lithuania. One unjust requirement of all adult male Jews was a forced 20-year conscription in the Russian Army. In the Army the Jews were subjected to the worst tasks, and continually harassed by the non-Jewish soldiers and officers. When the Jews were finally released from the Army, any opportunity for a civilian career, or profession, was gone.

These new arrivals to Trondheim were seeking not only religious freedom but also educational and business opportunity.

In Norway, the Jews were allowed to practice their religious beliefs without any interference from the government and were allowed to operate their own businesses so they could make a decent living.

Who could have guessed that only a few decades later, that small Jewish community would again face oppression and persecution, turning their security into disaster?

In those days Trondheim wasn't a very large town, with a population of no more than 25,000, including the outlying districts. But to the newly arriving Jews, having come from a small village, it was a metropolis. They stared at the streetcar as it rambled on the tracks placed in the cobble-stoned streets. In contrast, the roads in the village they had come from were covered with a mixture of dirt and clay. They had never lived in a town that had streetcars, and all were looking forward with great anticipation to their first excursion on this type of transportation.

Many of the streets were just as narrow as those in their native village. This made them feel right at home. But to their surprise and delight, the main streets in Trondheim, lined with trees, were wide and covered with the finest of cobblestones. They watched the horse drawn freight wagon leisurely delivering goods to the designated places. Seeing the freight wagons was also familiar to them and gave them another touch of home.

There were handsome coaches with mirror-like painted finish, lined with genuine, shiny leather, pulled by proud, well-groomed black horses. The coachmen wore silk top hats with bright, dancing plumes on the left side. This they hadn't seen before! They shook their heads in amazement and smiled with contentment at such an elegant sight.

As they walked around the town they found gas lights on every street corner. They watched as the local lamplighter lit each light, going from one streetlight to the next, performing his magic. (To my knowledge, at the present time, the only gaslights left are at the old drawbridge over the Nid river.)

The large warehouses along the river caused the newcomers to question why buildings were constructed so close to the water. My father asked some workers why they were built that way, and was told that the ships come up the river, tie up to the warehouse where they unload their freight. The cargo is then stored inside. When the goods were sold they were loaded onto the horse drawn wagons on the street side to be delivered around the city.

Before coming to Trondheim, my father had lived in Christiania (now Oslo) for two years, where he had worked as a traveling salesman for Feinberg's. It was there he learned to speak Norwegian. However, he never became fluent in the language, but knew enough to conduct his daily business.

As time passed, the Jewish settlers discovered that Trondheim, which used to be called Nidaros, was situated about 300 miles south of the Arctic Circle. Cold winters weren't new to them. None of the newcomers could find out why the name Nidaros was changed to Trondheim in the middle of the 17th century. However, they did learn that on April 18 and 19, in 1681, a fire totally destroyed Nidaros.

When the city was rebuilt, the major streets were widened and planted with trees and shrubs, giving the whole city a new and impressive look. This could have been a good time for a name change. (See note 3, Page 20).

Housing for the new immigrants was in short supply because most available space was too expensive and, also, many landlords refused to rent to Jews. The Jews were foreigners with strange customs, with a different language, and a religious faith that made the Norwegian Lutherans roll their eyes and shake their heads. Who knew what these foreigners were up to?

Salomon moved in with his brother Josef, who had come to Trondheim earlier with his wife Rosa and their son David. My father knew that Rosa had five sisters. The previous year they had arrived with their brother Abraham, from Latzkova, Lithuania. One sister, in particular, took Salomon's interest because she was so beautiful. Could this be my future wife? he thought. The other newcomers found lodgings in various Jewish homes, and they were greatly concerned about where they could obtain Kosher food. The already settled Jews provided the meals for them until other arrangements could be made.

Papa was born in 1877 in Sager, Lithuania, a small settlement of farmers and merchants. He never told us what kind of work he did before he left his homeland. Arriving in Norway with only the clothes on his back, it didn't take long before he became a successful businessman. Papa was a short man, not more than 5 feet 5 inches, with a small bone structure that made him appear to be weak and feeble. But that was far from the truth. He was physically very strong. After he and my mother were married and children started to come into the family he would often swim with one of the offspring sitting on his back.

He had an extremely powerful will that carried with it his strong religious convictions. His religious faith was the cornerstone and centerpiece of his life. Religion was infused into the depths of his soul. He talked, worked and slept in religious terms.

He had a full head of curly, reddish-brown hair that almost matched his eyes. That small mustache he had cultivated gave the impression that he was a well to do merchant; and caused him to appear older than his actual age.

There was a spring in his step, and a determination in his mind that he was going to make something out of himself. All this overshadowed his small stature. However, he had a temper that would make Attila the Hun flinch like a coward. If his plans didn't work out the way he wanted, his dark brown eyes would flash like instantaneous lightning. Those near him took several steps back and scattered like feathers in a windstorm.

Nobody knew what was going on in my father's mind except himself. What he wanted most of all was to have his own store and find a suitable wife. He had his priorities. He started first on building his business.

With the little Norwegian Papa knew, and the small amount of money in his pocket, he bought some overalls, work pants and shirts, put them in a burlap sack and swung his first inventory onto his back. He walked down to the ships where the merchant sailors were, and sold his entire inventory to them. He invested his profits in more merchandise, and made many more trips to the merchant vessels, whose crews had become his steady customers.

Although he had achieved success as a traveling salesman, Salomon had bigger dreams and plans. He just wasn't satisfied with what he was doing, because he had a towering ambition.

He knew he could do more, and would not remain a traveling salesman all his life. He wanted his own retail store with the finest goods to sell to the people in Trondheim. He didn't have the money to start such a venture, but while talking to his brother Josef he stumbled upon the solution to his dream.

"Josef, I want to have my own store, but I don't know how to get it. I also want to get married. I am already 24 years old and not getting anywhere."

Salomon could see his future being dashed to pieces if change, or improvement, didn't come into his life soon. By now the little patience he possessed had run out like water gushing out of a bottle. He felt like a juggler with too many dreams bouncing around in his head. He looked to Josef for advice on these critical, life important and difficult issues.

"You know Miriam, my wife's sister?" Josef reminded Salomon. "Remember you met her at dinner not long ago. There is your answer. You should get better acquainted with her." Josef looked at his younger brother hoping to have put an idea into Salomon's wonderful future. However, it didn't appear that Salomon was taking the bait. Josef wanted his brother to marry and start a family.

It was important for the survival of the Jews to get married and have children, especially boys. It was the sacred duty of the sons to pray for the father three times a day for 11 months after his death. This was a long-standing tradition. And the sons would carry on the family name, hopefully for generations.

Then Josef thought of something that surely would make an impression on his brother.

"You know, Salomon, Miriam has recently opened her own store. A fruit and tobacco store. From what I hear she is doing quite well."

"Yes, yes, I know all that" Salomon replied. He had been observing how she was doing. "Where did she get the money? It takes money to start a business. I know. How could she, a seamstress, know enough to have her own shop?"

"You're right, she worked as a seamstress for a number of years and then her two brothers, Aron and Abraham, helped her, of course." After a short pause, Josef continued. "Salomon, she would make you a good wife. Why not think about it? I have to go now, business is calling," he was ready to leave.

"Just a minute. Josef, I'm only a peddler. How could Miriam be interested in me?"

"She'll see that you're a good man, a hard worker with real potential. Besides, there aren't many eligible single young Jewish men in this town." And with a twinkle in his eyes, "There isn't anybody like you to be found for miles around."

"Think about it. Don't put it off. A beautiful woman like Miriam is a rarity, like gefilte fish and boiled chicken for dinner on Monday night. Don't wait too long or you'll miss out on getting a good wife," Josef encouraged his brother. "See you at supper." Then he called back over his shoulder; "Maybe Rosa can invite Miriam again." With that Josef left his brother to his own thoughts.

Josef was as short as Salomon, with a small mustache to give him a little dignity. The two looked very much alike, and from a distance people couldn't tell them apart.

The two brothers had been close since childhood, but even more so now. It was a matter of protecting and looking out for one another, especially since settling in this strange and unfamiliar country. They knew little of the language, and spoke with a thick, heavy accent. They knew even less of the culture and the people which made them feel very insecure. They took their new life very seriously.

In spite of all the strange and unfriendly surroundings, they tried to maintain a sense of humor in order to sustain a balance in life. They knew the importance of laughter, yet felt it was best not to laugh too much. Their religious faith and its diligent practice kept them aware that there was more to life than just buying and selling merchandise.

They worked very hard. Though they were used to life being a struggle, they enjoyed the challenge in their new country. Here there were good possibilities that there would be lots of mazel tov (good fortune) for them.

Up to this time Salomon had been so busy trying to establish himself that he hadn't taken the time to look for a marriage partner. Selling his goods, buying new inventory and counting his profits from the sales had kept him busy enough. Now it was time to find a suitable wife. He appreciated his brother pointing out to him a good candidate, and for encouraging him in this endeavor. It was like being served a big plate of Kugel.

As Josef left, Salomon had made up his mind. He would visit Miriam in her store and get better acquainted. It couldn't hurt! That very thought lifted his spirits. He felt like a spring flower breaking ground and waiting to bloom. The sun in his future was beginning to rise.

Salomon stopped for a moment outside Miriam's shop just long enough to gather his courage. He straightened his shoulders and stood as tall as he could. As short as he was that did little for his height. He lifted his chin, took a deep breath and with a steady hand opened the door. Without being too obvious, he quickly looked around her shop. He was impressed that she was with a customer.

The shop wasn't very large, he guessed about 15 by 20 feet. Just room enough for the little inventory of fruit, cigarettes and tobacco she carried. A coal burning stove was in the left rear corner. There was a wooden counter with a locked drawer that served as the cash register. He was surprised at what she had already achieved and found himself thinking, "How can I have a store, a real big one?"

This was her own business, and she was very proud of her accomplishment. It wasn't so long ago that she was laboring as a seamstress and worrying greatly about what her future held. Being a seamstress was not her cup of chicken soup. Above everything else she was dreaming of getting married. But to whom? There was a shortage of eligible unmarried Jewish men in this town, and she was hoping that her dream would soon come true.

It hadn't been easy for Miriam. Leaving Lithuania, her native country, had been exciting, frightening and traumatic all at the same time. After all, she had trusted her older brother Abraham to take her and her sisters to a place where there were no pogroms against the Jews; a place where she and her people could live in peace and security. Often she reminisced about her younger days in Latzkova, Lithuania, her family and all her relatives, the traditions that were observed and celebrated with religious fervor and inflexibility. Now her concern was for the security she longed to find in her newly adopted land.

Miriam's building had no insulation, and the cracks in the wall easily let in the cold air. Her store was located in the part of town where the "blue collar" workers lived, an area where the wealthier class seldom, or never, was seen. The buildings in this part of town were quite old, with wood frames and wood siding, and were known as the "Bazaar" district. Few buildings had indoor plumbing. The main street through this district was wide enough for the streetcar tracks, and with luck, if you held your breath, a horse drawn freight wagon could, with great caution, squeeze by the streetcar.

Salomon could see that she had reason to be proud of her accomplishment. He had watched how more and more people were discovering Miriam's shop. She must already be making some profit, he surmised.

Miriam closed the sale and her customer left the shop. She was aware that a gentleman had entered her store, but was too busy to recognize who he was. When she looked up she saw that it was Salomon. She could see that he was really a nice looking young man, though not very tall. His black suit was well pressed with a clearly defined crease in his pants. The dark gray spats almost hid a pair of brightly polished black shoes. He had already removed his derby hat, of course. She had not seen him look so well groomed. Even his hair was cut and his mustache trimmed.

"Good afternoon" she greeted him cheerfully.

Salomon answered in like manner. He felt a bit nervous. He knew that he had to be on his best behavior if he were to make a good impression on Miriam.

"What a nice shop you have," Salomon complimented her.

To impress her he bought one of her oranges, paid for it, and then gave it to Miriam for a present. She thanked him for it, and immediately put it back in her inventory. That way she could sell the same orange twice.

After that, they had a short and courteous conversation. He already had noticed when he was with the other immigrants that Miriam Fisher was something special. Her manner of speech, her behavior and the way she dressed made her stand apart from all the other Jewish women. Seeing her here in her store she was even more beautiful and stately than when she had come to supper at Josef and Rosa 's home. Her black hair crowned her head, and her milky white skin stood out in sharp contrast. Her features were those of a queen and she carried herself in an elegant and exquisite manner.

He had also noticed the kindness and caring that was written all over her face. With a petite elegance she walked like a feather floating in the air, seemingly never touching the ground. In the right places she could easily be taken for royalty. He was observing how comfortable she was with herself, no doubt because she had achieved the status of an independent businesswoman so early in her life.

Courting such a beautiful and stately woman would take finesse, diplomacy and patience. Salomon was deficient in all three, but he had a strong will and persistence. And she had the store.

His lack of so many virtues didn't discourage him. Instead he rose to the challenge that had presented itself, and determined that Miriam was going to be his wife. He remembered his brother's words "A woman like Miriam is a rarity---." The hope of tomorrow hung in the air.

It took quite a while to convince Miriam that she should marry him. He was the best choice, he told her, among all the eligible Jewish bachelors in town. "I would be a good catch," he said to himself. There seemed to be one drawback, though. She was taller than he. But he overcame that by paying no attention to it.

On October 12, 1902, the Rabbi performed the wedding ceremony. It was a traditional Orthodox service under a Chupa (canopy), the breaking of the wineglass under the groom's foot, followed by tears, laughter and lots of "Mazel Tov." Although there weren't many Jews who had settled in Trondheim at that time, there was still a sit-down wedding dinner followed by dancing.

Shortly after they were married, Mama encouraged Papa to start his own store. This was what he had longed to do all his life and now was the time to turn his dreams into action. With her experience in owning a store and his yearning to be a prosperous merchant, they opened their first store together in a rented space in hopes of attracting many customers.

Later, with two children in the family, and many more to come, my parents purchased a building for their business. With the store on the first floor, and an apartment on the second floor for the expanding family, my parents were on their way to establishing themselves as successful merchants in the community and loyal supporters of the Jewish settlement.

Notes for chapter 1

1. When on May 17, 1814, a new constitution was adopted, paragraph 2 stated "The Evangelical Lutheran Religion shall be maintained and constitutes the established Church of the Kingdom. The inhabitants who profess the same religion are bound to educate their children in the same. Jesuits and Monastic orders shall not be tolerated. Jews are furthermore excluded from the Kingdom."

This was a clear declaration that the prohibition against Jews to settle in Norway was to be practiced. Anti-Semitism was very much alive even in this small country. Norway, at that time, had only a population of 3 million people, and yet the majority members of Storting (Parliament) blocked any change to the constitution. Their minds were set like cement and their only concern was to keep the Norwegian population "Pure." It was doubtful if any member of the Storting ever had any personal contact with Jews, and yet they were afraid of how the Jews might influence the citizens of Norway.

However, I can't recall reading about any objections to other people coming from countries like Germany, France, Denmark and Sweden--to settle in Norway. As long as they didn't practice any other religious faith than the Evangelical Lutheran doctrines, all was well. For example, when Trondheim was destroyed by a fire in the spring of 1681, Major General Johan Casper von Cicignon, an architect born in Luxembourg, was commissioned to completely re-design the entire city. This project took several years, and all the while he enjoyed the hospitality of the

Norwegian people. Cicignon was a Christian, not a Jew.

My cousin, Dr. Oskar Mendelsohn, wrote an extensive work in two volumes describing the history of the Jews in Norway, and how they were treated over a period of 300 years. This was published in 1969 by University Press, Oslo, Norway.

[1]One case he related describes the prohibition against Jews. It was about two Jewish brothers from Amsterdam who had for some time conducted business in Norway. The orders for goods had been carried on through the mail and delivered by freight. However, the two brothers had difficulty making the customers pay for the goods. They decided on two occasions, once in 1734 and again in 1739, to travel from Amsterdam to Norway to collect what was due them.

When they arrived in Norway they were forbidden to leave the ship unless they could produce a special permit (which they didn't have) that was required for Jews. They were arrested upon going ashore, and placed in prison. After two months of incarceration they were finally released, but had to pay court costs before they were allowed to leave. They were never able to collect on their debt. They were also directed not to return unless they had special permission from the King of Denmark (Norway was under the reign of Denmark at that time) and they were instructed to tell this to all the Jews in Amsterdam.

That's the way the situation remained. Then a Norwegian author, Henrik Wergeland, took up the cause to have this ban against the Jews stricken from

---

[1] Oskar Mendelsohn "Jodenes Historie I Norge gjennom 300 aar" (History of the Jews in Norway through 300 years) Universitetsforlaget, Oslo, Norway

the constitution. It was a long and bitter fight against the prejudice and hatred directed toward Jews. After an extended and sharp debate in the Norwegian Storting, on June 13, 1851, a constitutional amendment to paragraph 2 was adopted. By a vote of 93 in favor, and 10 opposed, the ban against the entry of Jews to the Kingdom of Norway was lifted.

Unfortunately, Henrik Wergeland, who had championed the cause for the Jews, never lived to see his battle for equality accomplished. He died on July 12, 1845.

Every May 17, Constitution day, a wreath is placed on Wergeland's grave in Vaar Frelsers Gravlund (Our Savior's Cemetery) by the Jewish Community in Oslo in gratitude for his fight for justice on their behalf. The cemetery is located near the center of town where many famous Norwegian are buried.

2. Prior to 1921, travel between Oslo and Trondheim was long and tiresome. The journey could be undertaken by boat or by foot or horse. This was the only means of transportation available until, to everyone's relief, a rail line was completed in 1921.

3. Like many other European cities, Trondheim was a very old town, established in the year 997. Its founder, King Olav Trygveson, called it Nidaros because it was located at the mouth of the Nid River, which in a serpentine path, wound its way though the city. This was the same king who had sponsored Leif Erikson's journey to the New World. It was common knowledge among the Norwegians that Leif Erikson arrived on the North American continent in the year 1000. (Quite a few hundred years before Columbus!) In fact, Nidaros was the capital of Norway until 1380 when the government offices were moved to Christiania. (now Oslo).

Chapter 2

Life with Mama and Papa

Our family – March 30, 1926.
Seated: David, Papa, Abel, Aron, Mama, Heiman
Standing: Asne, Leopold, Beile, Jacob, Julius, Oskar, Samuel
Courtesy Fotograf Schroder, Trondheim, Norway

Salomon and Miriam were not among the first settlers of Jews in Norway. The first ones came to Christiania (now Oslo) about 1855, and to Trondheim in 1876. To the Norwegians, who were staid and traditional Lutherans, these new settlers seemed very different because of their customs, religious belief and language. These brought about a high degree of apprehension to the Protestant communities, which now had to adapt to having another culture in their midst. As with many people, a new environment means adjustments, sometimes big ones.

It was a difficult setting that met the newly arriving Jews. An environment faced them that bordered in some cases on hostility, distrust, suspicion and fear. The Jews were misunderstood and mistrusted by the Protestant population.

This, of course, caused the Jews to fear the Norwegians. The Jews had entered into a milieu where they were encountering trials and challenging experiences. It was difficult enough for the Jews to make a living without also having the obstructions of suspicion and distrust thrown on their paths and in their faces. Both the Jews and the Lutherans had much to overcome. Yet the Jews were very glad that Norway had opened its doors to them.

Adapting to new and different situations can be very difficult, sometimes impossible, to overcome. Living in a familiar environment is very secure. Nothing seemingly changes, everything remains the same. For those who do not wish to adapt, the most important priority is to maintain the status quo. The mindset of security must be protected at all costs.

Also, the Jews remembered only too well how the gentiles had persecuted them in Russia. How by orders of the Tzar their synagogues were burned, their homes looted, and at its worst, the church had executed many of them in the name of the Father, the Son, and the Holy Ghost. The charge against them was that they had killed Christ and thus were to blame for all the troubles and hard times people were experiencing all over the world.

Salomon remembered being taught that during the inquisition there was a great uprising against the Jews. At that time in the 1400s Spain was the cultural center of Europe and many Jews contributed to that status. However, jealousy and suspicion towards the Jewish population resulted in the Catholic Church forcing the Jews either to convert to Christianity or leave the country. The greater population in the Jewish Communities throughout the country left and settled in countries like France and Germany.

So now the Jews were in Norway, and yet, as in their old country, there was a deep-rooted fear of the gentiles. How were the Jews to know if the Norwegians could be trusted? Would these newcomers see a repetition of what they had already experienced in their native country? (I remember from my school days how other students had chased my younger brother Abel and me around the school grounds calling us "Christ killers." It was terrifying to us, but neither the teachers, nor the principal ever intervened.)

Centuries of hardships had taught the Jews that the only way to survive was for them to stick together, help each other when needed and concern themselves with making a living and providing an education for their children.

It was important to every Jewish family to have children - many children – especially boys. This would help facilitate one of the many religious traditions. For example, when the father died it was required to have memorial services for him three times a day, morning, noon and evening, for 11 months. In order to have a complete service a minyen was required. A minyen consists of ten men, all had to have reached Bar Mitzvahs, 13 years and older, so that the prayer for the departed father could be recited. Therefore to have as many boys as possible in the family was very important. In my family there were 9 boys, and with the help from one of our numerous cousins a minyen was guaranteed. (The Authorized Daily Prayer Book by the late Chief Rabbi Joseph H. Hertz, states that prayers for the dead are to be said for 12 months. However, if the deceased had been a good man, services could be held for 11 months. I never knew of services that lasted for 12 months.)

My parents opened their new store on Fjordgaten 1. The street was adjacent to the fjord. There was a small apartment upstairs and their first son David was born there. Later they opened a second store on Olav Trygveson's Gate, but it was a struggle to keep both establishments going. To find customers they would often go out in the street and persuade people to come into their stores.

In addition, in order to buy their inventory they had to become used to obtaining loans from the bank, and that frightened them. They had never had to do that before. Whenever they purchased anything they always paid cash. Being in debt was to them a sign of poverty, and they often questioned the necessity and wisdom of doing business that way.

They continually worried about how they were going to have enough money to pay the bank. They always met their financial obligations, but still felt uncomfortable about doing business this way. They soon discovered that that's the way business was conducted, but they never felt right about borrowing money.

In 1904 they purchased a building, where the two stores were consolidated, at Krambodgaten 9 (Merchant Street 9). Papa bought the whole building because it had a large apartment above the store. This was a major move for the family. Papa was 29 years old and with two small sons by then. We lived there until 1928. By then we were a family of 9 boys and 2 girls. At that time Papa had a men's clothing store, and the display windows were crammed full of merchandise priced to sell. It brought customers from the merchant ships anchored close by who recognized my father as the one who, a few years earlier, had brought goods to the ships to sell to the seamen. This in turn brought some residents of the community into the store.

Life with Mama and Papa   25

Miriam Fischer and Salomon Abrahamsen 1902
Courtesy Fotograf Schroder, Trondheim, Norway.

Mama and Papa
Silver Anniversary, October 1927
Courtesy Fotograf Schroder, Trondheim, Norway.

On Wednesday, October 12, 1927, my parents celebrated their Silver Wedding Anniversary. For this very special and important event my father and mother had bought for my younger brother Abel and me identical black velvet suits, from Paris, with lace collar and cuffs and short velvet pants. The long black wool stockings matched the suits, and our brand new shiny, patent leather shoes completed our outfits. For the occasion our hair was cut and we were given a bath (which I didn't think was at all necessary) before we were allowed to get into our new suits.

Asne, Samuel, Aron and Abel, 1927
Courtesy Fotograf Schroder, Trondheim, Norway.

Heiman, one of our older brothers, took Abel and me to the celebration in a taxi. By the time we arrived a large crowd had gathered outside to watch all the guests in their fur coats and formal attire as they entered the ballroom.

Inside, a huge room had been lavishly decorated for this outstanding occasion. There were three very long tables each covered with linen. Flowers were everywhere. Huge bouquets in tall vases could be seen throughout the room. Cut flowers had been placed in wall sconces, and every table was decorated with an abundance of roses. The aroma from the sweet fragrant roses floated leisurely throughout the banquet hall encircling all the guests with a festive welcome. Gracing the table at each place setting was an array of crystal stemware; one for water, one for wine and one for brandy. And there was a wide spread of sterling dinnerware. The tables looked elegant.

People were milling around, greeting one another, and talking loud and laughing heartily. The room, being filled with so many people, was very noisy. It seemed to me that there must have been several hundred guests present.

To my recollection, Heiman was the Master of Ceremonies. He rang a bell and invited all the guests to find their proper places at the tables. Fortunately a place card had been plaed by each table setting to facilitate the seating arrangements. My mother and father were seated at the head table with the Rabbi and other dignitaries. I sat with Abel and Samuel at the table to the right of the head table.

Now the main event was about to begin. A festive meal fit for royalty was about to be served. Suddenly, a number of waitresses dressed in formal attire with white aprons and white lace headbands appeared in the wide doorway. The serving of an exquisite gala dinner began.

The menu called for creamed cauliflower soup followed by poached salmon steak with boiled potatoes, whipped cream with horseradish for the salmon, melted butter for the potatoes, steamed carrots and green peas. Samuel, who was 10 years old, whispered to Abel and me that everything was very elegant. We three young ones observed it all with wide eyes.

The waitresses carried large serving plates filled with salmon. As they served they asked each guest what size steak was desired. Holding the plate in their left hand the fish was served by holding two serving spoons together and the selected piece of fish was placed with great care and very delicately on the dinner plate. This was immediately followed by other servers with potatoes and melted butter, whipped cream in horseradish for the salmon, and vegetables. Each dish was served with elegance and a refined style by the waitresses. Watching them carry out their duties was an exhibition of artistry in motion. It was obvious that these waitresses were well trained. A variety of desserts, such as delicious Napoleon cakes and a multitude of three and four layered cakes were arranged on large carts and rolled to each guest who then had to make the difficult choice. After dinner there were liquors, coffee and Aquavit for the adults. Instead of wine, the children, of course, received brus, (a soft drink) and vorterol, (like root beer), which was always welcome. Throughout dinner a small chamber quartet played waltzes by Strauss.

After dinner there were many, many (too many it seemed to me) speeches and toasts to my parents. Samuel, who is four years older than I, stood on a chair and gave a speech. What he said I don't remember, but I saw him taking many bows and smiling from ear to ear. We three younger children were sent home in a taxi, while the celebration continued. The next day I heard that my father had hired a big dance band that played till the late hours of the morning.

I have always been very grateful to my older siblings for explaining all the details to me of this special event as I grew up. I was only six years old at the time. What remained in my mind was the crowd outside the ballroom, our handsome velvet suits, the parade of waitresses serving so elegantly, and Sam standing on the chair to speak.

My father's business must have been good, for in 1928 my parents purchased a larger five-story building, and the whole family moved there. With 11 children and my parents, there were now 13 members in our family. The dining room table had "shrunk" quite a bit by now and it became a little too tight to sit around the table when everybody was present for a meal. It was obvious that a more comfortable dining arrangement was needed. Through an interesting circumstance that became a reality in our home.

In the summer of 1930 there was a big exhibition in Trondheim, that my father attended. The furniture section at this fair especially caught his attention. He saw a grand dining room suite that had 16 chairs set around a large dinner table. It could easily seat our whole family, plus a few more. In addition it came with an expansive credenza, as well as a large linen cabinet. He bought it and had it delivered to our home.

The whole set was made from solid oak and looked very expensive. When asked about the cost my father answered with smiling pride that it was expensive.

My parents provided a comfortable home for all of us. They wanted to give us security, something that they themselves never had until they arrived in Norway and started their own business. Security for them was providing a good home and a safe environment, and the way to get that was to work hard and long. Of course, they expected all of their children to work just as hard as they did. What else was there in life? Papa was secure and somewhat happy, depending upon how business was. He was proud of what he had accomplished: raising 11 children, educating them; being the owner of several buildings in the city, two of which housed his stores, and one large warehouse, as well as a three story villa by the fjord where I was born.

When he first came to Norway he had had a desire to go to America. But he kept postponing it and after many years he finally knew it had become too late for him. To uproot his family, sell his properties, and adjust to another culture was just too much for him and Mama to even consider.

My own experience in 1940, as an 18 year old, arriving in New York City by myself with nobody to meet me on the pier and not knowing the language, enabled me to understand their plight much better. I learned from being a stranger in a strange land that no matter where you are, adjustments are constant companions throughout life.

An education in a Jewish family takes the highest priority and Papa and Mama were determined to educate all their children as best as possible. But an education in a profession, like a doctor or dentist wasn't enough. "In case something should happen" I heard Papa say as I was growing up, "learn also a trade."

Like I mentioned earlier, our family consisted of nine boys and two girls. The oldest was David born in 1903. He was the tallest one in the family, with black hair, dark brown eyes and gentle facial features. He was educated in Berlin, Germany and at the University of Oslo, Norway, and became a medical doctor. Later he became a psychiatrist, specializing in forensic psychiatry, and an author of a number of books in that field.

Heiman, son no. 2, was born two years later. He was educated at the Business College and became the number two man in the store.

The rest of the children came like clockwork. Son number 3 was Julius, after him came Leopold, then Beile, their first daughter, followed by Jacob, Oskar, and Asne, their second daughter, who was followed by Samuel, making it almost a dozen. Oskar told me that a girl was born in 1919, but she was still-born. I was born 1921 and the youngest, Abel, in 1923. Twenty years spanned the birth from the oldest to the youngest child.

Heiman, who managed the stores, had a degree in business management. Being a good businessman, with great skills and diplomacy, he managed the three stores in Trondheim. Heiman's gray-blue eyes and dark blond hair made him look more Norwegian than Jewish.

Though his stature was small his will power and intent made him 10 feet tall. He also learned the art of playing bridge, and was an outstanding bridge player. He and 11 other Jewish businessmen formed an "exclusive" bridge club, which they called B-12. Heiman had a good sense of humor and was a man of great generosity. I considered him to be generous to a fault. He often came home with a new joke that he said he purchased for 10 cents from Mr. Garviloff's big joke book. Mr. Garviloff was a Russian, who owned the cigar store next to our building. I believed Heiman until I grew older and wiser.

Julius and Jacob became Dentists. (For details see Chapter 5, pages 86-88)

Leopold was a born window decorator. He had an intuitive feeling how to make the most attractive window displays. With the training he had received in Sweden, he did very well. Besides being the window decorator, he also had other desires - playing the violin, like our brother David. He was very sincere in wanting to play it well, but had great difficulty doing so. Leopold knew that the violin was no easy instrument to handle, but he never gave up. He had taken lessons for many years, but unfortunately his progress was not what he expected. Nevertheless, he received enjoyment from playing the violin. He became an active member in the Trondheim's Men's Glee Club.

He cared for the gardening and maintenance of the summer villa at Vikhammer, which was near Trondheim. Many long hours were spent weeding, fertilizing, planting and pruning. He was the only one in the entire family who took an interest in this work, and as a result, he had all the responsibility. The villa was kept beautiful, thanks to his labor and concern. However, we didn't fully appreciate his efforts in creating this beauty which all of us enjoyed. With his dark-blond hair, gray eyes and muscular body he could be taken for any of the natives in Trondheim. Like Papa, Leopold had a very short fuse. It didn't take much aggravation to make him go right through the ceiling, and very often somebody would have to scrape him off.

Oskar always found something humorous to say, to the extent that everybody expected him to be the one who told the jokes and kept the family and guests laughing. He was of average height, brown eyes, and dark-red hair and very short tempered.

He spent many hours in the store and like the others worked very hard. But when a certain young lady was in town, Oskar spent all his time with her. From his early years he had been in love with his second cousin Lilly. She lived in another city, Kristiansund. Whenever she visited relatives in Trondheim, Oskar couldn't be found except in her company. They were in love and perhaps the only thing that was on his mind was how he could marry Lilly.

Samuel was the philosopher in the family. He was very studious and had a logical mind. He could argue a point on both sides of the fence regardless of what issue was involved. He studied logic, Latin, literature and languages. His best language, besides English and German, was French. At one time he was going to become a Rabbi and in 1936 was scheduled to attend the Rabbinical Seminary in Berlin, Germany. When

Hitler came to power in 1933, it had become dangerous for the Jews in Germany, so Samuel's future plans were changed. He pursued studies in other fields. He was a very handsome young man with jet-black hair, dark brown eyes and a smile that would charm many a young girl.

Mama had great expectations for Abel, the youngest. She wanted him to be a medical doctor, like her eldest son, but Abel had other plans. From his early years he had an exceptional sense of timing, of being at the right place at the right time, especially when it concerned important personalities. Besides being a good student in school, he was also a very handsome fellow and was well liked by just about everyone, especially the girls.

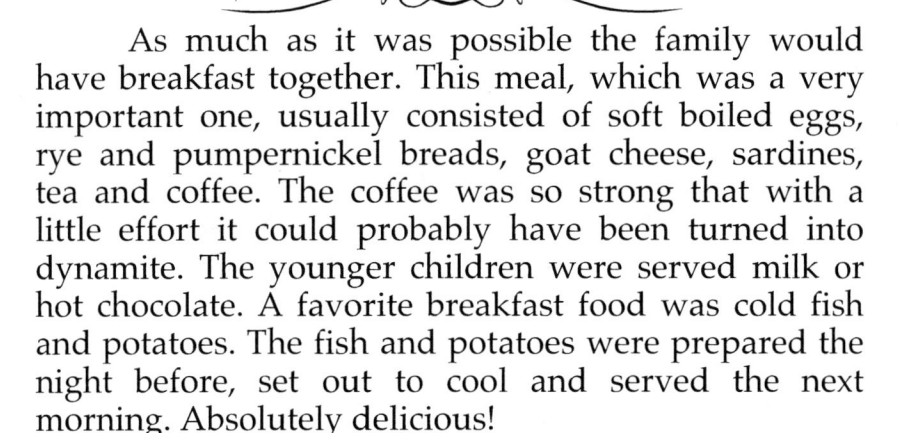

As much as it was possible the family would have breakfast together. This meal, which was a very important one, usually consisted of soft boiled eggs, rye and pumpernickel breads, goat cheese, sardines, tea and coffee. The coffee was so strong that with a little effort it could probably have been turned into dynamite. The younger children were served milk or hot chocolate. A favorite breakfast food was cold fish and potatoes. The fish and potatoes were prepared the night before, set out to cool and served the next morning. Absolutely delicious!

We bought fresh baked bread from a nearby bakery. Wilhelm Hoff's bakery carried a large supply of rye, pumpernickel breads, hard rolls and pastries. I was very fond also of his Napoleons. The crusty pumpernickel bread was a family breakfast favorite. Milk was purchased by the liter at the dairy outlet. I would carry our own milk pail, in which the dairy clerk would pour the desired amount of milk.

The younger children went to school at eight in the morning. While we were on our way to school the rest of the family went down stairs to prepare for opening time at our store. Family members who worked in the store never received a salary, but Heiman always came up with the money when we needed it.

For its time our store was quite large, occupying two floors. It featured a rich selection of yardage goods such as silk, brocade, cotton, woolens and linen that were imported from France, Italy, Germany, Spain, Egypt and England. This cloth was used for dresses, suits, overcoats, draperies and curtains. In those days many people had their clothing made by a tailor or seamstress, only the poor bought ready made clothing.

Salomon Abrahamsen and his brother Josef Kahn were very close. I was never able to learn why their names were different. The brothers had married sisters, Miriam and Rosa, and each had 11 children. We would visit each other's homes to chat and gossip. There was always a hearty and warm welcome in whichever home the visits took place.

In 1935 my family and the Kahn family, our cousins, formed a sports club called "AbraKa." For several years ski trips were arranged at Vassfjellet with ski contests between the families. It was necessary to carry food and coffee packed in large rucksacks. As soon as we arrived at the designated ski area the contests began. At the conclusion there were awards for the winners and runners up. After that, the food was brought out.

On one of the ski trips the following picture of my family was taken, though only 9 of the 11 children were present. Those absent were David, who practiced in Oslo, and Jacob, who was studying dentistry in Oslo.

From left to right: Heiman, Julius, Leopold, Samuel, Beile, Oskar, Asne, Aron and Abel (Easter 1935)

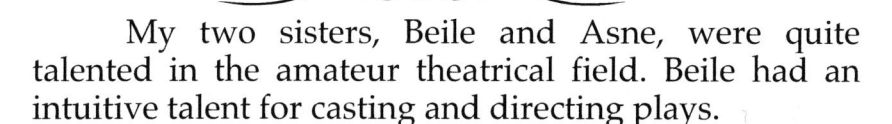

My two sisters, Beile and Asne, were quite talented in the amateur theatrical field. Beile had an intuitive talent for casting and directing plays.

Every year at Chanukah time, the Jewish community sponsored a children's party, followed by an adult party. A stage play was the center of attraction. Beile was always able to direct the plays that were either written, or adapted by my family from other stories, and then made into musical plays. She decided who would have the important roles and made sure the entire production came off on schedule. The best parts were usually given to the Abrahamsens and the Kahns. Minor roles went to those outside our two families. The whole Jewish community was outraged over such action and expressed anger towards us that lasted for several months after the play was over. Nevertheless, the ones who received the best parts were the most talented. The incident was forgotten by the next year when Chanukah was again observed. Then the entire process was repeated with the same outcome.

Almost every evening our family gathered in the living room to talk about what was going on in the city and around the world. True gossip was always welcome. Everyone had something to say, whether or not it was important or contributed anything of value to the issues of interest. We enjoyed being together as a family. The room was always filled with life and love. Vibrant laughter rolled over the ceiling and bounced off the walls like fireworks on a holiday.

When Hitler came to power in Germany, much of our conversation centered around the well being of the German Jews, but nobody knew what could be done to help them escape from the terror of the Nazi regime.

Evenings always included much music and laughter. There was usually someone who played the piano while some of us listened and others kept on talking.

Asne couldn't play the piano very well, but she used the little talent she had to her advantage. In addition, she could also sing and tell jokes. Together with her best friend, Sonja Meyer, (Jacob was in love with Sonja) the two made quite a musical team.

In that environment of enjoyment and smiles Mama always joined us. She carried a big basket of socks that needed to be looked after. One by one she examined each sock and then started to darn amidst the laughter, loud conversation and music that rang throughout the whole room. Mama had such great patience with all the work that was on her shoulders, and to alleviate her responsibilities Ingebjorg, our maid, would help her with the sock repair.

As the evening wore on, Ingebjorg would bring in coffee, hot tea, hot chocolate and snacks. It was like a spontaneous party. The hot tea was served in tall glasses placed in metal holders with handles so the tea could be enjoyed without burning the hands. It was common to add either honey or home made preserves to sweeten the tea. Sometimes it was very late before we went to bed. Tomorrow would soon come hand then school and work would be waiting for us.

There were times when our living room was empty and quiet. The family members had either gone to see a movie or were visiting the Kahns. Though I enjoyed being with the Kahns, I always felt much more secure when we all assembled in our own living room for another time of enjoyment and laughter.

On Sundays in the early autumn we would take long hikes. Our destination would be one of several restaurants situated on the outskirts of town. Among the most popular were Fjellseter and Skistua.

It would take us from one to two hours to reach these places and then we would order refreshments and rest for a long time enjoying the food and conversation.

The return trip to Trondheim usually took longer because we were tired by then and weren't able to walk as fast. Another place called Lian was more easily accessible because it could be reached by an electric train. The restaurant was built on a hill overlooking a lake. It was very pleasant to enjoy lunch in that peaceful environment. In the wintertime when the lake was completely frozen over we could ski across it.

During the winter, in the evenings we would often go ice skating on a public ice rink. There were no locker rooms made available and no restrooms, so we sat in the snow to put on our ice skates. These times filled us with happy memories.

In those years we didn't have any worries or concerns for the future. All of us had grown up in safe and secure surroundings. The outer world was far, far away. For the most part we only associated with Jews, being afraid to cultivate friendship with non-Jews. Our whole world revolved around the Jewish community, school and working in our family's store. Our life activities became routine and sometimes boring.

The thought had come to many in my family that it would be nice to have a change in the routine. What was wrong with cultivating friends among the non-Jewish segment of the population? The younger members of our generation believed it might be an amiable association. But there was ambivalence in the desire to find and develop new friendships. All of us had experienced being chased in the schoolyard as "Christ killers."

Such social changes predicated possible dangers and insecurities. This was too frightening, so we reverted to the status quo in our thinking. We became determined to prevent any changes from entering into our lives. It had been imprinted in our minds that the status quo had to be maintained to make sure that the future would be identical to the present. Most of us in the Jewish community dared not think what would happen if we were ever able to tear down the walls of suspicion and fear, and discover the world outside of our closed doors. Desirable as that was it could be too risky. Only a few had tried it, and the greatest risk at that time resulted in stern criticisms from the elders who were considered to be wise and all knowing.

We had non-Jewish business associates such as our attorney, a bookkeeper and the clerks in our stores, as well as Ingebjorg. There was always genuine respect between us. Of course, Ingebjorg had become like a cherished member of our family.

While Papa and Mama had a very large family, they also looked after the welfare of those less fortunate in the community. I didn't become aware of this until I was about 12 years old. One event that made a deep impression on me, and which I will long remember, took place in early December of 1933.

I was watching Mama and Ingebjorg, prepare food. They made lots of food, enough for a small army, I thought. I wondered who was coming to dinner?

Then Mama put the meat, potatoes, vegetables, and freshly baked bread into individual containers. There was so much food prepared that it filled four large baskets.

"Get your coat and cap," Mama said to me. "We're taking this food to a poor Jewish family."

I wasn't about to go out in the cold, snowy darkness, but she "persuaded" me. So finally I "joyfully volunteered." Mama needed my help.

We took the streetcar to the end of the line, and then walked through the snow for another 15 minutes, each of us carrying two baskets. The two I carried became heavier and heavier with each step, and I was hoping that the poor family would be home. Otherwise I would have to carry all this food back to the streetcar and home again. My arms, which I thought were stretched all the way to the street, were already aching and very tired from this heavy load. Mama couldn't have called them on the phone to make sure they'd be home. They were too poor to have one.

The aroma from the home cooked food, the freshly baked bread, the meat patties in thick gravy, boiled potatoes and steamed vegetables curled around my nostrils and made me very hungry. This food was needed for the poor family.

However, I knew I'd have a warm dinner and a warm home waiting for me when I returned.

Finally, Mama led the way to a house, rang the doorbell, and waited.

The door opened slowly as if the person inside was afraid of strangers. I tried to adjust my eyes to see who it was, but it was too dark. They were too poor to even afford a light bulb above the entry door.

The woman who opened the door recognized my mother and gave out with a loud "Oyh", and the conversation took off in Yiddish. We went inside and were led into the dining room that turned out to be almost as cold as the outdoors. The wooden floor was bare and showed a dire need of repair. The only food in the house was a piece of stale bread laying on the rickety dining table. There were children seated on wooden chairs lined up against the wall. The parents wept for joy over the food in the baskets.

Mama made herself at home in the small kitchen, found some pots and pans and transferred all the food to those containers. This was not the first time that Mama had brought food to this family. After a short conversation we left. We had to hurry home so that she and Ingebjorg could serve supper to her own family. (See note No. 1, Page 53).

This was just one of the many times that my parents helped the poor, including Jewish refugees from countries that had been occupied by Hitler's Nazi armies. These refugees told my father about the persecution of the Jews by the Nazis, and how they had been lucky to escape with just the clothes on their backs. My parents provided shelter for them and funds for their travel to a country where they would be safe – hopefully the U.S.A.

My parents kept a Kosher home in accordance with the strictest rabbinical traditions, and of course they observed all the high holidays. One of the most important religious observance was Passover.

The first two evenings of Passover were always celebrated as highly festive occasions, called Seder dinners. Our dinner table was dressed in its finest with sterling silver, beautiful china, and crystal. Two huge silver candelabras graced the table. For us Passover was probably the best of all holy days, much better than Yom Kippur when the family fasted for a whole day. All of us were dressed in our very best and sat at the dinner table according to seniority. My father was at the head of the table wearing a white skullcap. This showed his authority and that he was the patriarch of the family. David, the eldest, was next to him on his right, followed by Heiman, Julius, Leopold, and Abel. On the other side of the table were Beile, Jacob, Oskar, Asne, and Samuel. You will find me standing on a chair behind Asne.

Seder celebration in our family, March 30, 1926
Courtesy Fotograf Schroder, Trondheim, Norway.

Mama was seated next to Papa for the picture. Normally, she would be seated at the opposite end of the table. All the sons over Bar Mitzvah age had on black skullcaps. They were no longer boys, but men.

Before dinner could be eaten there were prayers for the food, and the reading from the Hagadah about the story of the exodus from Egypt. When the words "Now you may eat supper" were read, they were received with great anticipation and hungry stomachs.

Following a scrumptious meal, the last portion of the Hagadah was completed by singing several portions of it in Hebrew. I can still hear the melodies from many years ago. All I need to do is close my eyes and listen. The voices are still so clear, the singing in Hebrew ever so loud, and at times beautiful harmony fills the air. The Seder started at 7:30 and was finished around 11:00.

Years later, shortly after my arrival in New York, followed by Samuel almost three months later in 1940, we were invited for Passover dinner at the home of one of our newly found American cousins. During the reading of the Hagadah our cousin and her family wanted to know how Passover was celebrated in our family. With a little hesitation Samuel started to sing the passages from the Hagadah in Hebrew. My mind was suddenly flooded with memories from home. Though I had joined Samuel at the outset of the singing, I soon stopped. My throat choked up; my eyes filled with tears and soon I was crying like a baby. This was my first time away from home on a Seder evening. At that moment I missed my family and home more than ever.

Life with Mama and Papa

Sabbaths were celebrated in the traditional manner on Friday evenings. The table, covered with a white linen tablecloth, was set with better than everyday china, no chipped dishes were allowed, real silver flat ware, one silver candelabrum, two brass candleholders and lots of food. Before the meal, Mama would light the candles, and with her hands make three circular motions towards herself, and then cover her eyes. She would remain that way for 10-15 seconds, praying for her family and giving thanks to God that another Sabbath could be celebrated.

Then Papa and all the male members who had reached Bar Mitzvah stood up one at a time, and chanted the prescribed prayer for the occasion. When that was over we began eating. There was boiled chicken, zimmes, (candied sliced carrots), gefilte fish, kugel (noodle pudding), freshly baked challah, (bread), coffee without cream, tea and dessert.

After dinner there was prayer and thanksgiving for the food we had received. During that time I would sometimes sit on Papa's lap and watch him kneed a small part of the challah. He knew the prayers by heart and had the kneading timed so that at the conclusion of the thanksgiving prayers he had fashioned a small duck from the bread. With a broad smile he placed it on the table for all to see.

Mama, assisted by Ingebjorg, made her own noodles for the kugel. In those days this was done by hand. Once a month they rolled out large sheets of dough, cut them up in wide strips, put them on clean sheets and placed them over the furniture and all the beds to dry. On such a day there would be no place to sit. When the noodles had dried they were placed in large containers.

Early on Friday afternoon a portion of the dried noodles was cooked and then placed in a large, round, deep enamel pan. The remaining ingredients, which always had to include raisins, butter, sugar and cinnamon, were added and put in the oven to bake. When done, part of the top was usually burned because the oven browned unevenly. There was always a fight between us to get the burned parts because they tasted the best.

But that wasn't all the work for Mama and Ingebjorg. Among the many chores they had to do was to daily gather the family laundry. That was a constant reminder that on the first Monday of the month it was laundry day. It started at six in the morning. In addition to Mama and Ingebjorg two more workers were hired. They all climbed the stairs to the first attic where there was a large laundry room. A big copper tub, about four feet in diameter and three feet high, stood on a coal-fired cast-iron stove. On the wall above the stove was a long-armed water spigot that facilitated filling the tub. When the water was boiling, clothes were loaded into the copper tub until it was filled to the top, and then lots of soap was added. One of the workers used a big paddle to stir the clothes until they were "done." Then the clothes, using the big paddle, were transferred to three smaller wooden washtubs and scrubbed on a washboard. It was a question of who were worn out first, the workers or the laundry. Washing clothes was an all day job, but by early evening it was all finished. When the final step was put in motion, the laundry was hung up to dry on the clotheslines in the second attic. A few days later Ingebjorg had the "honor" to iron more than 30 shirts and many sheets and pillowcases. That kept her busy for many, many hours.

My father was a very religious man and one of the pillars in the Jewish community. Each morning, except Saturday, he would pray with his phylacteries, prayer shawl and skullcap as was the custom of every orthodox Jew. On Sundays in winter, when the hills were packed with snow and every one was eager to go skiing, he made sure all his sons prayed, like he did, before they were allowed to venture out in the snow. The three youngest, which included me, were excused from praying because we weren't of Bar Mitzvah age.

My older brothers had discovered that as soon as my father finished praying he didn't require any of his children to go through the ritual of the morning prayer.

So a clever plan was put into action. While the older ones stayed in bed they sent Abel and me downstairs to see if Papa had finished his prayers. As soon as he was finished, we carried the good news upstairs. Those in bed quickly got dressed and were ready for skiing.

As the number of Jewish families in Trondheim increased it became obvious that another and larger synagogue was needed. Up to this time a rented place was used for the worship services and with the many growing families the premises soon became too small.

A building was found that used to be an old railroad station. It could be remodeled to be suitable for a synagogue. Permission was obtained from the city council to change the old railroad station into a synagogue.

Then money had to be raised for the building and the remodeling, as well as for a parcel of land for the Jewish cemetery. The latter was obtained next to a Protestant cemetery.

Papa was the chairman of the fund raising committee. He made sure that the new synagogue would be large enough for all the Jews who lived in Trondheim. At its peak there were 40 families who had made their homes in this Norwegian city.

Being the head of the building committee he had

the responsibility of depositing all moneys collected for the building and keeping records of those who had contributed what sums. One day when he and Mama went to the bank to make a deposit on the account, she observed how carelessly the bank teller handled the money. Leaving the bank Mama stopped at the exit door.

"Salomon, I didn't like the way the bank teller handled the money you just deposited. I have an inner feeling that something is wrong with this bank." Mama looked at him sternly, and with her voice matching her looks, continued, "You go back to that bank teller and withdraw all the money in the account. Then go across the street and open an account there for the synagogue. That's the same bank you have your money in, isn't it?"

"Yes it is. But I don't see any reason for changing banks. It's a good idea to spread the business around. Don't you think so, Miriam?"

"Not at this time! Close the account here and open another one in the bank across the street. I'm not leaving until you do." Those were her final words. Mama placed herself between the exit door and Papa. She had no intention of moving until he had done what she believed was the right thing.

He looked at her and knew there was no way she would change her mind.

"All right, I'll do what you want, but I think you are making a mistake. This bank looks all right to me, so why change - - - I'm going, I'm going."

With that he slowly walked over to the bank teller, feeling embarrassed to close the account. But he did it. Mama and Papa walked to the bank across the street and opened an account there.

Three days later the bank from which the money had been withdrawn declared bankruptcy.

The local paper carried the news and the Jewish community was up in arms. For sure, they thought, the building fund was lost and they would have to start over again. The entire building committee descended upon Salomon and started to weep and lament and pounding their chest over the loss of the money.

"We are bankrupt! All our money is lost and we worked such a long time to collect that money. What can we do? What can we do?"

It sounded as if the end of the world had arrived, somewhat prematurely. Everyone appeared to be helpless, except for one.

Papa listened to them, enjoying their moaning and groaning as they agonized over the apparent financial loss. He waited until they had finished venting their feelings and smiling from ear to ear, he told them:

"All the money is safe! Don't worry, I knew the bank wasn't secure and I took the right measures to save our monies. I transferred the building fund from the bank in question and opened an account in the bank across the street. I had to act in a hurry so I didn't have time to consult with the committee. Besides, I got so busy in my store that I didn't have the time to let you know."

The committee could hardly believe what they heard, until Papa showed them the documents that proved the funds had been transferred. Then everybody smiled. Salomon had become a hero in the Jewish community. He later became a trusted officer of the synagogue. But he never told anybody that it was his wife's insistence that made him transfer the money to another bank. Years later, however, when some of the sons brought their wives home to meet Mama, she related the whole story to Becky, my brother Julius' wife, and Doris, my wife.

Except for the parties at Chanukah there weren't many social events in the Jewish community. At the few that were held, there was always an opportunity to hear the latest reliable, authorized and authoritative gossip. It was also an occasion for the ladies to "model" their new, and fashionable evening gowns and their matching jewelry and earrings. An affair such as a dance was a welcome break in the long winter dreariness, and, as should be expected, was always well attended.

On one occasion a formal dance had been organized. The invitation stated that it was expected that the men would wear tails and white ties. Nothing less than tuxedos would be allowed. That was a clear signal for the ladies to wear their formal gowns and the best jewelry.

Everybody was looking forward to that event and talked about it for weeks in advance. The evening of the party arrived, and as expected, it was cold with snow blanketing all the streets.

The men wore their heavy overcoats and their wives were dressed in fur coats that covered their finest gowns. It wasn't often that they had an occasion to wear their party finery, and everybody arrived in the best of spirits for this festive occasion. They were looking forward to a great evening of fun. An orchestra had been hired for the occasion and kosher refreshments were provided by the Women's Auxiliary. This was an evening that my father and his brother Josef wouldn't want to miss. Together, with their wives, they were among the early arrivals.

The men had put on their galoshes because the streets were covered with snow and slush. When they arrived at the party all the coats, fur-coats, hats and galoshes were placed in an unattended cloakroom.

As the evening wore on and it was getting towards midnight, Salomon and Josef were the first ones to leave. They got their overcoats and those for their wives. While they were putting on their galoshes both got an idea.

Quickly they changed the galoshes belonging to the rest of the people who were still dancing, so that there were either two right ones or two left ones, and in some places there was one left, while in others there were three. At no place could one find two galoshes of the same size. The stage had been set for total bedlam and confusion.

Then Salomon and Josef, with Miriam and Rosa, left.

All the way home they laughed. They wondered if they would ever know if all the others were able to find their own galoshes.

Back at the party when the dance was finished, there was pandemonium. All the men were searching for their pair of galoshes. By the time they found them it was three in the morning.

The next morning the phone rang very early in the homes of Salomon and Josef. Everybody in the Jewish community knew who had done it, but both of them denied it, of course.

This prank was never repeated.

The Jewish population had settled in. They felt secure having established themselves in a business, or a profession. As a whole, life was good to them. Some Jews had by now, under heavy critical glares and sharp words from the older generation, cultivated friendships among the non-Jewish population and a better understanding between the two cultures started to emerge. The suspicions towards the Gentiles that had haunted the Jews for so many years were beginning to fade away. A relationship of trust and integrity was being built. Many of the Jews were happy to discover that they could develop friendships with the Norwegian people. In the beginning no one dreamed it would be possible. Little by little, one step at a time, here a little, there a little, the curtain of misunderstanding and distrust began to lift. It seemed like a new day.

The Jews began to believe that they had found a safe home among all the Norwegians. It was good to feel secure and not have to live in fear and uncertainties. It was also good to know that you were welcome in circles that up to now had been closed. Doors of acceptance had begun to open and springs of hope for friendship and harmony were bursting forth in Trondheim. They were all looking forward to a wonderful and exciting future. But little did the Jews know what had been smoldering on the horizon of world events. Papa was aware of what had happened in and to Germany after 1918. He was greatly worried that Hitler would bring the war to Norway. (See note 2, Page 53).

As a whole, the family was very fond of all kinds of music in those days. We always had classical music in our home and attended classical concerts whenever possible. Of course, classical concerts were not in great abundance in this northern city. But that didn't stop us from learning to love the old masters. We were given as many cultural advantages as possible in this small town. Both Julius and Jacob played classical music and there were radio programs that featured classical music; of course we also listened to our classical phonograph records.

At that time, the early 1930s, a musical group called "Comedian Harmonists" skyrocketed to fame all over Europe. This group, consisting of six young men from Germany and Austria, performed for appreciative audiences. Obtaining a ticket to one of their programs was an accomplishment in itself, because all their concerts were sold out as soon as they were announced. They performed their concerts in a style typical of that era, in white ties and tails. On one of their concert tours they appeared for an evening performance in Trondheim. My father invited them to our home and played some musical recordings in Yiddish that were his pride and joy. I remember meeting them, and later that evening attended their concert. It was spectacular!

Unfortunately, this group stayed together for only five years even though they had had a meteoric rise to fame. Hitler's Nazi Germany was on the march, and with three of the group members being Jewish, the ensemble was forced to stop performing.

Several opera stars from Denmark and other countries performed in Trondheim during the early 1930s. Each time, the pianist who accompanied them was a gifted young man from Denmark by the name of Boerge Rosenbaum. On one occasion he was invited to our home before the recital. Many years later he changed his name to Victor Borge and rose to the pinnacle in the world of famous entertainers. Meeting these fine musicians in person and hearing them perform instilled within us children a great love and respect for good music.

My brothers Julius and Jacob, both dentists, played piano quite well and composed music in addition to practicing dentistry. One of Julius' compositions was accepted for the opening number at one of the musical revues (Studenter Uka) produced by the Technical University in Trondheim. My cousin, Oskar Bernstein, composed the finale for the same show.

Throughout the 1930s Julius had a number of his compositions on the Norwegian Hit Parade. After the war one of Jacob's songs, "En Liten Leilighet" (A Small

Apartment) became very popular in Norway. In 1948 it rose to number one on the Norwegian Hit Parade. Asne had the theater in her blood and with the proper training it is quite possible she could have become a very talented entertainer. In those days, however, girls were schooled in home economics so they could excel as wives and mothers.

All the Jews in Norway constantly followed the reports out of Germany about Hitler and his thirst for conquest of other nations. They were extremely distressed over what might happen to them should the Nazis attack Norway. On the other hand what would Hitler do with the tiny country of Norway? They dismissed these thoughts as having no foundation, but fear hung over them like a thundercloud ready to make its presence known at any time.

With all the treaty violations and threats of domination for world power by Hitler and the weakness of the Western Powers, my father saw this as a prologue to another war. He believed it wouldn't be long before Hitler marched into Austria.

Who knew what other countries would be Hitler's next victims? All the Jews prayed fervently for peace, but more than prayer was required.

Somewhere and somehow, my father thought, Hitler must be stopped and crushed. But at that time the Western nations had no planned opposition to Hitler, and Norway was not involved. Nevertheless, the frustration and despair grew every day and threatened to paralyze the Jews in Norway.

To ease his troubled mind Papa remembered the happy times with the family at the summer villa by the fjord.

Notes to chapter 2

1. This family had been citizens of Sweden. However, in 1936 they applied for Norwegian citizenship and relinquished their Swedish nationality. Looking back that was a fatal mistake. For in 1942 almost the whole family perished in a Nazi death camp. Had they maintained their Swedish citizenship they would have been exempted from deportation to Germany, because at the beginning of World War II Sweden had declared itself neutral.

2. There were those in the Jewish community, including my father, who remembered that at the end of World War I the Allies strapped Germany, who had started the war, with such heavy reparations it broke the back of that country. The German mark was devalued a number of times to an unbelievable low rate. In July 1914 the mark was valued at 4.2 to the U.S. dollar. In November 1923 it took 4.2 trillion marks to purchase one U.S. dollar. Savings accounts, insurance policies and other assets plummeted to such an incredible low value that they became totally worthless. The economy was out of control and the future for Germany was dismal. Unemployment was at a staggering rate. According to the Allies, though the situation was catastrophic, they didn't think it was too serious. However, there had been concerns by some statesmen on the Allied side, because they recognized that Germany needed help to stabilize its economy. But nothing concrete came from it. The Jews were worried about where these situations would take the world.

There was more to come that would worsen an already deteriorating situation.

French and Belgium troops occupied parts of Germany because the German government refused to pay those high-imposed reparations which were crippling their industries. To make matters worse the political arena was in shambles.

From 1924 the situation in Germany improved greatly until the depression in 1929 caused the country, like a ship without a rudder, to lose its direction. A number of political parties fought in the streets for dominance. Among the fighting factions was the National Socialists, known as the Nazi party, which was led by Adolf Hitler. Nobody took him, or his "Brown Shirts", seriously. Everybody believed that he would soon vanish into oblivion. But in 1933, Hitler became a frightening and gruesome part of history.

He had been arrested in November 1923 and was sentenced to five years in prison at Landsberg Castle, but was released after only eight months. While in prison Hitler wrote a book he called "Mein Kampf" (My Struggle) in which he called for a national revival, a battle against communism and Jews and their elimination from the world.

"Mein Kampf" became the manifesto in which Hitler gave to the world a blueprint of exactly what he was going to do. To Hitler, communism and Jews were the greatest menace to the stability of the world. On January 30, 1933, Paul von Hindenburg, the ailing, elderly president of the Weimar Republic, named Adolf Hitler to be Chancellor of Germany. This would make a dangerous situation explosive. Many insightful Jews could see the handwriting on the wall. They knew from Hitler's manifesto that there was enormous trouble ahead for them. Soon one disturbing event after another took place, like regularly scheduled episodes.

For example: One month later on February 27, The German Reichstag (City Hall) was set on fire and the entire building was gutted. A young Communist who was near the scene was arrested and charged with arson. On January 10, 1934 the young Dutchman Marinus Van der Lubbe was convicted of arson of the Reichstag and executed in Leipzig.

The government of Adolf Hitler wasted no time in linking the fire to a Communist plot to overthrow the government, and Hitler stated that "…now you can see what Germany and Europe have to look for from Communism." This was a clear signal that Hitler meant to take serious actions in eliminating any and all opposition to his dictatorial regime.

But there were many who believed that Hitler and his party had set the fire themselves, to create a "perilous" situation so they could claim to take control of the government and "restore" peace and order to the country.

With the world situation deteriorating from day to day, Hitler demanding more "living space" for his people, invaded the surrounding countries. My father became very nervous over what would happen to the European Jews. He didn't want to see a repetition of what had taken place in Russia for so many years. Remembering the large-scale [2]pogroms against the Jews that were sanctioned by the Russian government, Papa could see it happening again. There were enough Jewish refugees coming through Trondheim to convince him. He was visibly disturbed over the whole situation and fervently hoped that the persecution of Jews wouldn't reach as far north as Norway.

---

[2] An organized massacre of helpless people, as of Jews in Russia (Russian – devastation)

Chapter 3

Happy Days

Vikhammer, the place of my birth, where I spent many happy summers.

"Are we ready yet? I don't have any time to waste. Summer will be over soon. Is everybody ready to go?" I had run into the store all out of breath. My older brother Heiman looked up from his work, knowing what I was thinking.

"Hurry now, and pack what things you'll need for the summer. Are you excited about vacation time?"

he asked.

I nodded my head "Of course! What could be better than to spend the summer by the fjord! I'll pack my swim trunks, soccer ball and tennis shoes. That's all I'll need." and I started to walk off.

"Don't forget your toothbrush, toothpaste, and a bar of soap. You'll need that." Heiman called after me.

I ran upstairs, got my few things together in a suitcase and was ready to leave. But it took the rest of my family much longer before they were able to leave. Impatiently I waited.

At 2:00 p.m., on the last day, the school bell was heard in every building and throughout the schoolyard. With a relieved smile the teacher announced "Class dismissed. See you on Monday, August 20. Have an enjoyable summer vacation!" The students left the classroom in an orderly manner, as they had been taught.

Everyone was very excited. No school for two months! They all wanted to know how their classmates were going to spend the summer. They couldn't help being a little noisy about the forthcoming summer time as they "walked" across the playground. They all laughed looking forward to what the summer would bring.

The buildings reverberated with their laughter and joy, and if they could, they too would join in the chorus of all the happy sounds. The teacher, left alone, wondered what was going to happen to this bunch of kids he had taught for a number of years. He sat at his desk for a while, shaking his head and smiling, for he knew that everything would be all right. Looking over the classroom he studied each desk, which was made from pinewood stained in a light brown color. The inkwell in the upper right corner was now empty. As his eyes spanned the desks, the essence of each of the students passed easily through his mind. He knew them all by their first, middle and last names, where each of the 32 boys was seated, in what row and desk number. There were those boys who knew their lessons every time he called on them and those who never knew their lessons no matter how often he called on them.

The teacher didn't have many more years to teach. The end of the 1940 school year, he would retire and live on easy street. If he only knew what 1940 would bring.

He packed his books and other personal belongings in a large, well-worn leather satchel. As he left the empty, silent classroom, he felt a sense of satisfaction about the completed school year. It was a secure feeling to know that the classroom would be there when he returned in August.

Bispehaugen Folkeskole, our school, was situated high on a hill overlooking the city of Trondheim. Most of its wood frame buildings were built in the early part of the 1900's. There was one four-story brick building that had been completed in the early part of 1930. This structure can still be seen from many parts of town.

It is very large, and is quite impressive with a clock tower on the rooftop. Only the girls attended classes in this building. The boys were kept in the older buildings. There were no coed classes. The boys were not allowed in that building except to attend special classes, such as choir and natural history, but still without any girls present.

On that last day of school I ran down the many hills from the school and hurried home. There was no time to waste. I was eager to leave the city with two of my brothers, Abel and Sam. Abel was two years younger than I and Sam four years older. We would travel out to our country home to spend the whole summer together. Every year I looked forward to spending the summer by the fjord.

Once home I put my schoolbooks in a place

where I hoped somebody would find them and take them away. Or even better, that they would be lost forever. I didn't care much for school. The subjects didn't interest me, except for history, which I liked very much. The other subjects, such as geography and arithmetic, could just as well be outlawed as far as I was concerned. Maybe next year I would learn how to study these subjects and then I might appreciate them a little better. But for now the most important thing to be concerned with was summer vacation.

I brought home the report card for the whole year of class work and I wasn't very proud of the grades. But then, I had been told so often by my older brothers and sisters that I would never become a professor so there wasn't any necessity to apply myself. I showed my report card to my brother Heiman, he smiled, shook his head, and hoped I'd do better next year.

These were pleasant and peaceful times. Very few of the explosive and disruptive conditions emerging in Germany had reached us and we hoped that we wouldn't hear of them any more. We all felt very safe; believing that everything would remain the same as it had always been. This summer, like so many others, would be filled with laughter and fun. We were all looking forward to getting away from the city, enjoying lazy days in the sun by the fjord and doing only what pleased us. In our minds we couldn't imagine spending our summer any other way, and we were sure that there were many more enjoyable summers ahead of us. It was fortunate that we didn't know that in only a few short years everything would be changed. Our world, and that of many others, would be turned upside down.

Our store didn't close until 3:00 o'clock; we had to wait until then before we could leave. On Saturdays, in the summer time, all stores including grocery outlets were ordered by law to close at that time. Any stores remaining open past that time were fined severely.

Eagerly we counted every minute on the big grandfather clock in our living room. To speed up the time I was thinking of advancing the clock-hands to the three o'clock hour, but I realized that really wouldn't be of any help.

Ingebjorg, our maid, stuck her head into the living room.

"Aron," she said, "you and Abel come and eat your dinner now while you're waiting to go to the country. It will be at least another hour before they are finished in the store. Then the car will have to be packed. All that will take some time, so with good luck you might be on your way by five o'clock."

"Five o'clock? That will never come! I'll be an old man by then. We might not even live that long." Abel chimed in.

"If you eat your dinner you'll live long enough. And by the time you finish your meal it'll soon be time to go to the country." She opened the door wide to the dining room, motioned with her hand and urged us to have dinner now. She was used to our impatience. Since we were very hungry we hurried into the dining room.

Around three thirty I heard my parents and the rest of the family come upstairs from the store below. I gulped down the rest of my dinner, carried my empty plate to the kitchen to let Ingebjorg wash it, and hurried to my room, which I shared with two other brothers, and picked up what I was to take to Vikhammer. Halfway out the door I remembered my jigsaw. Crawling under my bed, I found it there among a number of pairs of shoes, and put it in the suitcase with my other "treasures."

In the kitchen Mama and Ingebjorg were packing food and clothing needed during the summer. Some food had been left at Vikhammer when we went there early in May to make the villa ready for summer. The grass had been burned to make it grow better during the summer; the windows were washed; and every room was aired out to dispose of the stagnant, musty air collected during the long winter months. After winter it felt good to see the place where we would spend the summer. These were happy days in our lives.

Ingebjorg Kommermo came to us after she had seen an ad in the local paper for a maid to work in a large family. She applied for the position and was hired on the spot. Ingebjorg had been with us for three years and from the beginning felt right at home with my family. She was born north of Trondheim in a place called Mo i Rana, where it was cold most of the time. She was almost six feet tall. Her features were fair, and with her blue eyes and blond hair she looked like a typical Norwegian. She spoke with a sing-song dialect which was common among those who were born in the northern part of Norway. It hadn't taken her long to relieve my mother of many of her duties and responsibilities. She made life much easier for Mama.

"Is everybody ready?" Leopold made his presence known. "I haven't got all day. Ready or not I'm leaving." He had gotten the family car out of the garage, and was waiting to load it with all the packages and clothing he expected all of us to have ready. My brother Leopold wasn't known for his patience. However, since it seemed to be a family trait, none of the rest of us were known for our patience either.

"Have a cup of coffee and some cookies Leopold, while we get everything together." Ingebjorg suggested.

"I'll give you thirty minutes, then I'm leaving. Ready or not I'm leaving."

"And what will you have to eat when you get to Vikhammer?" Mama looked at him with a smile. She knew how eager everyone was to get to the country.

"I'll wait." Leopold mumbled to himself, though

he wasn't happy about it. "But," he continued, "who will go in the car? With all that stuff you're making ready there probably won't be any room for anybody, including me. Anyway, hurry up!" Satisfied that he had complained enough, he went into the dining room to enjoy his coffee.

By five o'clock everything was packed in the car. As Leopold had predicted, there wasn't enough room left for all of us. A nice selection of mother's plants took up considerable space in the back seat and she protected them like children. When she had them sitting in the window sills and the sun was shining directly on them, she would shade them by placing newspapers, printed in Yiddish that had come from America, in front of the plants. When Leopold spotted that, he would rip the papers from the windows and told my mother not to do that again. He was ashamed to have Yiddish newspapers seen by passers-by. Mama never listened to him.

Prior to our move to the country a loyal worker named Trygve, had used his big truck and transported a lot of our stuff to the country. He unloaded his truck and placed everything where mother had told him, locked the doors to the villa and returned to Trondheim. At the end of summer he would move it all back to our apartment. He was always reliable, always on time, and always smiling.

With Mama taking the front seat next to Leopold, who was driving the car, Abel, Sam and I squeezed into the back seat. The rest of the family would take the train. Amidst "good-byes" and "drive safely" the 1931 four-door Studebaker sedan moved slowly away from the curb and we were on our way. Soon we'd be at Vikhammer.

The Studebaker was a much quieter car than my father's first automobile, a Stutz open roadster. I think it was called a Stutz Bear Cat. The steering wheel was on the right side and the engine made so much noise that a horn was not required. The Stutz didn't have a fuel pump. The fuel was transferred from the main gasoline tank to a container above the engine by moving a rod on the dashboard in and out. Gravity allowed the gasoline to flow into the carburetor and it would be at least another 15 minutes before the same procedure had to be repeated. The driver, who was either Heiman or Leopold, would dress in a large trenchcoat wearing a cap turned backwards. Large goggles and gloves completed the outfit. They looked very impressive.

    The Studebaker was smaller than the Stutz. The drive to Vikhammer took around 30 to 45 minutes, depending upon the mood of the driver; in this case it was Leopold. During the trip everybody riding with him had to remain silent, otherwise Leopold couldn't concentrate on the driving. The slightest disturbance would make him very agitated and send him through the roof.

    At one time during the journey Mama got warm and took off her hat. Looking for a place to hang it, she found a knob on the dashboard and pulled it out. That was perfect for her hat. A couple of minutes later the engine started to cough and sputter and was about to stop. Leopold became very nervous, and began checking all the gauges. They showed normal. Then he looked to his right where Mama's hat was hanging. In a flash of anger he yanked the hat off the knob, threw it in Mama's lap, and pushed the knob into the dashboard. The engine revived and all returned to normal. Poor Mama, she didn't realize that the knob she had pulled out was the choke. Her doing that had just about stopped the engine. To us, the event was hilarious. Not daring to make a sound, we muffled our sounds as best as we could and laughed heartily on the inside. There were no more mishaps and we finally arrived at Vikhammer.

I was the first one out of the car, crawling over packages and plants Mama had brought along. I found my little suitcase and headed down to the villa.

"What's the hurry? Don't go empty-handed. Take some of the packages with you." It was Leopold who had stopped me in my tracks. Reluctantly, I returned to the car and took a few of the bundles and carried them down to the villa.

"Don't spend too much time down there." he called after me. "There are many more bundles and plants to carry down."

"Yes, yes, I'll be back." But I didn't tell him when.

Leading down to our summer place was a narrow path consisting of pure clay, which on a rainy day became slicker than an ice rink. As a little boy, to me, the path seemed to be many miles long, but it actually was only about 200 feet.

On both sides of this trail a wire fence enclosed the properties along the path. A white house was on the right and a red one with a thatched roof was on the left. In season, the red house had the best apple trees. I remember we were allowed to pick only the apples that had fallen on the ground. When we didn't find any apples on the ground we just shook the trees. Presto! Apples covered the ground like manna from Heaven.

At the end of the trail I made a left turn, and our villa was another 100 feet away. When Papa purchased the summerhouse in 1918 it was one of the largest homes in the area. I was born there and spent every summer at the villa. From the outside it was quite an impressive structure. It was constructed from heavy timber and stained a dark brown. The window frames were painted white, which made an interesting contrast. The roof was covered with slate tile. From a distance it looked like a church because it had a tower that could be mistaken for a steeple. At the top of the tower was an iron banner with the date "1918". The tower provided a clear view across the railroad tracks and across the fjord. The villa's front faced the road above, and it was the back of the house that had the view of the fjord.

The house was dark and damp because the trees on the hillside surrounded it, except for the left side where the villa was very close to a granite hill.

There were two entrances to the villa. The one, (straight ahead and on the same level as the path) takes you up a few steps and across the porch with white painted woodwork. This brings you into the kitchen. From there you enter the living/dining room. The other entrance, (at a lower level of the path) was reached by a steep stairway of 17 steps that takes you to an entry-hall/game room. Inside there, a door to the left brings you into the living/dining room.

Considering this was only a summer home, the kitchen was quite large with a walk-in pantry, and an electric cooking stove with four burners and an oven. There was also a large wood burning stove and oven. In addition, there was an abundance of cupboards and drawers so that dishes and flatware could be stored when the house was closed for the winter. There was also a small cast iron-enameled sink on the wall next to the door leading to the living/ dining room for washing dishes. There was no water heater so we had to boil water for dishwashing.

In addition to being used for the preparation of the meals, the kitchen was also a meeting place. It was a favorite spot for a small gathering. We kids would bring our special friends there. Our sisters would slip into the kitchen to share secrets and the latest "news." Here, we three boys had all our meals during the summer time. After each meal the dishes were washed- -paper plates and cups, not yet an option in Norway, would have been a dream come true.

The kitchen was a friendly place. I always felt at home there, and there was no other place I'd rather be than the kitchen. I loved to watch Ingebjorg make lefse and potato cakes on the electric burners. Whenever Mama felt that my two brothers and I, had suffered long enough from our own "cooking" she would send Ingebjorg out to the villa, and for a few days we would have delightful meals. To top it all Ingebjorg would also wash the dishes, but insisted that we help her. It was either that or no breakfast.

At other times, at home in Trondheim, Mama prepared the most delicious meat cakes in heavy gravy, boiled a lot of potatoes and cooked fresh peas and carrots. Adding freshly baked bread she put all that food in separate containers. Then she placed this heavenly food in two baskets and carried them to the railroad station. When the train arrived she convinced the conductor to take the food on the train and drop it off at the Vikhammer station.

We eagerly waited at Vikhammer for the train to arrive. The conductor always carried the two precious baskets off the train and delivered them to Abel and me. He would smile "This food smells awfully good, and if you hadn't met the train I would have had a wonderful lunch and dinner with probably something to spare."

We hurried back to the villa before all that wonderful food got cold and feasted for a few days.

Just beyond the kitchen was the living/dining room. It was about 20 feet square, with a fireplace in the middle of one wall. This had been added after the villa had been completed. It protruded four feet from the wall into the living room. It was made of brick that had been painted bright red, and the grout between the bricks was coated with a bright white paint. It was very colorful.

This being the only source of heat on cold days, and there were a number of them during the summer, we usually gathered very close around the fireplace. Neighbors would drop in on those cold days and we'd wind up the gramophone, and soon there was dancing and laughter ringing through the room and flowing throughout the villa. Obtaining firewood was always a problem. The only wood we could find was "green," and sometimes it smoked more than it burned.

A piano occupied part of the opposite wall. It was a good instrument as long as you didn't touch the keyboard. If you did, no matter how well you played, the piano would ruin the performance and make the melody sound like a honky-tonk tune played in the "Last Chance Saloon."

A large dining room table in the middle of the room could seat 14 people or more if you insisted. An old sofa with a genuine imitation leather covering was next to the fireplace. Next to it was a bookshelf and a tall china cabinet. A few odd chairs scattered around the room completed the furnishings. The floor was covered with linoleum. Next to the ceiling and going all around the room, there was a wide white border on which Leopold, with great patience and skill, had painted the traditional "Rose Paintings." It made the room very colorful and gave it an interesting look.

On the far wall and to the right was a little room that was used for private conversation or as a reading room. There was space for only two chairs and a small sofa. Here, if you listened really hard, you could hear the latest edition of the best "news" and gossip, told with captivating, glib tongues. It was related in a very confidential and very authoritative tone. Believe me!

Entering the living/dining room from the kitchen and going through a door on the right you would come into another small room that doubled as an entry hall and game room. This was the main entrance at the top of the long stairway. Here we played bridge and chess when it rained or when there was nothing else to do. These games became a challenge to all of us as we honed our skills to defeat our opponents. Sometimes a friendly game could turn into a tournament of knights on spirited stallions. What fun!

Directly across the room from the entrance was a narrow wooden stairway that had a sharp curve close to the top, and that led you to the second floor. A turn to the right brought you into a small hallway with a very large bedroom on the right, and my parent's bedroom on the left. Their bedroom suite, which was quite large, had two single beds, each against opposite walls on one end of the room, and a large table with several comfortable chairs, and a small sofa on the other end. By the door was their own private sink. There was no bathroom inside. But we had a fine outdoor plumbing unit built from the finest pinewood, and made to look like a guesthouse.

To get to the outdoor bathroom facility you would go out through the kitchen and down the porch stairs. Turning right from the foot of the stairs you entered a heavily wooded hillside. There, hidden among the trees was the outdoor "resting-place." You would have to climb several wooden steps to reach the door. It was quite a walk, and a very, very long one if you were ever in a hurry.

From my parents' bedroom another door took you out onto a large deck which was directly above the entry hall/game room. From this deck you had a view towards the fjord, over the surrounding large trees. Mama enjoyed doing her mending out on the deck. Whenever the sun could break through the clouds in the morning, this became a very comfortable place to have breakfast.

The other larger bedroom contained five beds. Those who retired early were fortunate enough to find an empty bed. One bed was so wide three people could sleep there at the same time. It was known as the "family bed." The latecomers had to climb one more flight of stairs to the third floor, where there were two rooms. The first one had two beds and was occupied by our two sisters. The second one, had three beds, and was for when our sisters had their girl friends stay over. These two rooms had sloping ceilings. The one room window looked out over the porch, and the room of my sisters had a great view over the fjord.

To reach the tower area, you had to climb the wooden circular stairway from the second floor. This brought you to the lookout, which was the highest observation point in the villa. It was an area no more than four feet square with a wooden bench all around the walls. Here the view was spectacular. You could see all the way across the fjord, a distance of 25 miles.

On Sundays a number of relatives would come to visit us at the villa. Sometimes there could be as many as a dozen additional people coming for dinner. My parents were always generous, and showed sincere hospitality to all who came to visit. Fortunately, Ingebjorg was available to help Mama prepare the meals. Both of them worked so hard on those Sundays, and by the time all the visitors had left, Mama and Ingebjorg were worn out.

In the midst of my reminiscing I heard Leopold calling from the road. Expecting trouble from him for not having returned to the car to help unload, I hurried downstairs, through the kitchen, out the door and ran as fast I could. All the way up to the car, I hoped the packages had already been carried in by someone else. But they hadn't.

"Where have you been? You better realize that you have responsibilities. You will be out here all summer and there will be much for you to do, so you might as well start now."

I had heard that same old tune many times before. "Yes, of course, I know, I know," I mumbled as he loaded me up with the rest of the bundles. "Hurry up with these and carry them carefully to the house. Mama will have supper ready in a few minutes. Before you run down that steep narrow path, try to remember you are carrying, among other things, eggs for Sunday morning breakfast. They are in that brown bag on top of everything else. Good luck and don't fall." For a change he smiled as if he knew that I'd break every egg in the bag.

Very cautiously, I walked sideways down the first approach to the narrow trail leading to the villa. With a great deal of grunting I managed to get to the kitchen without dropping anything, not even the eggs.

"What's in the sack?" Mama asked.

"Eggs! I didn't break one." I was proud of that.

She opened the sack and took a look. "No wonder you didn't break any of them. There are no eggs here, only a few rocks, in the shape of eggs. Where are the eggs? I'll need them for breakfast in the morning." She looked very disturbed and started to look all over the kitchen counters and in the pantry. "Could I have forgotten---?"

"Here they are," Leopold stood smiling in the doorway proudly holding up the bag of eggs. He took a delighted stance, as if he had single-handedly captured a wild lion. "I wasn't about to take any chances with you." He looked at me with a frown. "The way you ran down the path you could easily have broken all of them."

"But I couldn't because I didn't carry any eggs. You sure know how to discourage me!" I walked out of the kitchen in a huff. I was angry at him and Mama as they stood in the kitchen laughing at the incident. But it wasn't funny to me.

On the outside I saw the woodshed that was right under the entry hall/ game room. I remembered that a few years earlier my brother Abel and I took on a project that had a disastrous result. The idea was good, but the planning was almost nonexistent.

We were building a toy tank from what we thought was scrap wood. It was a tank that, according to the design, would fit over a young boy like a tent, and could be carried with ease. But we made the tank bigger than the design called for, and from wood that had been left out in the rain for years. The end result was a "toy" tank so heavy that ten grown men couldn't have lifted it. But we had fun building it anyway.

It got even funnier when Leopold discovered what we had done. It was Leopold's responsibility at the end of the summer to cover the steep stairway to the front entry of the villa. This cover protected the steps from the heavy snow and ice during the harsh winter. He used the same wood for this protection year after year. This was the "scrap wood" we had used to build the tank. Upon being discovered, Abel and I ran off in opposite directions to escape Leopold's wrath. Our tank building days were over for good!

I started to walk towards the beach, which was down a narrow footpath covered by grass and tree branches, through a wooden gate built by the railroad company, across the railroad tracks, through another gate on the other side, and there was the beach. Several adults were readying the float to be towed out from the shore and anchored in deep waters. It was used for a place to swim to, sunbathe on, and then swim back to shore. At high tide the distance out was about 200 feet. The structure was kept afloat by six empty steel drums. The week before, repairs had been made and an undercoating of tar had been applied. It was now ready to be turned right side up and "launched" for another season.

With great effort and a lot of "Push!," "Lift!" and "Watch out, here she comes!" the float was finally turned over. Now the men had to carry, push and pull it, to get it down to the water, about fifty feet away.

"Stay away, Aron, you'll only get hurt if you try to help. This is too dangerous for you. The best way you can help is to stay away." I wanted to give them a hand, but didn't realize it was for my own good that they didn't let me. With loud grunting and "Everybody together now: one, two, three - - lift!," the float was carried over a number of boulders to the waters edge. "Hurrah! We made it on the first try!" they congratulated themselves.

"Get into the rowboat, Olaf, and tie a rope to the float. Don't forget to tie the other end to your rowboat," one of them teased.

"Of course, you think I was born stupid?"

Large rocks were carried onto the float for an anchor. A rusty old anchor chain was wrapped around the rocks and held together with some wire.

"We need three more strong fellows in the boat. This thing is heavy, rowing is gonna be tough. Who'll volunteer? Not you, Aron, you aren't strong enough."

Within seconds the boat had the necessary complement, and out to sea they went. There was a little arguing about how far out to take the float, because they had to consider how close to shore it would be at low tide. Finally they all agreed on a place. Two of the fellows from the boat jumped on to the float and dropped the "anchor." They untied the rope from the float and rowed back to shore. The float would be there for the whole summer for all of us to enjoy.

Seeing that my "help" wasn't needed, I decided to explore the rest of the beach in hopes of finding some of the boys I hadn't seen since last summer. I walked past a shed that had a dirt floor. It was used for a boat storage during the winter. But it wasn't in good condition. The sway backed roof and the way the structure was trying to maintain its composure, clearly indicated it had seen better days. It had turned that way when, over many years, a number of people climbed up on the roof to sunbathe. It was probably more than the roof could support. Fortunately it didn't collapse during my years there.

I followed a narrow dirt lane to the other part of the beach, and to my disappointment all was quiet. I looked in both directions, sort of studying the area. From where I was standing there was a stretch of grass for about 30 feet. Beyond that there was a space of various sized boulders that extended to the waters edge. At high tide most of the boulders would be under water. At low tide not only were the boulders exposed, but to us kids it seemed like we could walk for miles with the water not getting any higher than our armpits.

As I stood there and looked over the water I remembered the time I almost drowned and was rescued by Asne.

It was a warm summer day, and I was going to practice the swimming instructions I had learned earlier. Being only 10 years old I had carried my inflatable "wings" out into the water, which was at high tide. I hadn't told anybody what I was doing, but Asne saw me and followed. She watched from a big rock that extended out into the water near me. I slipped the "wings" under my arms and stepped into deeper water. But for some reason the "wings" got away from me, and I went under. Twice I came up, each time I yelling for help, and was going down for the third time when Asne reached out, grabbed my arm and pulled me out. I was glad that she had saved my life. After that incident I practiced constantly, and finally became a good swimmer.

The thought of how much fun we kids would be having here this summer filled me with anticipation and excitement.

Little did I realize that in a few years this happy time would only be a memory.

Turning back toward the villa I heard the familiar sound of the train whistle coming from around the bend. It would stop at a small station, not more than just a platform, and then the next stop was Vikhammer.

Waving to those on the train I spotted the family members who had "volunteered" to take the train instead of trying to squeeze into the car. Running down to the train station, I crossed the tracks and met them just as they were getting off the train.

It was a typical country station. A small, wooden building painted in a buff color with dark brown trim. A big sign on the front of it read "Vikhammer." Inside, was a spotless waiting room with shining, clean linoleum on the floor, and hard benches for those who wanted to wait inside for the scheduled train. A loud, rhythmic, "tick-tock" came from a clock, encased in a highly polished cherry wood case, displayed on the wall. There was a station mistress who opened the ticket window just 10 minutes before the arrival of a train. That gave you just enough time to buy a ticket to your next destination. When she wasn't busy selling tickets, or taking care of the incoming freight, she planted a flower garden. This made the station area look more like a home than a public facility. If you walked to the back of the building you'd see a small apartment where she lived -- all year.

"Sure glad you're here," Asne spoke up, "Now you can carry the milkpail, the potato sack and the bread," she pointed to them on the station platform. The conductor had helped carry off the luggage they had brought along, and much of it was food.

"What are you going to carry?"

"These." and she pointed to a lot of Napoleon cakes and pastries.

"But they are light."

"That's why I'm carrying them. You are stronger than I, and it won't hurt you to use the muscles you've got. Hurry now, so we can catch up with the others." She pointed down the fenced path that followed alongside the railroad tracks. With that she picked up her responsibility and walked on ahead. I followed her with the milkpail in one hand and the bread and potatoes in the other.

"But what would you have done if I hadn't come? You would have to carry it all. Wouldn't you?"

"No, I knew you'd be here. You always met us at the station last year."

She was right. I would often meet the family at the station. When they came by car, I would be up on the road waiting for them.

"How was the train ride? Did you see anybody else?"

"I talked to Martin and Otto Mikalsen. They're looking forward to being here this summer." Asne knew I'd be glad to know they were coming this year.

"The way you run around all day when they are here, don't eat properly, swim for hours and don't get out for a rest -- it can be dangerous! So take it easy. You need to preserve your strength for school when it starts in August. That isn't far off, you know. That'll be your last year; and then what'll you do?" She kept on talking until we came to the villa, and then she dropped the conversation and concerned herself with what to do that evening. Asne could talk at 500 words a minute with gusts up to 800.

Otto and Martin were my age and were well behaved and nice to be around. (During the Nazi occupation Otto was sent to a concentration camp and worked to death by the Nazis.) Their parents had a large villa close by, which they used only during the summer as we did. They also had a large barn on their property, and when it was filled with hay all the children in the area (and there could be quite a few) got to play there. We had lots of fun! The barn became a field of exploration and imagination -- pretending we were on a big game hunt and waiting in silence for the "game" to make its appearance. Whoever turned up, after we had taken our position, became the target, provided it wasn't an adult.

There was no bailing machine on the property so the hay was placed loose in the barn. It was great fun to play in the freshly dried hay, feel its coarseness and inhale its friendly aroma. The hay would stick to our perspiring bodies, but that was soon washed off when we jumped in the fjord to cool off.

This was Saturday, our first weekend at the villa this summer, and it was time for supper. Asne led the way into the kitchen, still talking as if her life depended on it. She was in a hurry to talk with the rest of the family about summer plans. However, there was another, important subject that had forced itself on the family as well as all of Norway, the world situation.

More and more the uncertainties in the world were being discussed openly. There were rumors about the possibilities of war breaking out, and we kids found security and protection in the family structure. The newspapers had carried reports about the re-armament of Germany that was contrary to the surrender agreement Germany had signed in 1918. There was a worldwide outcry, but nothing more. No one at that time thought there would be another war, certainly not in our lifetime.

Supper, which Mama had prepared, consisted of open-faced sandwiches, milk, and fish that had been cooked before we left home. Poor Mama, whether she was in the city or in the country, it was work for her. She didn't get much rest.

The meal finished I wondered what to do next, when I heard Leopold's voice, "Aron, come and help me with the garden. There is so much that needs to be done, and Monday I'll have to return to the city."

Reluctantly I agreed to help him, but my heart wasn't in it. I'd rather sit and listen to the family talk about this and that, but Leopold was insistent so I followed him.

Outside I was told to get the rake and shovel and to "start digging there," he pointed to an area overgrown with weeds. "When you have eliminated all the weeds and raked the area smooth, we can plant flowers and vegetable seeds."

"But it'll take me all summer to get the weeds

out, and by that time it'll be too late to plant anything before school starts."

"Quit complaining and start working." With that he went to take care of other chores.

I had to admit that it was Leopold, out of all the rest of us, who made certain that the villa was well kept. It was he who did all the repair work, the weeding and spraying, caring for the berry bushes, and we had many of them--with four varieties of berries. He even tended to all the trees we had on the property and saw to it that they wouldn't overgrow the land.

I have many fond and happy memories from our times at the villa. Memories of security and peace. Memories of protection, and that somebody cared for me. One such memory stands out, and it has been a constant reminder during all these years.

One morning during the week, when only Sam, Abel and I were there, I was sleeping in my father's bed. I was awakened by a sound that I shall never forget. As I listened closely I recognized it as clothes being washed on a washboard. It sounded so good. To me it was a very secure sound. I knew that somebody cared. Ingebjorg had come out to the villa early that morning and was busy with the chores. That sound of clothes being washed on a washboard, has always been with me, and has continued to give me a secure feeling, as it did so many years ago.

Summers at the villa were coming to a close, and 1937 was among the last years my family spent by the fjord. Sooner than expected a great tragedy, followed by enormous difficulties and uncertainties, came to all.

Chapter 4

Tragedy Strikes

Fortunately Papa didn't live to witness the rape of Norway by the Nazis and the deportation of a large part of Norway's Jewish population to German concentration camps and certain death. This was Hitler's "final solution to the Jewish problem." (Of the 767 Jews deported from Norway only 26 came back alive after the end of the war. Those who were not deported had already escaped to Sweden or other countries.)

On January 7, 1938, Papa passed away. What I remember about him is that he was a hard and consistent worker, whether in his store or in the Jewish community. He was a stern man yet at the same time, very generous. At one time he gave a large gift to the Tuberculosis Center (he had been suffering from that disease for many years.) He asked me to deliver that gift, a check, to their office. When the clerk opened the check she exclaimed "Oh my, such a large contribution." I also remember when I was 10 years old he bought two tricycles, one for Abel and one for me.
But I didn't know much about my father and nothing about his life in Lithuania before coming to Norway. To my recollection he never talked about the early years in his homeland, and I didn't have the courage to ask him. In those days a youngster never

engaged an older person, especially one's father, in a conversation concerning what took place in his earlier years. I'm sorry that I knew so little about him. I suppose he was so busy with his business he didn't take the time to talk about it.

During his lifetime in Norway he had managed, without even trying very hard, to provoke most of the Jews in the community to dislike towards him for one thing or another. It was obvious that diplomacy and patience were not his strong points. He would often make fun of and belittle others whenever he had an occasion and would also intimidate many people in a disgraceful and hateful manner. Why he exhibited such an inconsiderate behavior towards the other Jews was perplexing to many. He was a man who many feared, and many respected him.

Through all his life he was a hard worker. He labored at all times, except on the Sabbath and during the high holidays, and he expected everybody in our family to be as occupied in the store as he was. With nine sons and two daughters, plus a few hired clerks, there was enough help for all the work at hand. He never encouraged any of us children to take up any other career, except for the eldest, the doctor, and two other sons who became dentists. The rest of us had to work in Papa's stores and be content with that.

Papa suffered from several complications in his illness, and at the time he passed away he was in a tuberculosis hospital in Lillehammer, at that time a 10-hour train ride from Trondheim. The day before he died, the hospital called Mama and reported that Papa had suffered a setback and that the prognosis was not good. Mama then called David, a practicing physician in Oslo. He caught the first train to Lillehammer. For him it was less than a two hour trip. He arrived in time to see father alive but very weak. Nothing could be done now to save Papa's life.

A few hours later he watched as father slipped away. David remembered the many happy times he and Papa had spent together as he was growing up. Tears came to his eyes as he realized that the old days were gone forever. All he had now were the memories.

Mama took the first available train to Lillehammer. Heiman traveled with her. The train left Trondheim at 8 P.M. and arrived in Lillehammer at 6 A.M. On the way Mama fell asleep and had a dream in which Papa appeared to her. He stretched out his hand to her and said, "Come with me Mary," as he often called her. She reached out to him, but discovered that his hand was cold. Immediately she withdrew her hand, for she knew he was dead. On awakening Mama was certain that Papa had already died before she could get to him. Mama was right.

The same day Oskar was sent to Mr. Rognmoe, the carpenter who for over many years had done a great deal of work for Papa.

"My father has died." he told Mr. Rognmoe, "We need a pine casket for his burial. Make sure you use wooden dowels to hold the boards together, our religion doesn't permit the use of nails. Father's body will arrive by train from Lillehammer tomorrow. The funeral will be in two days. Do you think you can have it ready by then?"

"You can be sure I'll have it ready, and I'll deliver it to your home." After a short pause, "So old Mr. Abrahamsen has died! He was a good man. I'm sorry to see him go. Your father and I had become good friends." He turned away to wipe away a tear.

In Lillehammer Papa's body was placed in a casket borrowed from a local funeral director. The lid was not placed over the top because there was a cross on it. This was a typical casket used for a Christian burial. Instead, a white sheet was placed over the body. On arrival in Trondheim, the casket was brought to our apartment, the body was transferred to the pine casket and placed over two sawhorses in the salon, and the door was closed. The borrowed casket and its lid were returned to Lillehammer.

As soon as Mama and Heiman arrived home, Mama went to work sewing funeral clothes for Papa. She called in some of the other Jewish women, and all of them went downstairs to the store. There they took a bolt of white cotton cloth, cut it to the size they thought was right, and started to sew. It was a very simple garment, a pair of pants and a shirt.

While that was going on, several Jewish men entered the salon where Papa's body had been placed; and with the Rabbi in charge, they began to wash his body. My brother Leopold asked if he could help. After a few minutes he came out with tears flowing and said, "I can't do it any longer. It is too difficult for me." When the washing was completed Papa was dressed in the newly made burial clothes. The white yarmulka (skullcap) was placed on his head. An important part of the burial preparation is the placing on the body the phylacteries that is in two parts. One part of the [3]phylacteries was wrapped around his left arm and the other part was placed around his head. These Papa used in his daily morning prayers for many years. Finally his frail body was wrapped in his large prayer shawl. The pine lid was then placed on the casket.

In our apartment all the mirrors were covered with a thick white cloth. All of us boys had a cut made in our garments, and after the funeral we had to sit [4]Shivah for seven days. During that seven days we were not to shave and we had to sit on hard wooden stools.

---

[3] Narrow leather bands, called Tefillin, wrapped around the left arm and around the head during morning .prayers. Attached to the band is a small square box containing Old Testament text including the "Shema".
[4] Traditional period of mourning among Orthodox Jews

On the day of the funeral several strong men carried the casket down two floors to a waiting horse drawn hearse. (According to Orthodox rules the body had to be placed in the grave 24 hours after death. But because Papa's body had to be transported from Lillehammer, the burial could only take place as soon as possible.)

Mama and my two sisters hurried into a waiting taxi. All nine sons gathered behind the hearse for the long walk to the Jewish cemetery. All of us had black armbands on our left sleeves. We were positioned in two rows. Starting on the right, David, the eldest son took his place, and on his left the next in age until the first row was filled with the five oldest. The four youngest were in the back row.

In January the days are very short. If the funeral was to take place during daylight hours there was no time to waste. In less than two hours it would be dark and very cold.

At one o'clock the funeral procession, led by the hearse, began. Through the large, highly polished windows one could see the outline of a casket draped with a black cloth. There were no flowers. The Jewish religion did not permit that.

With great caution and measured steps we moved slowly and carefully over the icy streets. There were no spectators along the route. Only a few passers-by stopped for a moment in the frosty afternoon, took a quick glance at us and hurriedly moved on before the cold, damp air got to them. They had to move on to keep warm.

The sun, low on the horizon, hung like a faded piece of yellow paper ready to disappear at any moment. There wasn't much warmth coming from it on this day.

Snow had been in the streets since mid-October. With all the snow that had blanketed the city since then, the cobblestone streets were heavily snow packed, making them very slippery.

It really wasn't a good day for a funeral.

At the cemetery ritual prayers were said by the Rabbi. After prayers the casket was lowered into the grave. Then a shovel was passed to each of us brothers, and we cast a small amount of earth on the casket. As each shovel of soil hit the casket we heard a muted "thump." To me it sounded like both a tribute and a final goodbye to Papa.

I remember walking home with Leopold who commented on how low the sun was on the horizon. It would soon disappear, and darkness would swallow up the city. It wasn't even 2:30 in the afternoon.

After Papa's death a number of global events took place that eventually caused our entire family to be pulled apart to various parts of the world, completely changing the future for all of us.

Everything was rapidly changing for the worst.

Chapter 5

Before the Storm

Changes were in the air!
Everybody suspected that something was going to happen but they didn't want to say what; they were afraid to think that far. Government officials as well as the entire population felt it. Tempers easily flared up. Women and children cried over nothing. The atmosphere was explosive. Nobody knew when it would happen. But all knew it would happen sometime - - perhaps too soon.

The quiet tension, the feelings of instability and the uncertainty brought about a sensitive apprehension that unsettled just about everybody. It was like a conspiracy of silence. One day it would explode - - - and then what? The government officials and the military knew that too, but were reluctant, in a diplomatic way, to do anything about it. "It is too big for us, too much that can't be done. The events must take the course they are destined for."

With Hitler in charge of Europe's destiny everybody speculated, and rightly so, that the unwelcome guest of war was coming. But when, how and where would it start? Who would be involved in this next war and whenever it started how long would it last? It became obvious that a violent political action, a war, was the only solution that could be seen on the horizon.

Above everything, the Norwegians desired to continue living in freedom, and with a measure of stability--even in the midst of great uncertainty. Naturally, in spite of all their concerns life went on. People wanted peace, some wanted peace at any price. How could a small country like Norway defend itself with outdated equipment and untrained soldiers? Besides, what would Hitler want with such a small country?

The Norwegians and its government were in complete darkness about Hitler's agenda. If they had only read "Mein Kampf" and believed what Hitler had written, they might have been better able to defend themselves. But like so many other nations, Norway was naïve and not "street smart" when it came to dealing with dictators like Adolf Hitler.

Shortly after Papa's death Mama took a more active part in the store. After her children were born she had more than enough to do, even with the help of Ingebjorg, to take care of the household and her family. During those years she hadn't spent much time in the store. But now, with most of her family grown, and a full-time maid to take care of all the chores, she decided to become more involved again in the business.

Afterall, this had been her first career and she had opened her own store long before my Papa did. Mama believed that working in the store would be a welcome diversion for her and she looked forward to it. When she discovered that the store carried a large debt she was horrified. She had forgotten how the financial side of business was carried out. Debt to her was identical to poverty. She cried and wept, believing that all she had worked for was ruined and that she would have to sell her home and all her possessions in order to get out of debt. Being in debt was to her a disgrace and a black mark on her character. She cried and moaned for a long time, and worried constantly night and day over the debt.

Heiman explained to her over and over again that being in debt was no disgrace. That was the way business was done these days. Mama still couldn't understand why we had to be in debt. And when she realized that the store and all the properties were in her name and that she was responsible for paying that debt, she cried a whole lot more. She was reminded that in order to buy inventory, and that happened several times a year, money had to be available to pay for it. The bank advanced money for these purchases, and the loan was paid back over several months with interest favorable to the bank.

That made Mama greatly concerned. For if she also had to pay interest she would be losing money. But Heiman explained that the amount of interest she had to pay, including the freight for the purchased goods, was added to the retail price of the merchandise. Mama felt better for a while, but continued to worry about the debt the stores had to assume for their operation. After several months she got used to it; however, at no time did she ever like it or feel comfortable with it.

In the spring of 1938 Heiman obtained a loan from the bank, using our warehouse as security, and purchased a very fine gift shop in the central part of town. He asked Oskar to manage it. This was Oskar's opportunity to provide a living for himself and Lilly whenever they got married.

Two of my brothers, Julius and Jacob, were dentists and practiced in Trondheim. They were doing very well, except for a problem that could have become quite serious unless it was nipped in the bud. Both of them were known as Dr. J. Abrahamsen, which caused a mix-up in the minds of their patients. Patients of Julius would turn up in Jacob's office, and vice versa. This caused Jacob to take an action that resulted in changing his name from Abrahamsen to Ilevik. He hadn't told anyone about what he planned to do, and no one could persuade him to reveal why he chose Ilevik for his new name. From then on there was a Dr. J. Abrahamsen and a Dr. J. Ilevik in town. The mix-up of patients no longer occurred.

These two brothers were very different in nature as well as in character.

Julius, being five years older than Jacob, was a happy-go-lucky fellow. He was always smiling and took life in easy steps. But he had a "short fuse" when things didn't go his way. Many times it seemed as though he didn't think other people had feelings, and didn't care how much he had hurt them. Julius was the only one in the family who had the fortuitous luck of a gold miner. I am sure that he must have had legions of angels watching over him, and I suppose he kept them all very busy. He was very generous, in that he took care of the dental needs of the family. It wasn't easy to get started in his practice, but after a few years he was doing very well. Of all my brothers he was the shortest one. He was born two months pre-maturely and that might have been the reason for his small stature. Early in life he lost most of his hair, which was a family trait, and he was prone to be overweight; which was not a family trait.

In contrast, Jacob was a refined, quiet gentleman who spoke only when he had something worthwhile to say, for he was a deep thinker. He took great care to be dressed meticulously. He always looked as though he had just stepped out of a showroom. To be in the latest style of fashion was important to him, and he dressed well for every occasion. With light brown hair and gray eyes he could be taken for a Norwegian and not a Jew.

He was an excellent dentist and built his practice with a running start from the beginning.

Patience was his hallmark, while the rest of my family, including myself, had no time for patience. Like the rest of the family (except for Julius) he was slender.

Meanwhile, Hitler managed to stage many more atrocities that unsettled my family, and all the Jews in Norway.

On March 14, 1938, only two months after the death of my father, Hitler invaded Austria, and took that country under his "protection."

To prepare for Hitler's arrival, the Nazis had conscripted the Austrian Jews to scrub the streets of Vienna where Hitler and his entourage would enter the city. While the Jews were on their knees having been forced to do this work, the non-Jewish population was laughing at the Jews and humiliating them to no end.

On that day a Jewish medical student from Vienna, Austria, was a guest in our home. We all listened attentively as the news from Austria was reported over the radio. When the Nazi troops entered Vienna our guest started to cry, his body shook with fear and his face lost all its color. In a hoarse and frightened voice he said that he had to return to his home immediately to be with his parents. Though my family tried to persuade him to stay in Norway where he would be safe, his mind was made up.

"What can you do when you return? You'll be arrested with your family and sent to a concentration camp where your lives will be swallowed in death." my family warned him.

That same evening he boarded the train that would take him to Vienna, Austria.

We never heard from him again. (See notes Pages 96-102).

However, life had to go on in the midst of the turmoil and threats encircling every free democracy. People went to work, planned their vacations, read the local and foreign news and shrugged their shoulders, feeling there was nothing they could do to change the dangerous situation. Many people, like my sister Beile, were still looking forward to getting married.

It was summer 1939!

"Beile, hurry, hurry, there is no time to waste!" Asne insisted. "The wedding coach will be here soon, and you aren't dressed yet." Though it was only 5 o'clock and the wedding wasn't to take place until 7, Asne was very excited. To make sure that she'd be there on time, Asne had been ready for the wedding for several hours. Now she was trying to help Beile get dressed. Neither Asne nor Beile were calm enough to get much accomplished.

"It isn't every day that my sister gets married." Asne said excitedly. "And now," she kept on, "you get a chance to get away from this town and see other cities. Living in Amsterdam will be very exciting for you, and there will be so much to do." She dreamed on out loud. Then she asked, "Will you go to the theater often? There must be a ballet and opera season there. I hope you can attend. Promise me you'll write me all about it. Here in Trondheim, we never have operas or ballet." she complained.

"Asne, you can be lucky there are no operas or ballet in Trondheim, I think they are both boring and meaningless. Now, give me the theater, a drama, and you can have the rest of what you call culture."

Beile started to wave her hands and move her head to give greater emphasis to her convictions about culture. But all it did was to disturb the hairdresser who had been engaged for this occasion. She had to stop until Beile quieted down.

The two sisters were making small talk. As close as they had been all their lives, two girls among nine boys, it was going to be sad to be away from each other. They tried to act as cheerful as they could. Asne was always the outwardly happy and carefree person, so it was natural for her to start and end the dialogue. On this occasion she didn't have to think of what to talk about. This was Beile's wedding day, the oldest of the two girls in our family. It was difficult for either of them to think that after today they would no longer have time to talk for hours on end as they used to do.

"Well, Beile, I don't see any future for myself in this town," Asne continued. "Do you suppose I'll ever have a chance to get away, too?"

"You'll find the right man someday, and get married and have children."

"I hope you're right." Asne sighed quietly. "There's so little to do here. The young people are getting older, and the old people aren't getting any younger. The way I see it there isn't much hope for improvement."

Each knew that the world situation was serious, but how serious none of them realized. Neither of them could fathom that in a few short months their secure world would be history. But they also knew that after today they would be living what seemed like a world apart --- Beile in Amsterdam and Asne in Trondheim.

After a long silence Beile said thoughtfully "Asne, what do you think will happen in the near future?"

"There probably will be war," she answered, "but I hope it will be a short one. War makes everything so inconvenient. The men are in uniform, and the women are left at home. Very inconvenient, very scary and lonely."

Suddenly the door opened "What? - Aren't you ready yet? With all the time you have taken you should have been ready two days ago."

"You're right Mama, I should have been ready, but I'm not. I won't be long," Beile promised. You could hear from Mama's voice that she was getting nervous and upset.

"Let me help you." Mama started to do whatever was necessary. She too was excited but tried not to show it. She had told half of the Jewish community about Beile's wedding, and the other half heard from those she had told. She was so proud and happy.

As she tried to help, memories moved swiftly through her mind. She was losing a daughter and the house would be a little emptier. No longer would she hear Asne and Beile discuss what clothes to wear, who "borrowed" the 4711 perfume and on and on. But it hadn't been so long ago that David, her first born, had moved to Oslo to set up his medical practice and then her husband had died in 1938. "The family is getting smaller. The children will be living so far away." Mama sobbed. She wished they could be closer, or even better, that they would all stay home. Nevertheless, she was glad to have a lot of pictures of the children to remind her of her family.

She began to sing softly "Gedenkt sach kinderlach - - -" a verse from one of her favorite Jewish folk songs. Then she started to cry.

"What are you crying about, Mama?" Beile gently patted her mother's hand. "I'm no longer a little girl. I am a grown woman. Today I'll be married. You are not losing me, Mama. I'll always be your daughter. I won't forget you, even though I'm going away. Benno and I will establish a new home in Amsterdam, and you will come to visit us there!"

"But Beile, it's so far away. Who will look after you?"

"Remember the time when you and Papa sent me to Germany to learn to cook? Well, I know a lot about caring for a home. When you come to visit us I'll make you a Kosher dinner that you'll long remember. So stop crying now, let's enjoy all the excitement!"

"I wasn't crying. I was eating some onions before I came into your room. That's why the tears." she fibbed. Mama was known for eating onions and garlic as if they were candies, and if she were true to her reputation she probably had an assortment of these "delicacies" in one of her dress pockets.

"Listen, - - listen." Asne stood by the open window and pointed down the street.

"What is it, Asne?" Beile asked impatiently. "Don't you hear it? Listen!"

KLOP Klop, KLOP Klop, in a steady cadence through the pleasant summer afternoon. KLOP Klop, KLOP Klop, it came closer. You could hear the difference. The regular horse drawn wagons didn't sound like that. There was no mistaking what it was. The bridal carriage was near.

Traditionally the bride would ride in a specially made carriage. It was made from wood, painted black and highly polished to a mirror-like finish. It was upholstered with black velvet, and had short lace curtains draped across the two large side windows and the very large one in front. Fortunately, and on purpose, the curtains were short enough, only a few inches down from the top, so that they didn't cover too much of the windows. This way the town's people would be able to see who the lucky bride was. The bride would ride alone to the wedding. There was room for only one.

The carriage was pulled by a well-groomed black stallion outfitted with the finest of decorations to suit this festive occasion. The coachman was dressed in his best black suit, a bow tie and silk top hat with a merry plume waving in the air. To make the ride for the bride smoother, the carriage was outfitted with narrow rubber tires, thus the coach, carrying its precious cargo in comfort, toured through many streets on its way to the wedding. Oh yes, it had to be reserved far in advance, because there was only one coach of its kind available in Trondheim.

"Can you hear it, can you?"

"Yes I can."

"Oh my. It's the wedding coach, and it will be arriving here in less than a minute. Ready or not here it comes."

"Oy!"Mama called out as she rushed out of the room to get her hat and coat.

"She thinks she will ride with me to the synagogue. But she'll be surprised. There is room for only one person in that coach, and that one person is me, THE BRIDE." Beile said to Asne.

"Just a minute and I'll check your hair once more." The hairdresser had waited to make last minute adjustments to Beile's curls.

Beile gathered her train and with Asne's help the two walked downstairs holding on to each other.

Each knew these were the last moments they would have together. Both tried to smile and laugh, hoping nobody would notice their tears. It was difficult to leave a secure home where all is peaceful and protected, and to wander out into the world to a strange city, meeting strange people whose language you don't understand. It would be equally difficult to become used to strange customs. Asne and Beile knew from now on they would be far apart. Both living in two different worlds.

The bond between the two, developed over many years, had served as a protection and security against the outside world. Each was quick to defend the other when needed. They had spent hours on end discussing how to find a husband, all about clothes, boy friends, books, movies, people and current events. Finding a husband was discussed more often than any other subject. They agreed that finding a spouse wasn't the easiest task in the Universe, especially with an acute shortage of eligible men in their own town. Beile had found her husband-to-be. Now it was Asne's turn.

They were both greatly concerned about the reports in the newspapers of Germany's fierce persecution of the Jews and like so many others in the Jewish community hoped it would never show its ugly face in Norway. They were both afraid of the future, but that didn't mean they had to stop living.

The carriage had been waiting for only a few minutes when mother came out, followed by Beile.

"My good man, this carriage doesn't look like it can hold two people?"

The coachman saw Mama, with hat in hand, ready to step up to the coach and seat herself inside.

"There is room for only one person, mum, and that's for the bride."

"I am the bride's mother and I want to ride with her to the synagogue." and she started to cry.

"Here comes the bride now." the coachman exclaimed, and gently led Mama away from the carriage, and made room for Beile. Beile and Mama embraced and together they had a little cry. Someone has said that crying is good for the soul. So with tears in their eyes they looked at one another, touched each others face, and looked again as Beile stepped into the carriage.

If Mama had any insight into the immediate future she would not have wanted to know - - - there would be many more of her family, including herself, leaving home sooner than she would have believed.

With a quick tug of the reins the wedding coach was on its way.

The synagogue was filled to capacity. Under a canopy decorated with flowers Kantor Jakobson, who was also the Rabbi, performed the traditional orthodox ceremony that ended with the breaking of a glass under the groom's foot. Laughter and joy filled the synagogue followed by lots of "Mazel Tovs."

Afterwards there was dinner in mother's apartment for over 50 guests.

Though the ominous threats of war had become louder, the ears and eyes of most people in our Jewish community were closed. They didn't want to know what was coming. Only a few saw the signs very clearly and started to prepare for what might come.

Notes for chapter 5

In October 1933, Hitler's Nazi army marched into Sudetenland; that was a hotly disputed border area of Czechoslovakia.

Then another gruesome event took place. On November 9, 1938, the infamous "Kristallnacht" ("Crystal Night" or "night of broken glass") was unleashed. This was an attack by the Nazi troops who were encouraged by their officials to vandalize and destroy all Jewish stores and synagogues. Many buildings were burned while the police stood by and offered no protection for the Jews. The Jews weren't even allowed to defend themselves, nor their properties.

Hitler had already taken away their citizenship making them ineligible for any protection under the new German Constitution. The Jews were declared enemies of the state, and received the same treatment as traitors. Thousands of store windows were smashed, and more than 90 people were killed, most of them Jewish merchants.

The violence was unleashed after a Polish teenager, Herschel Grynspan, assassinated the third secretary of the German embassy in Paris, Ernst von Rath. The teenager said that he was avenging the treatment of his parents in Germany. The Nazis used that incident as an excuse to launch their belligerent attack against a helpless and defenseless people.

The next day the morning paper in Trondheim reported the violence. Hitler issued a decree that levied a fine of 1 Billion Mark against the Jews. He made them responsible for the destruction of the properties and those who were killed during the night. There was an enormous outrage among all the Jews throughout the world, including the two Jewish communities in Oslo and Trondheim, but there wasn't anything they could do against the ravages of the Hitler regime. The Jews could protest all they wanted but that didn't make any difference with Hitler and his Nazis.

The Western powers remained passive and issued a feeble protest. Justice, decency, law and order had vanished from the German world ever since Hitler became its dictator in 1934.

The world was moving towards another raging war at an uncontrolled, staggering and breakneck speed.

Hitler marched to his own violent, treacherous and insidious cadence while the leaders of democracy were cowering to a very different course, one of appeasement and accommodations.

Fear and anxiety overshadowed the hope and aspirations of all nations for a better world. The dream of ending all wars, when the League of Nations was formed after World War I, had vanished like raindrops on the desert floor. The whole world found itself in a situation that seemed to be like that of a pressure cooker and a time-bomb combined. A strong world leader to defy and defeat Hitler's terror was needed. But who was capable of such an undertaking? Only one person showed this resolve and determination. A few years later Winston Spencer Churchill was asked by the king to assume the leadership of Great Britain, and from then Great Britain marched to a drummer of singleness of purpose to defeat the dictatorial Nazi reign of brutality.

Prior to that, Great Britain had been for a number of years on the course of disarmament. A great majority of the people, including many in government circles, had become Pacifists. The population and many of its leaders believed it was immoral to have a strong defense force. Some openly stated that the reason for Hitler's aggression was that Great Britain hadn't disarmed enough. In 1933, a movement that had its start at Oxford Union, under the leadership of Mr. Joad, passed a resolution "That this house will in no circumstance fight for its King and country." (Winston Churchill "The Second World War," Volume 1, P. 77.)

Great Britain had an albatross around its neck. Neville Chamberlain, Britain's Prime Minister, declared "Peace in our time" when on September 30, 1938 he returned to London after a visit with Hitler. Chamberlain was also heard saying "We can do business with Herr Hitler." He was only fooling himself, and in the process deceived his country as well as the entire free world.

Adolf Hitler had promised Chamberlain that Germany had no additional territorial demands after they annexed Sudetenland. However on March 15, 1939, Hitler's army overran Czechoslovakia and took it under their "protection." By now it was evident to the Western European leaders that Hitler and his regime couldn't be trusted. In spite of all this the leaders of France were dangerously indecisive, and were still hoping that an accord with Hitler could be reached.

Meanwhile, they didn't want to antagonize Hitler, and postponed any military action until a more opportune time. They firmly believed that a peace accord with the German dictator would be far better than a prolonged war. "Tomorrow would bring good news" was the common slogan. They just had to wait. They waited and waited for such an accommodation, and the waiting brought about their own demise. [5]

The Allies were playing with a firestorm. It was easier for the Western leaders to procrastinate, allow circumstances to make their decisions and do nothing, thus placing their countries in harms way, instead of

---

[5] In retrospect it is appalling that those who had assumed the responsibility to lead, protect and serve the country and its people, could be so negligent and reckless with their sacred and sovereign duties.(Winston Churchill)

developing and implementing clear plans on how to defeat the Nazi scourge. They seriously wanted to appease Hitler, and through that appeasement scheme they nearly walked right into Hitler's trap and almost sealed their own doom.

At that point Winston Churchill stood virtually alone, facing the oncoming storm as he tried to convince some leaders about Germany's true intent. In May of 1940 he finally was able to swing them over to his side, just before the "cyclone" hit.

With all those threatening events taking place it appeared that an invasion by Hitler's Army was coming closer to all free nations surrounding Germany, including Norway. But most Norwegian believed that this would never happen. However, had they known what was being planned behind their backs they wouldn't have felt so secure in their uncertainties. Norway was going through a phase of denial; yet there were clear signs that should have made the people, and their leaders, think otherwise.

An era of destruction of human dignity had entered upon the scene of world events. Fear and suspicion were building at a rapid rate. Who could be trusted? What could be planned for the future? These were times that called for all free nations to have the determination of their convictions. Finally, the West started to awaken to the terror at hand and was aghast at what they saw when their eyes were opened.

Amidst all this tension and uncertainty the Norwegian people tried to live as if nothing were about to happen. Regardless of the events taking place around them they couldn't stop living. On the one hand there was the hostility and aggression occurring in the countries south of them, and on the other hand there was the necessity to follow human needs and desires, hoping the terror wouldn't reach them.

On August 23, 1939, to add more bewilderment, perplexity and uncertainty to the world situation,

Germany and Russia signed a non-aggression treaty. Had Stalin taken the time to know what Hitler had written in "Mein Kampf" the Russian dictator wouldn't have been so eager to be party to a treaty with him. The deceptive stand that Hitler had assumed was that [6]"One makes alliances only for fighting." A non-aggression pact between two leaders like Hitler and Stalin was an enigma clothed in lies, parading as truth and sincerity.

The Western democracies were at a loss to understand what could be behind such a pact and how it could ever be implemented. A few years earlier Hitler had declared war on Communism, and had made them the enemies of the third Reich. So why had Hitler now changed his mind? Or had he? It turned out later that Hitler had a secret agenda.

Hitler had ulterior motives in getting Stalin to sign such a treaty. No doubt he wanted Stalin to feel "secure" in the "friendship" of his gigantic war machine. At this point Hitler had maneuvered himself between Stalin and the Western Allies in hopes of discouraging them from any counter offensives. He wanted Stalin on his side, for the time being, to give a signal to the West that they were licked, and that he and Stalin would destroy them. His show of power worked.

Hitler was determined to make treaties, and keep them only as long as they would serve his purpose. The Allies gave no sign that they were determined to fight, instead they ran for cover. However, Hitler was also salivating after Russia's rich oil fields in Caucasia. He needed petroleum for his mechanized war vehicles so that he could carry out his ruthless agenda to enslave the whole world. Hitler also had to neutralize Stalin so that Stalin wouldn't interfere with Germany's attack on

---

[6] Klaus P. Fischer "Nazi Germany; A new History"

Poland. The German Chancellor had other plans for Russia; its elimination from the face of the Earth.

This pact came as a blow to the leaders of Western Europe because that treaty, between the Soviet Union and Germany and ill-gotten satellites with such enormous resources, would impede Paris and London from restraining Hitler. At that point it was obvious to all that Stalin was not on the side of the Western Democracies. This alliance gave Hitler free reign, and he could do whatever he wanted without anyone stopping him. He didn't disappoint the Allies, for he lived up to what they feared and suspected. At that time the Allies were vacillating in their decision making. They hadn't made up their minds whether they liked Communism more than Nazism and therefore had made no overtures to Stalin concerning an alliance with them.

The Allies, who had seriously disarmed themselves prior to this, had caved in to Hitler's threats of violence, and felt completely helpless. Numerous meetings and conferences were conducted between Great Britain and France without any resolve. For the time being The United States had decided to stay out of the conflict, and had determined to leave Europe to the Europeans.

[1]Like Pancho Villa, Germany was armed to its teeth. The Western democracies had been maneuvered into a helpless situation. Adolf Hitler with his superiority in men and war machinery had masterminded himself to look like a ferocious lion circling its victims.

The free world was facing a frightening and devastating future. All hope for peace had evaporated, and a curtain of despair and defeat was rapidly descending. The free world didn't realize, nor did they

---

[1] Pancho Villa, orig. Doroteo Arango – Mexican guerrilla leader –(1878-1923)

want to know, that the Nazis planned and practiced the overthrow of human liberty and dignity.

Chapter 6

September 1939 – World War II

When September 1st arrived, the whole world was thrown into the horrors of another war. It turned out to be a war of horrendous proportions, involving most every nation, and millions of people, with catastrophic destruction. Like a nightmare the Nazi forces marched forcefully, and with arrogant violence, on to the world scene.

I was still in Norway. How can I forget it?

Hitler's Army had overrun Poland. This was an "extension" of the summer maneuvers of the German Army, so Hitler declared. Everybody in Norway expected the Polish cavalry to save the country from the invasion. Each day new hope was raised for the Polish people, expecting their famous and efficient cavalry to attack the Germans. But they never did. Little did the Norwegians and the Poles know about modern warfare, and how completely useless a cavalry unit would be against German tanks and fighter planes.

The Polish people had neither the equipment nor the quantity required to be a deterrent against the invasion force. Their military tactics were poorly planned and executed in as much as they had their forces extended all along the frontiers of Poland. With what they had available they had spread themselves dangerously thin. That wasn't all, the Polish military had no central reserve units. The Polish government had a similar attitude as other Western democracies in that they were afraid to mobilize fearing it would provoke Hitler.

Thirty divisions, or two-thirds of the active Army, were almost ready to meet the enemy. However the speed of the invading force and the blitz of the German Air Force made it impossible to sustain an effective defense. 900 Polish airplanes were taken by complete surprise and a number of them were destroyed before they got into action. (Winston Churchill 'The Second World War" Volume 1, P.396)

On September 29th Poland surrendered, the day after Britain and France declared war on Germany. World War I, the war to end all wars, including the League of Nations, had become nothing but a myth. The dream of President Woodrow Wilson had vanished like smoke from a chimney.

But in the minds of the Norwegians, Poland was so far away that few would allow themselves to believe that Hitler would ever invade Norway too. What would Hitler want with their little country? The Norwegians continued to be in denial, believing that everything would remain the same, in spite of what they knew was taking place on the world scene.

As if that weren't enough, a heat wave had hit Norway. It was a very unusual weather pattern. By this time of the year it should be cold and windy --- but not this year. The heat was stifling. The air stood still. There wasn't even the slightest breeze to cool the intense hot air. Everybody remarked repeatedly about this unusual hot, hot weather. Nobody could even remember ever having experienced this kind of tropical weather, particularly in the early fall. This oppressive heat wave was like a prophetic message, "If you think it's hot now, just wait."

Throughout Norway tension continued to build like a storm brewing out of control. This tension was not because of the hot weather, but because of the fear of a Nazi invasion of Norway that would lead to war.

It hadn't been so many years earlier, when in 1934 David had visited Papa in Trondheim. They discussed the rise of Hitler in Germany, and Papa was badly shaken and visibly depressed. He knew what it meant for the Jews and believed Hitler would treat the Jews the same as the Tsar and his government had. A few years later he was to be proven right.

Besides, there was Beile's experience in Germany, when in 1936 she returned there for the second and final session of the cooking school she attended. The train, as usual, stopped at the border, and a German border guard came through the train checking passports. Looking at Beile's passport he asked, "Are you Jewish?"

"Yes. I am Jewish."

Within seconds and with swift contempt he gathered her luggage and in a stern voice told her to follow him off the train. She was taken to the Police station, arrested and then placed under house arrest in a nearby home. For two days she was detained in a small room, where every day she was bombarded with military marches and Hitler's speeches blasting at full volume from the radio. Hitler had ordered all loyal Germans to keep their radios on full volume so as not to miss any of his speeches. To disobey this order was punishable by a fine and prison sentence.

After two days she was placed on the train returning her back to Norway. Anti Jewish propaganda raging through Germany like the black plague made it impossible for her to complete her course in food preparation. This experience made a deep and very frightening impression on Beile.

The people rightfully anticipated that something ominous was about to take place, but when it would come about, and in what form, was unknown to most people, and in many ways that was very fortunate. Sometimes it is merciful that everything isn't known. This would give rise to more worry and more concern as to what events would take place and the timing of these assaults. There were those few however, who not only "knew" what was coming, but who also had made some preparations in case they needed to escape. Among those were my family and a few relatives. They had followed Hitler's rise to power and saw what he was up to. With him in charge of the world events it didn't look very promising for the future of the Jews.

In all this, the people of Norway needed to prepare for any eventuality, if that was at all possible. But not knowing what in particular to prepare for, it became increasingly difficult to do so. They all knew for certain that a war, with Russia or Germany or both was possible, and that was all they had any knowledge of. It was the same old story that had been repeated time and again throughout the history of civilization, that if you don't know what the game is, it is next to impossible to become an active participant.

Towards the end of October 1939 Norway started to mobilize her forces and called up all men who were born in 1920 or earlier. The old cannons were put into operational condition; the military went through drills and mock attacks. The civilian population was instructed about what to do in case of an invasion, be it from land, sea or air. Provisions were stored, first aid courses were given throughout the country, and blackout rehearsals were staged at frequent intervals. But these exercises were not taken seriously. The Norwegians wanted to file the possibilities of war towards the back of their minds. Christmas would soon arrive and that was enough to prepare for.

Rumors were circulated that German merchant vessels had cast anchor in the harbor of Trondheim, and the same rumors were repeated about ships in the harbors of Oslo and Bergen. There the ships lay while Norway was scurrying around getting organized. Some international law prohibited the Norwegian government from boarding and searching these ships.

If the Norwegian government and the military officials knew what was onboard those ships they would have been greatly alarmed.

The situation became very tense as each week passed, and still nothing out of the ordinary happened. It was like walking a tight rope, expecting the line to be cut at any time. The people were clinging to a flimsy hope that the world situation would change for the better any day. Hitler could change his mind about world conquest; he could pull his troops back; he could declare peace with Britain and France, and the world situation would return to its former status quo. Surely tomorrow would be better, much better. There would be security, peace, no worries, and no anxieties. Only peace and tranquillity would reign. Obviously those who hoped for that hadn't read Hitler's "Mein Kampf."

But the big question was what about today? What do we do now? It was as if everyone was waiting for the game to start. The players were on the field, the spectators were in their seats, the cheerleaders were on the sidelines and so were the marching bands. But the referee hadn't arrived and there were no programs available.

In spite of all these uncertainties people managed to keep a cheerful attitude. Business went on as usual. People were preparing for Christmas – a happy season. As November approached, the population became more and more apprehensive and they couldn't help being concerned about how long Norway would remain a free nation.

There was great anxiety among the Jews in Norway. They were aware of all these infamous events taking place so near them. The newspapers were filled with reports of what was taking place, and the Norwegian Broadcasting System gave daily news of the latest events. The Jews knew that it might not be long before the Nazis would attack Norway. They could feel the Nazis breathing down their neck. Still they hung to a thread of hope that the war wouldn't get near them. It was easier to do nothing than to think of where to escape to in case that became necessary. They discussed the events over and over only to make themselves the more nervous and agitated. Like the Western leaders, the majority of the Jews made very little effort to plan for the safety of their own lives.

But this was only the beginning of what was coming. A number of enormous and distressing events took place in the fall and winter of 1939, among them were:

1. On November 30, in a lightning attack, Russia invaded Finland. It was a brutal deception on a peace-loving nation, and all of Europe was enraged over such a barbarous aggression. This was an assault by sea, land and air. Helsinki, the capitol, was left in flames after heavy bombardment by low flying Soviet planes. Fierce fighting broke out along the 50 mile Karelian Isthmus front. (Chronicle of the 20th Century, p. 500.)

With Finland on the northern border of Norway, it was expected that the Russian Army would overrun Finland and one day come marching on down the whole length of Norway. That prospect didn't set well with the Norwegians and the tension started to escalate like a volcano ready to erupt.

2. On the third page of the daily newspaper in Trondheim an article appeared about the theft of the membership register of the Jewish Community from an unlocked car. The president of the Jewish Community had left it in his car while he hurriedly ran into his store to pick up some papers. He hadn't been gone for more than five minutes.

When he returned, the register was gone. At the time it didn't appear to be very important. Probably somebody was playing a prank on him, and the register would surely be returned shortly. It never was. We learned later that members of the Norwegian Nazi party had stolen the register. It was turned over to the Gestapo after the invasion on April 9, 1940, and that information was used in conjunction with other registers that had been generated to round up the Jews in Trondheim, and deport them to one of their many extermination camps. ("Of the 767 Jews that were deported from Norway to Auschwitz, Poland, only 28 Jews survived." Kristian Otteson "I slik en Natt.")

That winter, another weather extreme set in. As hot as it had been in the fall, the month of December delivered an intense and fierce cold front. An excessive and unwelcome deep freeze settled over the city. The old-timers said that they had never experienced such penetrating and paralyzing cold weather in over 30 years. The river flowing through the town was frozen from shore to shore. Snow hadn't fallen yet and that made the cold more intense and piercing. The air was so still and quiet it made the cold feel like an ice sheet had covered the whole area. The cold went to every fiber in the body. The intensity of the cold stood out like a frozen picture in 3 D.

In an atmosphere of tension and uncertainties the events that took place, would in time drastically change the destiny of every member of my family. My parents had lived together for 40 secure years in Norway, but at my father's death everything started to turn to the most difficult events in the history of my family.

The main reason for this turn of events was Hitler's rise to power, his re-arming of Germany, his persecution of the Jews, and the so-called "final solution" to the Jewish problem. These, coupled with the war between Russia and Finland, were the problems and few were the solutions. For those who were able to anticipate the future, a partial solution was quite simple --- prepare!

Mama must have "known" what was coming. Otherwise she wouldn't have been so persuaded to make plans for the immediate future. Her intuition had given her clear guidance on a number of occasions and each time she was proven right.

When Russia attacked Finland on November 30, Mama became very concerned for the safety of her family and her valuables. She decided, towards the beginning of December, to pack all her valuables and ship them to America. She believed they would be safe there, in case Russia should come marching down from Finland to invade Norway. On the other hand, what if Germany attacked and occupied Norway? And there was no telling whether Sweden could remain neutral during the oncoming conflict. If Sweden were neutral, she could ship her valuables there. But no one could give any assurance of her neutrality. Having no guarantee of that, her decision was to ship all of her valuables to America.

It was difficult for my Mama to make that decision. She and Papa had worked for many years saving their money and planning to buy a "few" nice items for their home. Over the years they had accumulated a sizable collection of valuables, which were kept in the salon. These occupied several large credenzas that my parents had purchased in Paris during one of their business trips. Her home would seem so empty without these treasured items. She had a very large crystal chandelier hanging in the salon. She didn't know what to do with the chandelier, because packing it would be an enormous task, and too much to think about right now. She would have to deal with the chandelier at a later time.

Mama was speculating if Norway were invaded by the Nazis, and the family was able to escape to America, they could sell these valuables and live from the income until they could establish themselves in the new country. Another contributing factor for Mama's decision to pack and ship her valuables to America was that, as Jews, it was wise to try to be one step ahead of our enemies, if possible.

On December 4th the packing started. Four large trunks were used to hold all of the valuables. These trunks were 2 feet wide, 3 feet long and 2 ½ feet high with rounded lids. All the trunks were made from wood, covered with metal, with wood slats nailed over the metal. Solid brass hinges and locks finished the exterior. Inside, the trunks were lined with thick colorful paper.

Leopold, was an excellent packer, and was put in charge of this task. Every night, for several weeks, every piece was carefully wrapped, and tenderly placed in the trunk with adequate packing material, as if it were a valuable museum piece right out of Tutankahmen's tomb.

Nobody in the Jewish Community knew what my family was doing. If our plans were made known, the people would start believing that we knew something they didn't, and a panic might break out. My family wouldn't want to be responsible for such an occurrence. On the other hand if nothing happened my family might become the laughing stock of the whole Jewish community. It was the better part of wisdom to keep the packing of the valuables a secret. Even if the Jews were told, only a few of them would admit that they truly understood the seriousness of the situation at hand. This was not the time for negative comments from fellow Jews. So the packing proceeded according to schedule, and in extremely deep secrecy.

By Christmas time everything that was to be shipped had been packed and the trunks locked. All of Mama's valuables were safe in the trunks. But before they were closed and the lids locked, she had quickly put several mothballs in each trunk. "Just in case the American moths liked her valuables." It was her practice to put mothballs in with everything, including fresh baked cookies --- just in case.

Christmas 1939

Christmas Eve 1939 fell on a Sunday. It had started to snow early in the morning, and by mid-afternoon there was over two feet of snow in the city. The stores had closed the previous afternoon at 5:30, and the law prohibited any business to stay open on Sunday. There was no shopping to be done at all on that day.

At five that afternoon, on Christmas Eve, the streetcars stopped running, all restaurants and movie theaters were closed. It was still snowing. There were no taxis available, because cab drivers also remained at home with their families.

At 7 P.M. the church bells embraced the city with their deep, muffled, sounds, like a shroud of security and protection. The call for the parishioners to assemble in their neighborhood churches for worship service was heard by all. Many trudged through the deep snow to the Christmas Eve service. The 8 P.M. train from Trondheim to Oslo was virtually empty. On Christmas Eve no one traveled, everybody was home enjoying the family.

Little did the Norwegians know that it would be six years before another Christmas in a free Norway would be celebrated.

And the snow continued to fall ever so silently through the deep, dark night.

All over the country the people looked forward to a festive holiday in hopes it would lift their fears of being occupied by a Nazi or Soviet Army. The

Norwegians focused on what gifts they had bought, and kept their doors open for expected visits from friends and family.

But behind closed doors and in the shadows of a world that was fraught with fear and anxiety, treacherous plans were made. Agents of a conspiracy, in clandestine meetings, were methodically, and with calculated and sinister skills, were making the final plans for Hitler's barbaric "New Order" for Norway.

[7]"Shortly before Christmas, Rosenberg, German Chief of Foreign Office, dispatched special agent Hans Wilhelm Scheidt to Norway to work with Quisling, and a handful of officers from OKW (Oberkommando der Wehrmacht) who were aware of the pending invasion. They began working on "Study North" as the plans were first called. The code name for the eventual attack was named "Weseruebung" (Weser Exercise.)

While the Norwegians celebrated Christmas, and delighted in being with family and friends, the collusion was taking place behind their backs. Detailed plans were laid to turn over the Norwegian government and its people into the zealous claws of the Nazis.

In Norway, December 25th and 26th are both celebrated holidays. The first day all public entertainment, including restaurants and stores are closed. On the second day everything but the retail stores are allowed to open. This provides an extra day for the people to observe and enjoy the holidays, as they did with great enthusiasm.

That Christmas Eve in our home began as a very quiet time. Some of us spent the evening reading, and others conversed. Then our cousins, the Kahn's, came for a visit, and the party began instantaneously. The gathering went on till late at night until they had to rush home before the snow got too deep. Our two

---
[7] William L. Shirer "The Rise and Fall of the Third Reich"

families were very close, and we spent a great deal of time together. We laughed and talked and laughed some more. Over the years the relationship developed to such a degree that it was normal to find the Kahn's wherever the Abrahamsen's were.

The Christmas season passed. Life went back to normal. Well, as normal as could be. It was still very cold, and the snow stayed in the streets like stubborn slabs of granite.

People looked forward to spring and summer. Everything would be so much more pleasant then.

But not in 1940!

Chapter 7

Just in Time

Monday January 15, 1940, four trunks full of the family treasures were ready to be sent by train to Oslo, where they would be taken on-board a ship for America. But who could take them? It probably wasn't possible just to ship them to a storage place in New York, and then send for them at a later date. There was no telling how safe they would be, and how much would be stolen. Besides, nobody in the family knew of any safe storage facility in New York. Mama's concern was to find someone in the family who could take them to America, and make sure they were stored safely.

That someone had to be available, someone who didn't have great responsibilities at home, and who could act in a mature way in taking care of these trunks full of heirlooms. Going down the list there wasn't much choice. David was a practicing physician, married with two small children and living in Oslo. Since Papa's death, Heiman was managing two stores and Leopold was also involved in the stores. Oskar managed the gift shop. Samuel was pursuing graduate studies, while Abel attended gymnasium (Junior College) to graduate in the summer of 1941. Asne was busy in the store. Beile was married to Benno Hess from Amsterdam and Julius and Jacob were practicing dentistry in Trondheim.

I was the only one available. I was 18 years, could hardly speak any English, and had never been away from home alone. Not a likely candidate to carry out such a mission, but I was all that was available. Though I managed another family store, somebody else in the family could take over my duties because the merchandise was similar to that of the main store.

My responsibilities consisted of opening the store at 8:30 every morning, place the cash for the day in the cash register, and wait for the two clerks who reported for work shortly after the doors were opened. In the winter I emptied the ashes from the stove and started a fire to make the store warm and welcome for the customers. By law the store had to close at 5:30 in the afternoon, at which time I locked the doors and rolled the blinds down over the glass in the doors. My brother Heiman came over to the store to make up the cash register and record the sales for the day. It really wasn't too hard or backbreaking to manage that store.

I certainly wasn't overly enthused about leaving my home, seeing how unprepared I was, and with the background I had. I was very frightened at the thought of such a long journey. My despair reached to the depths of my soul. Out of great fear I cried often not knowing what my future would be, and because I knew how empty-headed I was for such an undertaking. Nevertheless, I would obey what Mama decided.

Mama pondered for some time before she gave her permission. She was concerned that I might lose everything, or that I might fall prey to robbers and that she might never see me again. She was still struggling with the decision. She felt that I was so young and inexperienced. Mama was right. What if he came down with eczema again? She remembered that I had been born with it--my entire body was covered with a red scab. It was so bad she couldn't put clothes on me for some time. Just a few years ago, she remembered, I had come down with rheumatic fever. Mama wondered if she should send such a frail child all the way to America by himself. I was hoping that she would change her mind about sending me so far across the seas.

I knew how strong willed Mama was. When she had made up her mind about something nothing would change it. We had all witnessed her determination in action, and trying to persuade her to change her decision was like talking to a wall. Though she was of average height, her strong will was ten feet tall.

"Well, he can go," she finally agreed, "but not by himself. Somebody will have to travel with him."

Samuel had applied for a scholarship at the graduate school of the University of California, Berkeley, California, which made it possible for him to travel with me. But he hadn't received confirmation of the scholarship yet. He was hoping to start the fall of 1940. If he received the scholarship in time we could travel together. Mama was assured that confirmation for the scholarship would arrive before the ship for America departed on January 24th.

But there were other complications, and big questions for me that nobody had given any thought of or even discussed. No one told me where I could stay in New York. Mama had decided not to let any of her distant relatives in New York know that I would arrive there on February 3rd. She didn't want any of them to know that I was bringing along all the family treasures--that was to be kept a guarded secret. Besides, she didn't really know them; they were just strangers to her. Neither did anybody in my family give me an address to a storage company in New York where the family valuables could be stored safely. What was scary for me was that I didn't know where I would live when I arrived in New York.

According to the schedule from The Norwegian America Line the ship would arrive in New York on a Saturday, and who knew if any storage place would be open on that day? To me it was all very confusing and disturbing. This only frightened me the more. I cried a great deal during those days, knowing that I soon would leave my home and might never see it again. I was hoping that somebody else would take my place, but there wasn't any sign of that. So I resigned myself to travel to America.

Then I had to obtain a passport with permission to leave the country. I went with my brother Heiman to the police station, the only place where an application for a passport could be made. Before processing the application the police officer made a call to the commandant of the local military unit to determine if that document could be issued.

"There is a young man in my office" he said, "applying for a passport with a permit to travel to America. What is the latest information you have?"

He waited for a few minutes which to Heiman and me seemed like hours. "1920 you say. Well -- no -- this fellow was born in 1921. You say we can issue the necessary papers for his travel then? Fine, I'll follow your directive."

He turned to me "Just talked to the commandant's office. A new order was issued yesterday that prohibited all male citizens born in 1920 or earlier to leave the country. They'll be needed for possible military service. The only exception is for those going abroad to study, provided they have been granted a bona fide admission to an approved University." Now I knew why my older brothers couldn't travel to America with the family treasures.

Heiman and I breathed a sigh of relief. I also thought of Samuel. He would be able to leave Norway if his scholarship from the University in California came through. My birth year made me acceptable for travel, this confirmed to Mama that I was the one to go. It was Thursday January 18th, 1940 when I received my passport validated for travel to America. The day drew closer to the time of my leaving home.

On Sunday, January 21, at eight p.m. Mama, Heiman and I boarded the train to Oslo, where I would catch the ship for America. All the trunks, having been shipped ahead, would be waiting for us there. I wondered when I would see my family and hometown again. For the hundredth time I checked to see if I had the envelope containing my travel documents. Though I knew I had put it in my inside coat pocket, I constantly kept touching it to make sure it hadn't disappeared.

Inside that envelope was my passport and a letter of credit for $775.00, which my mother had given me prior to leaving for the railroad station. The instructions were that whenever I needed money I could go to a designated bank in New York and draw out the cash, but only up to the specified limit.

On Monday morning, next day, the train arrived in Oslo, and Heiman assisted me in obtaining the remaining necessary papers for the journey. He did all of the work and I just followed along. If he hadn't helped me I wouldn't have known where to start, nor would I had known what to ask for. January 22, 1940, I received from the American Consulate at Oslo, Norway my temporary visa, valid for 12 months, for travel to America.

Every day I cried a little. I was very scared. During the following three days we lived as normally as we could, in the mornings we walked over the ice and in the afternoon, as it warmed up, we walked through slush. Before we finished in the late afternoon, it had turned back to ice. The dark gray clouds hung low over the city. All of this added to my dread. I wished so many times that somebody else could go instead of me, nevertheless, I resigned myself to my fate.

On Wednesday, January 24, the round-trip steamship ticket to America was given to me by Heiman with express and serious instructions to take good care of it. I promised to keep it with the passport and the letter of credit, which I had received a few days earlier. I noticed that the round trip fare was $350.00. I had to have a roundtrip ticket otherwise there would be no guarantee that I would return to Norway. Mama gave me $50.00 that would last me for a while, which she told me to pin on my under shirt with a large safety pin. She admonished me to take good care of that money and not to spend it foolishly. The cabin assigned to me was 162b, and it was to be shared with another man. I was hoping it would be my brother Samuel who was supposed to join me in Bergen.

At 8:30 in the evening the three of us took a taxi to the dock. All along the way I was very nervous. What would become of me? How would I get along in America, when I knew so very little English?

"Don't be too worried," Mama encouraged me thoughtfully. "Samuel will join you in Bergen, and together the two of you will travel to America. Samuel has been in foreign countries before so he will know what to do." But with the encouragement she was trying to give, I still detected the fear in her voice.

She remembered that two years earlier Papa had died, and now two sons were leaving home. Would she ever see them again? What would happen to them? America was such a large country, and the language was so foreign. Inwardly she cried, agonized, and was extremely worried, but knew she had to encourage me. She wanted to keep me at home, but understood that she had no other choice. She wished she had other options, but none came to her mind. These were such unstable and uncertain times. It reminded her of 42 years earlier when she had to leave her native land and journey to Norway, a country with foreign customs and a strange language. Besides, she reminded herself, somebody had to take the family treasures to a safe place.

At nine p.m. the taxi arrived on pier 1 that was reserved for the ships belonging to The Norwegian-America Line. There the ship was waiting for the departure time. (On November 26, 1942, at 3 P.M., 767 Norwegian Jews, men, women and children, were deported to Germany, from the same pier, on the ship "Donau" destined for Stettin, Poland. Final destination was the gas chambers in Auschwitz, Poland.)

Because of the tense political and military situations, and danger of war, the Norwegian government had ordered a total blackout. The scheduled Departure time for the "SS Bergensfjord" was 10 P.M. Hurriedly I said goodbye to my brother and kissed my mother. Tears of concern and worry rolled down her face. Softly we said to each other, "Shalom." I can still hear her say "Goodbye, mein kind - - - take care of yourself. Stay well."

Quickly I walked onboard the ship and found my cabin. I didn't take time, then, to unpack my personal belongings. Instead, I hurried back out on deck.

There was no one else there as I waved good-bye into the darkness. Though I couldn't see them, I knew my Mama and my brother were on the pier – no doubt waving to me. I knew they would watch the big ship leave the harbor. But in the darkness I couldn't see them. I squinted, as if that would improve my night vision, but still couldn't see anyone on the pier.

Under the cover of blackout, at ten p.m. the "SS Bergensfjord" left Oslo, Norway, on its regularly scheduled voyage to the USA. The blackout was complete. No lights were visible from the pier or the ship. Slowly and cautiously the giant steamer, having cast its mooring lines, slipped out through the Oslofjord. It would carry me away from those who had made my 18 years so secure.

As it turned out, this was one of the last three sailings it would make to the USA before the invasion by Germany on April 9, 1940.

Two days later, I arrival at Bergen which was the last stop before setting out across the Atlantic. I decided to visit a person who had worked in the family store, Paula Helberg, who was now living in Bergen. On returning to the ship about an hour before its departure, I received a telegram from home.

"Samuel can't come STOP Travel alone to New York STOP Samuel will take the later ship STOP Mother."

With panic in my heart and the telegram in my hand I left the ship and ran to the telegraph office. Somewhat out of breath I was able to explain to the agent that I needed to place a long distance call to Trondheim.

"This is an emergency call!" I exclaimed, hoping that this would enable me to obtain an immediate connection to Trondheim.

In those days it wasn't easy to make a long distance call in Norway. Usually one had to order the call through a long distance operator, and when a line was open the phone-company would call you. Sometimes the wait could take 2 or 3 hours or more. But I didn't have 2 or 3 hours to wait for a long distance call. The ship was leaving in 45 minutes. The call and the connection had to be made immediately.

Fortunately a line was open and within minutes I was talking to my mother. "I can't go to America all by myself." I declared frantically. "If Samuel can't travel with me I'll take everything off the ship and come home. Perhaps I can try again when Samuel is---"

"No, no, no!" Like lightning Mama quickly interrupted. "You go back on the ship and let it take you to America. It will be the best thing for you. Go mein kind," I could hear her crying. There was nothing else to do but to obey her. "One day we'll meet again.

Remember to ----"

The operator broke in "This line has been requested for a high priority call." The connection was immediately broken. I listened to the silence in the telephone hoping that Mama's voice would return. Finally, with great disappointment, I placed the receiver in the receptacle, went over to the cashier and paid for the call.

Slowly, so very slowly, and reluctantly I walked back to the ship in a state of shock. A couple of times I stopped and looked back to the telegraph office, wondering if I shouldn't try to make another call home. But it was probably impossible to obtain an open line. Even if I did, what could I say to convince Mama to let me come home? It was obvious that she was as upset as I was, and why should I upset her more. But I still wished I could call her back. Perhaps, if I could be more persuasive then she might change her mind and tell me to bring everything back home. No, there really wasn't time, and Mama would give me the same message as she did before - "You go back on the ship and let it take you to America. It will be the best thing for you. Go mein kind."

I heard the blast from the ship, signaling that it would be leaving soon. As I returned to the ship my legs felt so heavy that it was difficult for me to move them. Thoughts of despair ran through my head. I tried to keep an outward, confident composure in spite of how terrified I felt inwardly. Samuel wouldn't be there. It would be a very lonesome journey. There would be no one to talk with, and I was so shy I didn't know how to begin or even maintain a conversation, especially with strangers. And the ship was filled with strangers. I felt very much alone and very much frightened - - - scared from the top of my head to the bottom of my feet. If only I could have stayed home. I felt like an eaglet that had been pushed out of its nest by the mother eagle. It was time now for me to learn to fly.

It was getting close to departure time for the ship, so I tried to walk a little faster. The closer I came to the ship, the more terrified I became. I would be traveling all the way across the Atlantic Ocean--and to a foreign country whose language I didn't know--- all alone!

In the cold air I could feel perspiration starting under my hat and beginning to roll down my face. Quickly I got out my handkerchief and wiped my face and the inside of my hat. I tried not to allow others to know that I was so scared. Though it must have been written all over me, I'm sure, in my voice, in my eyes and in my behavior. I could almost hear and feel every bone in my body clatter as I walked towards the ship. I was shaking so badly I hoped that the passersby didn't hear my bones rattling.

I didn't know it then, but I was the first one in my family to leave Norway prior to its invasion by the Nazis. In another ten weeks my native country would be occupied by them. While I was greatly occupied with the uncertainty of my future, fierce fighting continued between Russia and Finland. The newspapers reported that the Russians were baffled about how defiantly the Finns fought defending their country. Their courage was the legacy of the unbridled carnage of war.

During the crossing I met some fellow voyagers. Since the passengers were busy with their own problems, for the most part I kept to myself. It was a very lonely journey for me. How I wished that some of my brothers were with me, then I wouldn't be so scared and lonely. Sometimes a few of the passengers talked with me about things that travelers talk about to pass the time of day.

A recurring theme was about life in America.

As I listened, I began forming an opinion about the country I was going to visit.

One day a Norwegian-American said to me: "In America, nobody will help you; you are on your own the moment you set foot on land. America is a tough, hard country. All people are busy caring for their own needs. They don't have any time to help others. You must help yourself from the moment you arrive."

I felt like jumping off the ship and swimming back to Norway. What was I to do? My prospects for the immediate future didn't look promising.

I went to sleep with those thoughts and woke up with them.

Outside, an Atlantic winter storm raged; inside of me a tempest of discouragement, fear, misgivings, and doubts literally roared. Days passed as the ship drew closer to New York. I wished the vessel would stop and stay off shore. My mind rang with: "---in America no one will help you; you're on your own; you'll have to help yourself."

For several days during the passage, that angry winter storm was raging at full speed. The ship rolled and pitched at a severe angle and the dining room chairs and tables were chained to the floor. To assure that the dishes and the silverware stayed on the tables the table linens were soaked in water before they were placed on the tables. For two days most of us passengers were seasick. On the third day I had become accustomed to the erratic movements of the vessel and was able to eat again. I wished that the storm would delay our arrival in America.

On February 2[nd,] because of the discouraging remarks about America that had been made by some of the passengers, a panic began rising in my stomach. I knew that the ship would arrive in New York the next day – the end of the journey. Though this was the end of the trip from Norway, years later I saw it as the beginning of a wonderful and eventful discovery of life for me.

On that day, however, I wished that the ship would remain at sea, that way I would never arrive in America. Afterall, on board the ship there was someone to cook for me and to serve my meals. I had a place to sleep, it was warm inside, and it was someone else's responsibility to supply the heat to the cabins and the dining rooms as well as all the lounges. Though I hadn't made friends with any of the passengers, I felt secure as long as I didn't have to leave the ship. I had found a home – even if only a temporary one.

In spite of all my childish fantasies the ship arrived in New York at 6 in the morning on Saturday, February 3. It was a huge city, bigger than anything I had ever seen. All this made me only more frightened.

With the usual ceremonies and formalities when a foreign ship enters another country, the national anthems of each country is played by the ship's band. When I heard the Norwegian National Anthem "Ja, vi elsker dette landet" (Yes, we love this land of ours) my eyes filled with tears and I wondered when I again would hear this anthem that I held so dear to my heart.

I watched the long-shore men on the pier put the heavy lines around the huge pilings and place the gangplank in its proper place so that the passengers could begin to disembark. I felt I was watching my own execution. Soon I had to leave the ship, whether I wanted to or not.

Shortly thereafter the first passengers left the ship. I saw them on the pier being greeted by friends and loved ones with lots of hugs, kisses, tears and laughter. Many people on the dock called out to those still on the ship whom they knew, and were eagerly waiting for them to arrive in their midst. But nobody was waiting for me.

Before I could leave the ship I had to appear before the immigration officials, who had come on board as soon as the ship docked. They examined my passport, asked several questions of which I understood only very little, and finally they placed a stamp in my passport allowing me to stay in America for six months. I was crestfallen – six months? That seemed like such a long time before I could return to Norway. I couldn't imagine what was about to happen in less than two months, much less in six. I was such an amateur at traveling I thought I had to remain in the USA for 6 months, where in reality I could have returned on the next ship.

I still didn't want to leave the ship. But I knew what my mother would say. Besides, the family valuables were my responsibility now. With all those scary and unsettling thoughts flying around in my head, I was in no hurry to leave. There would be no one waiting for me on the pier so what was the hurry?

Finally, all the passengers had left, and I was the last one off the ship. I walked very slowly down the gangway, frightened at this strange city that was so huge, and a foreign country whose language I didn't know, and feeling very much alone in the world.

After some searching on the pier I located the trunks with the valuables and was able to communicate, in broken English, to the customs inspectors that these trunks belonged to me. When they opened them and saw what was there, they became very suspicious.

Here was a young man, who could hardly speak any English, traveling with treasures packed in those trunks. How did they know that I hadn't stolen them? I didn't know enough English to tell them that they all belonged to my mother, and I was bringing them to America for safety.

In the end, they kept the trunks and all the contents, put them in safe storage at the custom's warehouse, and gave me a receipt for them. I could claim them when I could convince the inspectors that the trunks belonged to my mother. I would have to wait for Samuel to arrive for that, and then we could reclaim the trunks and put them in safe storage. Samuel spoke much better English than I. (Even if I had been able to get the trunks released I wouldn't know where to store them. And it was now Saturday afternoon.)

Ashamed that I lacked the authority to claim our trunks, I took the receipt, put it in my wallet, found my personal suitcases on the pier, had them taken to the street and looked for a taxi--still not knowing where to go. Fortunately I met Miss Rasmussen, who had operated a café on the second floor in one of our buildings in Trondheim. She had traveled on the same ship to America to get married in America. She stopped me on my way to the street and asked where I would stay. "I don't know." I replied in a shaky and frightened voice.

She turned to her fiancee, who had met her on the pier, and asked if he knew of any place where I could get a room. He wrote an address on a piece of paper and told me to give it to the cab driver. Then they caught a taxi and left me standing there – all alone.

I felt abandoned. Here I was in this big city. I gave the address to a taxi driver and he took me to Sloane House YMCA on 34th street, where I rented a room for 75 cents a night.

Well, it wasn't really much of a room. It was too large for a telephone booth, but if I should walk in too fast, I'd fall out the window. Nevertheless, for awhile this would be my home. A far cry, and cry I did, from what I had in Norway. But then -- here I was.

Sitting alone in this small room I was thinking of

my home and family. What were they doing now? How was Mama? Were they still having blackout exercises? How was the fighting between Russia and Finland going? Was Hitler still on the march swallowing up countries like a hungry tiger? I wondered what to do. I looked around at the sparse furniture. A black, steel bed frame with a thin mattress, a plain dresser and one wooden chair. No telephone, no gramophone or radio. The narrow room took me back many, many years to a wonderful event.

"Oskar, build me a snow hut. There is so much snow in the courtyard it's a shame to let it go to waste." I was only a small boy then.

"What would you do with a snow hut? Besides, I don't have time for such things as that." Oskar replied.

"It really won't take you that long. I promise I'll help you build it by staying out of the way."

Oskar finally created the magical snow hut for me. When it was finished there was only room just for me. A burlap sack was laid for the carpet, and another burlap sack was hung for the door, and a small candle, that I had begged from Mama, gave enough light for me to see in the darkness as I sat in that little hut for several hours at a time. This was my private place. My first one. A home away from home. As long as I occupied it no one else could come in. How I enjoyed sitting in my private home. All alone in my ice "castle." I felt very secure.

Reality jogged me back to this small room. Here I was a continent away with a great ocean separating me from my family. In the security of my ice "castle" I had no worries. In my YMCA room I had constant worries about what was in my future.

First, I had to contact those relatives whose names Mama had given me. It didn't occur to me to phone them, besides I didn't know how to use the American phone and my English was so poor that I didn't know what to say to the other party. My only thought was to meet someone connected with my family.

The clerk in the lobby was very helpful. He explained patiently in great detail how to find my relatives' home. Because of his kindness I was able to spend my first evening in New York with relatives, albeit, a new and unfamiliar link of the family. We were new to each other, and I was related to them because of Beile's recent marriage to Benno. This couple I was about to visit was Benno's sister and brother-in-law. I shall forever be grateful to this lovely couple for extending to me their kindness when I was a stranger in this country.

In February 1940, Samuel received a letter from the University of California, Berkeley, that he had been accepted in the graduate division beginning in fall of 1940, and with an urgent recommendation that he should arrive for the summer session. Upon inquiring about passage to America, he was informed that between Oslo and New York there was only one ship going, the "SS Bergensfjord," with two sailings scheduled to leave April 5th and May 7th. My brothers David and Heiman urged him to take the April sailing. On the pier, as he boarded the ship in Oslo, Friday April 5th, were Heiman, David and his wife Lova, and their daughters Inger and Anne-Marie.

Winston Churchill in his "Memoirs of The Second World War," the abridged version, reports that on April 5, the same evening Samuel sailed to America, the German minister to Norway, Dr. Curt Brauer (in Oslo) invited members of the Norwegian Government to a film presentation at the German Embassy. The film traced the German blitzkrieg on Poland, and it climaxed with an exposé of horror scenes during the bombing of Warsaw. The party broke up in silence and dread. The Norwegian Government officials left the embassy frightened, wondering why this movie was shown. They wondered if this meant that in a few days the Nazi Army of Adolf Hitler would invade Norway.

[8]This film prompted Dr. Halvdan Koht, Norway's foreign minister, to state that "it was intended to show neutral Norway what would happen if Germany attacked."

After leaving Oslo, The "SS Bergensfjord" stopped at some of the cities in the Southern part of Norway and finally arrived at Bergen on Sunday April 7th. Samuel wanted to call Mama in Trondheim. There was no phone available on board the ship, so he had to walk through the streets in a snowstorm to Hotel Norge to make the call.

He had just started to speak to her when the operator interrupted them. All telephone connections over the mountains had been canceled because of a snowstorm. Samuel returned to the ship, which left Bergen early the next morning - Monday, April 8, 1940, with Captain Mathias Anzjon in charge.

The next day, April 9, the ship received some weak radio messages that Nazi Germany had invaded Norway. These were considered rumors and no one on board believed that this could be true. Why would Hitler invade Norway? For sure the newscast must be

---

[8] Taken from Samuel Abrahamsen's book "Norway's Response to the Holocaust" Page 59, Holocaust Library, New York, NY

in error. Perhaps it was another country that had fallen under Hitler's iron hand.

But when the ship came north of Scotland, and heard clearly the hourly reports from BBC about the German invasion, it became clear to all passengers that Hitler's army had indeed invaded Norway. It was also reported that Allied troops were on their way to repel the German Army in Norway. They arrived in the middle and northern parts of Norway but after a few weeks were withdrawn because they were needed in France. As it turned out, the Norwegian forces surrendered to Germany on June 12th ,1940.

On Monday April 15, 1940 Samuel arrived in New York. I got up early that morning and took the subway to the pier where the ship would dock. I arrived long before the ship did and could see it in the morning mist a short distance from the shore, with tug boats taking it to its assigned berth. My heart started to beat fast in anticipation of seeing my brother. I would no longer be alone and lonely, I thought, and with his help I would know what to do with the four trunks containing Mama's valuables.

The passengers started to disembark, and I stretched my neck in hopes that my brother would be among the first ones off the ship. What if he weren't onboard? What if he had decided to take a later ship? What if he had changed his mind and traveled to England to study and had given up his scholarship from the University of California? All those thoughts went through my head and I started to become discouraged when finally, after waiting for many hours, I saw Samuel coming down the gangplank. I was happy to see him, a familiar face for a change.

Both of us had left Norway - - just in time.

We then took the subway to the place where I had found a room with a family named Trepp, who lived at 717 West – 177th Street. We were able to obtain the release of all four trunks with the family valuables, and had them transferred from the customs house to a secure storage place under our control.

For the next few weeks we talked about the invasion of Norway, and what preparations the family had made. Both of us were greatly concerned about their well-being. We listened attentively to the radio reports, read the newspapers and were hopeful that the British and French troops would challenge the Germans in Norway, in hopes that the Nazis would retreat from our homeland. This was just wishful thinking. The Germans held steadfast and remained in Norway until the end of the war.

Because of the invasion of my homeland there was no way now for me to return to Norway. The fact that my visa wouldn't allow me to work in America, Samuel and I decided that I should obtain immigration papers to America. In addition, the letter of credit that was given to me by Mama had been frozen. No money could be drawn on it, and fortunately Samuel gave me some of the money he had.

On Sunday May 5th I left New York City by Greyhound Bus and arrived in Miami on Tuesday the 7th. There I caught an overnight ship to Havana, Cuba, where I received my immigration visa. That evening I left for Miami on the same ship that had brought me to Havana the day before.

Early the next morning the sound of the ship's air horn heralded our arrival once again in the United States. The immigration officials boarded the ship immediately. I knew they would interrogate me and inspect my papers before allowing me to leave the ship.

Breakfast was served, and I remember that I ordered a waffle. But I was so anxious and fearful of all the uncertainties facing me that I couldn't eat it. I left the table and nervously waited my turn with the immigration officers. It was at times like this that being alone was so frightening. Fortunately, my visa was in order and everything went fine with the immigration personnel.

While I traveled to Cuba to obtain these papers, Samuel would travel to California to start his studies at the University. After a month we finally met again in Berkeley.

I learned later that after I had left for America Mama was very concerned for me. She cried a great deal and worried that I might fall in with the wrong people. What if all the valuables packed in the trunks were stolen? Often she wondered "Why did I make him go to America - - alone? And he has never been away from home before. Who will take care of him? Who will prepare his meals, Kosher of course, and who will make his bed and do his laundry?"

Mama knew that when she decided to send the trunks to America there wasn't anybody else available but me, and somebody had to take the family treasures to America. On the one hand she wanted to find a safe and secure place for them, and on the other hand she wanted all her children to remain at home. Though she had every wall in her apartment covered with family pictures she still wanted all her family to be near her.

Mama didn't like any changes at all in her life. As far as she was concerned everything should always remain the same. Yet there were changes in Mama's life when Papa died in 1938; changes when her nephew, David Kahn died suddenly from an enlarged heart; changes when we moved to another place of business.

Changes were the worst things that could happen to her, so she thought. Changes meant insecurity and instability, and if she could she would postpone indefinitely any changes that might enter her life. All those changes were necessary, but that didn't mean she had to like it. Nevertheless, when looking back on those changes she had to admit they were all for the best.

Daily, and hourly, she convinced herself that it was probably the best thing for me to leave home. How right she was! Though the present situation didn't appear promising, she was hoping that I would be able to make something of myself. To become, as she often would say, "A Mensch," (a man.)

As if Mama didn't have enough to worry about, the events leading up to and including the invasion on April 9, 1940 gave her many more reasons to be greatly alarmed.

Though Sam and I were safe from the Nazis, my family in Trondheim faced grave dangers, having been caught in the disastrous web of the Nazi invasion force. Their problems were beginning to mount, and sooner than expected they had to consider that the only way to survive was to escape.

Chapter 8

Invasion

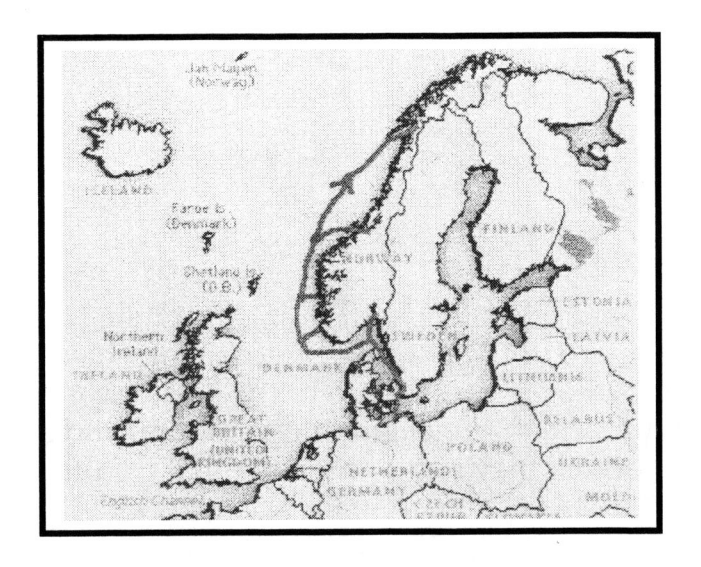

Germany's assault on Norway.
Five cities occupied: Oslo, Stavanger,
Bergen, Trondheim and Narvik.

Like a vulture circling over its prey, the Nazi forces, in a blitz, swept down upon the sleeping population of Norway. Just as several other strategic cities, like Oslo and Bergen, my hometown of Trondheim was suddenly awakened before sunrise by the alarming drone of low flying aircraft from the Luftwaffe. The people of Trondheim were not accustomed to having aircraft of any kind flying over the city. The small airport at Vaenes, and the flight path of the few planes landing there, was east of the city. The deafening sound of the Luftwaffe had a terrifying effect on the towns-people. They rubbed the sleep from their eyes believing at first that this was just a frightening dream, hoping that it soon would be over. It didn't take them long to realize that a brutal unprovoked attack by Germany was in progress.

It was April 9, 1940. I had been in New York City for two months by then, all alone and not knowing the language. I was greatly worried about, and for, my family. I didn't know what was happening to them, and I was anxious to have some news about their welfare. For many months I didn't hear anything about them. At the end of 1941, I received a letter from my sister in Sweden, saying that most all of the family had escaped from Norway and were now safe in Sweden. (See chapters 11 and 12.) During the war I had very little contact with any members of my family who were in Sweden.

A few months later I learned that under the cover of darkness the invasion forces had managed to land troops on Norwegian soil, and had started to occupy all the vital buildings and offices in Trondheim.

A cloak of fear, like a sinister spine-chilling cloud, hung over the city. The snowfall from the previous night, which had turned into sleet and then rain, added to the paralyzing spell that engulfed the town.

The German ships, masquerading as merchant vessels, anchored in the harbor for several months, now sailed to the docks and unloaded troops, guns and ammunition. (See Note 1, page 153.)

There were a number of Nazi sympathizers on the waterfront in Trondheim welcoming the ships and their "crews." Among those in the "welcoming committee" was a Mr. Knobloch, in full SS uniform, a native of Germany, who had operated a furrier business in Trondheim for a few years. My parents used to take their furs to him for repairs and storage during the spring and summer months. My family had no idea that he was such a strong Nazi supporter. It became evident that he came to Norway with the express purpose of spying for Germany, and had sent all information he obtained down to the Fatherland. But he wasn't the only person in Norway who acted as a spy on behalf of Germany.

It was Vidkun Quisling who, during the previous year, had conspired with Hitler to invade Norway. As soon as the invasion had taken place he executed a coup d'etat;' and declared himself Prime Minister of Norway. However, he was rebuffed by many Norwegian community officials and leaders, as well as the German occupation forces, who refused to work under him. With Vidkun Quisling's treacherous actions a new word for traitor, or treason, was coined. Since then, the word "Quisling" has become internationally known for its intent, and wherever it is used it means "a traitor."

In his earlier years, Quisling was a career army officer, and later Norway's minister of defense (1930-1933); he organized the Norwegian Nazi party in 1937 (Nasjonal Samling). Under the German occupation of Norway, he was the head of the only legal political party, and most of the time he held the post of Ministerpremier.

By 1937 many of us knew that for several years a swarm of German students and vacationers had come to Norway on so-called "goodwill" tours. They had really been sent from Germany to spy on us, and to find out everything they could about Norway. We had been almost overrun by these German "Wandervogels" who went everywhere, took pictures of everything, bought postcards by the thousands and sent them all back to the Gestapo headquarters in Berlin. I remember in the summer when these German "tourists" visited our villa, they played a few melodies on the accordion they carried in hopes of being invited in for a meal. Those who entered our villa seemed to be very friendly, and soon discovered that we were Jews. Everything they heard and saw was sent back to Berlin. When the invasion came about there was a strong possibility that these so-called "tourists" were part of the assault force.

As soon as the invasion had taken place and the ships had unloaded their "cargo," the Nazi soldiers assembled at the dock along with the German military band that had accompanied them. They paraded up Munkegaten (one of the main streets), their metal heels making a jarring sound on the cobblestones, and marched directly to the city hall; surrounded it, and took over every office, and confiscated all the official records. The swastika was immediately displayed from the top floor of the building.

At the same time, another detachment surrounded the police headquarters, took over all its offices. The Norwegian flag was removed and replaced with the swastika. By high noon all the Norwegian flags throughout the city had been removed and replaced with the swastika; a flag that was hated and despised by the loyal townspeople. Seeing those flags hanging on their buildings was like a dagger of betrayal to them on that cold and fearful morning.

The Norwegian government discovered, after the invasion had taken place, how well planned the German assault had been. The Norwegians had no idea that plans for an invasion of their country had been in the making; nevertheless in the fall of 1939 they started to prepare for an eventual invasion from Germany. But Norway had only an arsenal of small and outdated weapons with which to defend the country. The Norwegian people knew that they had been betrayed, but it was too late to do anything about it.

There was complete co-operation between the German high command and the Norwegian Nazi party. At the designated time they were to turn over to the Germans the radio stations in various cities throughout the country. Thus the Nazis would have control of a very effective and important communications media. It was later learned that the German warships that appeared in the harbor, after the "merchant" ships had landed the German soldiers, had left Germany on the 5th of April for Oslo, Stavanger, Bergen, Trondheim and Narvik. (See Note 2 page 153.)

Loyal Norwegians went about their business utterly stunned. They kept shaking their heads and saying to one another "How could this have happened?"

What was so perplexing to them was that since Norway was such a peaceful land, and so insignificantly small, surely Hitler couldn't be serious about wanting to occupy this tiny country. They quickly discovered that Hitler was not only very serious, but had certain plans for Norway and its Jews. Within 18 months after the invasion, Norway was turned into an armed camp of horror. The Nazis lived up to their reputation of persecution and tyranny.

A storm of terror, like a cloudburst, had forced its way into this peaceful country. The curse of war had fallen upon Norway, whose people had been betrayed. They found themselves frustratingly defenseless.

The Jewish community refused to look at the situation realistically. They were hoping, of course, that the Nazis would leave them alone. But they had overlooked that it was only a few months earlier that the register, with the addresses of all members of the Jewish community, had been stolen. They were unwilling to face the seriousness of the circumstances. (See Note 3, Page 158.)

Most of them expressed a startling passivity in relation to their dangerous situation. It was obvious, however, that the Nazis knew the names and whereabouts of all the Jews, and would come after them when they received orders to do so. It was only a matter of time before the clock ran out for the Jews, and then there would be mass arrests.

My family in Trondheim was in shock. In hopes of obtaining some information about this unbelievable event, they turned on the radio and heard an announcement from the mayor of Trondheim, Mr. Skjaanes, who said that the German Army has occupied our city this morning, as well as Oslo, Stavanger, Bergen and Narvik. I urge all of you to remain quiet, don't fight against the Germans. It is useless. They have an overwhelming force, and any opposition will antagonize them and cause bloodshed. Stay calm, go about your daily work. Do not panic. It will all turn out for the best.

When they heard the mayor speak they were confused, and skeptical, not knowing what to believe or what to do. The mayor's words had not instilled confidence that all would turn out for the best. There were many unanswered questions in their minds. What if the RAF dispatched a number of planes to bomb the German positions in Trondheim and other cities? (See Note 4 Page 159.)

What if a British expeditionary force landed in Norway? It they launched a counter-offensive preventing the Germans from proceeding up the valley from Oslo that would hold back the invasion force. All this was a possibility, and that's all that it was.

The first thought my family had was to get out of the city. They were thinking seriously of escaping to Sweden. To remain at home might be very dangerous, and they didn't want to take any chances. But how could they know whether or not the Germans would also occupy Sweden? They knew how Hitler had terrorized the leaders of Austria, Czechoslovakia, and Poland before occupying their countries. Why wouldn't he follow the same strategy in dealing with Sweden?

Should the family try to escape, they could contact a relative in Sweden. Nevertheless, escaping presented another problem. How could they preserve their personal properties in Trondheim, as well as the buildings and the store inventories? There were problems on every side, and there didn't seem to be any practical solutions. No one knew what the future would hold for them.

"I'll call David in Oslo and see what's going on there." My brother Heiman spoke up. "Afterall, we live in a civilized world. This is the country of Edvard Grieg, (Famous Norwegian composer,) Henrik Ibsen, (Norwegian dramatist,) Fritjof Nansen (Norwegian explorer, Scientist, statesman, author and Nobel laureate,) and Henrik Wergeland (Norway's national poet.) Don't believe all the things the newspapers are printing." He went to the phone, talked to the telephone operator and placed an order for a long distance call to Oslo, for Dr. David Abrahamsen. There would be a two-hour delay before a phone line would be available.

There wasn't anything they could do but wait. The family was aware that David was well informed about the ways of the Nazis. Perhaps he might have some advice on whether or not it was wise to escape at this early time of the invasion. They were all hoping that there would be no need to consider such an action, and they all wanted to be assured that their decision was prudent for the time being. They were all concerned and greatly worried. The security they had enjoyed for so many years had vanished like a ship in the morning fog.

Finally the phone rang. Heiman took the receiver. "Ready for your long distance call to Oslo, for Dr. David Abrahamsen. Please go ahead." The phone on the other end rang and rang and rang. After a minute or two, Heiman signaled the operator and explained that there was no answer. "Can you call his office in Oslo? It is listed under his name."

The operator obtained his number and told Heiman that she could make the connection, "Hope you are able to contact him." Then she got off the line. Here again the phone on the other end rang and rang and rang. Finally Heiman hung up the receiver and walked into the living room.

He told the others that David wasn't home. "He was neither in his apartment nor at his office. I hope he and the family have escaped," he declared. "It wouldn't be safe for them to stay in Oslo." Heiman was obviously worried about their welfare.

"David isn't home?" Mama cried. "Or in his office? Have they arrested him already? The next thing is he'll be sent to a concentration camp, and if that's the case I'll never see him again." Mama was very upset. She paced from the living room through the dining room, to the kitchen and then back. All the while weeping and talking with great anguish about what could have happened to her son and his family. Then she stopped, and thought for a while. Her face brightened up, she smiled and said in a loud, confident voice: "I'm sure he has escaped. He had friends who would have warned him. By now, David and the family are probably on their way to Sweden, if they aren't there already."

But still Mama feared the worst. What if the Germans catch them while they're trying to escape? But in the midst of all her fears for David and his family she was hoping for the best. She remembered how difficult it had always been for the Jews, but no matter what dangers they faced, they always survived.

"Calm down, Mama," Heiman urged. "The Germans haven't started to organize themselves yet. It's too early. Maybe in a few months, but not right now. David may have driven his family somewhere out in the country to get away from the Gestapo. That's probably what he has done. Soon we'll hear from him." Heiman hoped to comfort his mother and calm her down.

It was at this point that my family took the train to our country villa at Vikhammer, which is just a short distance east of Trondheim. At least, for a while, they thought, they would be safe there, and hopefully they could make some plans for the immediate future. Who of them could know what kind of danger they might be in? Being at the villa and away from the presence of the Nazis might help them think more clearly.

The month of April was still very cold and we normally didn't open the villa until May; the only heat for the entire three floors came from the fireplace in the living room. Snow was on the ground, and the family was hoping that they wouldn't have to stay very long. However, they remained at the villa for a few days.

Having talked to the neighbors who had come out from the city, they discovered that nothing had changed in Trondheim, and everything seemed to be normal.

On Saturday the family decided to return. The apartment in town would be much warmer than the cold villa. They packed up everything they had brought along and took the train back to town. The only conclusion they had reached at the villa was that if they didn't feel safe in Trondheim they would go to Sweden. They had a cousin living in Stockholm.

The Nazis hadn't troubled the Jews at all--as yet.

This lulled most of them in the Jewish Community into thinking they were safe. It was very confusing for them. They could choose to conveniently forget the track record of the Nazis and their atrocities against the Jews, or accept the fact that the Nazis are Nazis no matter where they are.

However, the record was clear from what they knew about the treatment of the Jews in Germany,

Poland, Austria and other countries and regions under the Nazi reign of terror.

Then Mama spoke up, "Do you think that we are in any danger here? If we are, wouldn't it be wise to leave right now, before it is too late?" Mama was worried about what the next few days would bring. Nevertheless, she was very stubborn and had a defiant attitude. She was willing to fight the Nazis in a unique way--by ignoring them.

"We are in great danger," Heiman responded gravely. "Only time will tell how desperate our situation will be. Anyway, Mama, you can't ignore the Nazis. They are all over town."

After a pause she said, "As long I stay at home I will be safe. I can ignore them from here." Little did she realize that the Nazis wouldn't allow anyone to ignore them. The time would come when the Nazis would show how brutal they were.

Nevertheless, at this time in Trondheim, people went to work, students went to school, the stores were open and it was business as usual. Seemingly, the daily routines had not been disturbed.

Yet, the family still felt uneasy about the situation, and wondered what to do next. They could stay and wait to see what the Germans would do. Afterall, the synagogue was intact, and services were still held every Friday night and Saturday morning. That was a positive sign. Everything might improve for the better and they believed that they shouldn't look on the negative side. That would for sure bring about disaster.

Tension among the Jews in Trondheim was high. Many were greatly concerned about what to expect. The leaders of the Jewish community met with my brother Heiman, immediately after his return from the villa. He recommended escape to Sweden. Even England at that time was an option, but would escape be right? They discussed the pros and cons. All of the

Jews knew that they had to escape—but not right now. Everything was safe for the time. We'll see how it goes; we are in no danger for now. Who knew for how long their safety would last?

"Why be alarmed, the whole danger may be over soon," someone spoke out. "The Nazis have no right to occupy our land. I'll watch how the situation develops and then we'll take any action that is needed. If we do make plans to leave Norway, they would have to be made in secret, otherwise the Nazis will discover them and all of us will be arrested, and then we will lose everything we have worked for. We must do nothing for now."

"What if we stood up against the Nazis?" someone else took the floor. "We have to show our determination in the face of the danger we are in. The Nazis respect force and strength. Don't give in to them. The Nazis had better know that we are humans, and that we have a right to live in freedom. They surely would listen to reason. This is the way to approach our situation."

"They will not listen to us. We are Jews, enemies of the Nazi regime, and as such we have no right to live. We can't stand against the Nazis. Nobody can at this time." Heiman blurted out. "We have to be ready to escape at any moment. We are in grave danger. At any time we can be arrested and sent to prison, and then it will be too late. We must not make ourselves visible, say nothing to the authorities and we may live longer."

Was it morally right to escape without a fight? Why should the Jews have to flee, leaving behind all they had worked for over so many years? What would happen to their homes and businesses? If they did escape, they reasoned, all of their properties would be confiscated; and the Jews wouldn't receive any compensation from the Nazis. Some refused to believe that their lives were in danger at all, and closed their eyes and minds to that probability. Others knew that something had to be done; that remaining in Norway might not be safe for very long. They talked and talked, but few could bring themselves to do what they knew they should do.

Many of the Jews in Trondheim, and probably in other towns as well, had resorted to the state of denial not believing that their lives were in mortal danger.

It was difficult for them to come to a rational decision, because the sacrifice seemed so great. But the loss of their lives would have been the ultimate loss by default. They just couldn't face that possibility.

Over the years the Jews had become accustomed to consider themselves to be Norwegians and not foreigners. They were all Norwegian citizens, and they were proud of their new heritage. The first generation of Jews had finally found a secure home in Norway, and with the second generation entering professions like medicine, judicial and engineering, the future for the Jewish population was as bright as sparkling diamonds. However, they were not to forget that they were also Jews. And didn't they see the Nazi atrocities against the Jews which were reported in the newspapers almost daily? This was taking place in all the Nazi occupied countries.

"I'm going to Stockholm!" Asne announced the next day. "It is now the 14th of April, and as long as we remain here we will all be lulled into a false sense of security. If anybody thinks it is safe to stay, they don't know how the Nazis operate. One day when we think we're secure, mark my words, without any warning they will come to our door and arrest us. Our properties will be confiscated, and we'll be sent to a concentration camp. That will be the end of us."

"Why don't you wait a few more days?" Jacob urged. "We might know a little more by then." Though he didn't see any change in the status quo, he expected the worst. He almost agreed with his sister, but had to think of his dental practice and all the equipment he had in his office, purchased through the bank. What was going to happen to all that, if he escaped to Sweden?

"What more is there to know?" she shot back.
"The Nazis are famous for their brutality, especially towards the Jews. Their mission is to rule the world, and in the process of gaining world domination they will exterminate all the Jews." Asne began laying the grounds for her reasoning.

"You saw what the newspapers reported from 'Mein Kampf.' Hitler has put it all there. Besides, remember how in 1933 he made null and void the Weimar Constitution; and then re-wrote the German National Constitution so that the Jews would be denied their citizenship. That way the Jews couldn't claim any protection from the police. Weren't they forbidden to enter or remain in any profession? Hitler ordered them to wear a yellow Mogen David, (Star of David) on their outer garments; he had their identification cards stamped with a big red "J," and confiscated their passports. Remember that? That wasn't so long ago. That is what will be done here too, you can be sure. (See Note 5, Page 160).

"I'm not staying! And I hope none of you do either. Tomorrow I'm taking the train to Storlien, (the border station) and from there to Stockholm. I'll call cousin Rakel, and through her I'll find a place to stay." After a short pause, "It's simply too dangerous to stay here!" and she emphasized every word. By now Asne had become agitated and very emotionally upset. She feared for their lives. Then she explained with relief, "Aren't we glad Beile took the baby to Amsterdam before the Nazis came here."

"Ooooh!" Asne turned to Mama with alarm. "Will Amsterdam be safe? Will any place be safe now?" She asked quietly. It was as if she was afraid to speak those words. Afraid that if she spoke them too loud her words would surely come true. Asne and Beile were the only girls in our family of 11 children. Naturally my sisters were very close. Beile, who had married a man from Holland, had chosen to have her baby in Trondheim, where Mama and Asne could help her.

"Calm down, Asne." Heiman spoke up. "Is it really wise to run away at this time?" Heiman was greatly concerned, of course. Since Papa's death he managed both stores, was responsible for their daily operations, did all the banking, made sure that there was sufficient inventory in both stores, did the monthly payroll, and consulted with the CPA on matters of finance. There were loans on the inventory to be paid, and in addition he was also in charge of the inventory in the free zone. What about all the cash in the bank, in the office safe, and in the store's cash registers? What about the inventories in the stores? What was to happen to all that? What if they escaped, and never came back, what then?

My mother's apartment was full of furniture including the huge crystal chandelier that was suspended from the ceiling in the salon. "What was to happen to all that?" Mama was thinking. Having to leave behind so much would delay her from making the life-saving decision.

During the afternoon my brother Julius came up to the apartment and asked what was the latest news. He had his dental office across the street from our main store, and like Jacob, was concerned about his practice and the dental equipment he had signed notes for. He also wondered if he should leave now or wait.

Asne snapped at him immediately, "Wait for what? For the Germans, or the Norwegian Nazis to come and get you and send you to a slave labor camp?

That's not what I want!" The air was filled with apprehension. "You've heard what the refugees tell us," she warned.

Then Mama spoke up, "We don't have to do anything - - - right now. When, or if, the time comes that we have to leave, we'll make plans then." She was thinking also of all her sisters. What about their welfare and security? She was very close to them. Some years ago they had all left their homeland in Lithuania and journeyed to Norway. To leave her adopted country now was very difficult for her. Here she had come to feel secure. This was her home now. It had been her home for over 40 years. "So that's what we'll do!" She had to talk to her sisters to see what they were going to do.

Nobody tried to oppose her, because they knew how stubborn she was. When the time to escape came, she hopefully would leave with her sons.

Asne having made up her mind to leave for Stockholm, walked to the railroad station and purchased a second class ticket. She was hoping that the border was still open, because she was determined to leave the next day. "Everything is happening so fast now," she thought, "I'll have to be one step ahead of the Nazis." On April 18th, two days after Asne's departure, Mama, Julius and Abel followed by train.

The train left the main station and traveled east toward the border. About 20 minutes after it had passed Vikhammer the passengers heard gunfire, and several bullets hit the train.

"Why are they shooting at us?" one of the passengers shouted. "We're just ordinary citizens! Can't the Nazis leave us alone?"

Bedlam turned into panic when one of the passengers, seated several rows from them, was killed from the flying bullets, and there were several others who had been wounded. A frantic call went out for a doctor to help bandage those who had been hit.

"I'm a doctor." Julius called, not clarifying that he really was a dentist. He figured, as long as those in charge didn't know, he could function as a doctor. He was put to work right away caring for the wounded.

When the train reached Storlien, (the border station,) they were met by Asne who had come up from Stockholm. She told them that there weren't any rooms available in Storlien, because the Swedish military was occupying the entire Storlien hotel. In addition to the Germans being ready to close the border to Sweden, the Swedish government thought it was important to watch their border for any unwanted refugees who might come over from Norway.

Julius informed Asne about the excitement on the train. Later he learned that Norwegian soldiers, who were operating in the area where the train had passed, believed that there were German troops onboard the train. They were almost right. Several miles back, the car occupied by the Nazi soldiers had been decoupled from the train leaving the German troops behind.

Asne assured Julius that they had a place to stay when they arrived in Stockholm. Rakel, knowing that Asne was going to the border to meet the family, insisted they come and stay with her when they arrived the next day. At least the family would have a roof over their heads until they could find their own apartment.

Like a frightened child overcome by a fearful storm, Mama frantically insisted, "But we need a place now to stay for the night. Where else can we go? We mustn't allow the soldiers to send us back to Trondheim. Heiman and the rest of the family will hopefully follow soon." She was greatly agitated and very disturbed. Thoughts of having to sleep in the woods, or someplace outdoors in this cold weather, flooded her already frightened mind.

"Mama," Asne assured her. "I know what to do. We can take the train to Ostersund--one of the stops on the way to Stockholm--and stay there for the night. From there we can continue on to Stockholm."

They boarded the next train and arrived in Ostersund early in the evening. There they found a small Pensjonat (boarding house) and stayed overnight. The next morning they called cousin Rakel to let her know when she could expect them to arrive. Rakel assured them that she would be waiting for them at the railroad station.

The next morning, on the way to the train station in Ostersund, Mama saw some radio towers and thought that they were masts from ships. Believing that, she told Abel "Go down and find out if this ship goes to America." She was now determined to escape to America, the only really safe place she knew. Abel told her, with a little chuckle, that what she saw were not ships but radio towers that took on the appearance of ships' masts. She was disappointed, but consoled herself with the anticipating arrival in Stockholm where a relative was waiting for them. At least they had a place where they could celebrate Passover, which was fast approaching.

When they arrived on April 19th Rakel and her husband Arthur welcomed them. The first evening of Passover was on April 21st. Mama asked if any of her sisters had escaped out of Norway. But Rakel said that Mama was the first one of all her sisters to cross the border. Mama also asked if there was any word from David and his family.

"Haven't heard anything about them. I hope they're safe."

"So do I," Mama replied. She wondered and worried about where David could be. Had he escaped to Sweden, or was he still somewhere in Norway? "He certainly must be hiding somewhere so that the Nazis can't reach him," Mama consoled herself. All she could do now was to wait and hope for the best.

And there was no word from David.

Notes for Chapter 8

(1) Towards the end of August 1939, several German merchant vessels tied up at the piers in Trondheim. After the invasion of Poland, these ships were ordered by the Norwegian government to move away from the piers and secure the ships some distance away from the wharf. The local newspapers covered this incident, and further reported that since there was a state of war between Germany and Poland, and because Norway was neutral, Norwegian government officials were not permitted to board these ships. Food, beverage and water were supplied to the vessels. We didn't think to take this event with any serious thought. What harm could a few merchant vessels do?

(2) [1]However, plans for the occupation of Norway were in the minds of the German administration several years earlier. On October 3, 1939, Grand Admiral Eric Raeder, Chief of the German Naval staff, suggested to Hitler that military bases should be obtained in Norway. This was to give them preferred strategic and operational abilities, and thus improve their position for an invasion of Great Britain. Besides, Admiral Raeder believed that the British might occupy Norway, which would be a setback for Germany.

[2]Alfred Rosenberg, the foreign affairs expert of the Nazi party, who also was responsible for propaganda activities in foreign countries, agreed with

---

[1] Winston Churchill "Memoirs of the Second World War" Page 198
[2] Winston Churchill "The Second World War" Vol. 1, Pages 483-484

the Admiral. But they needed a sympathetic Norwegian contact person.

Early in 1939 he had discovered an extreme political group in Norway called "Nasjonal Samling" (National Unity) led by Vidkun Quisling, a former Norwegian minister of War. Connection was established and he was "linked with the plans of the German Naval staff through Rosenberg's organization and the German Naval attaché in Oslo." Quisling and his assistant, Viljam Hagelin, who was a Norwegian businessman who had spent several years in Germany, and had established contacts with the Nazi party leaders, arrived in Berlin on December 12th, 1939. Admiral Raeder had arranged an audience for them with Hitler on December 14th to discuss political strategy in Norway. Quisling brought with him detailed plans, including maps, for an invasion of Norway to show to Hitler.

During the meeting, Hitler exhibited great caution in expressing any interest in Norway; and officially voiced his desire for Norway to remain neutral.

Yet, according to Admiral Raeder, it was on that day that Hitler gave the order to the Supreme Commander to prepare for the eventual invasion of Norway. It was on March 1, 1940, that Hitler decided to occupy Norway before attacking France. Two weeks later, the invasion was set for April 9. (Winston Churchill "Memoirs of the Second World War" Page 204)

The Norwegian government was unaware of Hitler's invasion plans. However, Quisling and his associate traitors knew all the details, but kept them under cover.

As the time approached for the invasion an episode took place that should have been a wake-up call for the Norwegian leaders.

[3]It happened on February 26, 1940, and became known as the *"Altmark* affair." This gave the Norwegian government and the military officials their first hint that something sinister was in the offing. They couldn't imagine that an invasion of their country was being planned, but felt it only wise to exercise caution when dealing with the German Ambassador to Norway.

[4]The German tanker *Altmark,* an auxiliary ship to the battleship *Graf Spee,* had broken through the British blockade, and anchored near Bergen. However, by wireless, a British agent contacted the British Admiralty who was determined to capture the tanker.

The British destroyer flotilla, under the command of Captain Philip Vian, of H.M.S. *Cossack*, intercepted the *Altmark,* that had steamed into the Jossing fjord, a narrow mile long inlet surrounded by snow clad mountains.

The British destroyers were met by two Norwegian gunboats whose commanding officers reported that they had inspected the *Altmark* and had not found anything of importance onboard. The Norwegian officer in charge also said that the ship didn't carry any armaments. However, the British destroyers ignored the Norwegian officer, for they had received orders from the British Admiralty to board the *Altmark.* In doing so they found several hundred British prisoners there. In addition, they also discovered that the *Altmark* carried heavy armaments. During the scuffle that ensued six Germans were killed.

This incident caused a jolt of terror among those of the top ranking Norwegian government officials.

---

[3] Tape recorded conversation between the author and Abel Abrahamsen June 12th 1987
[4] Winston Churchill "Memoirs of the Second World War" Pages 202, 203, 204

On April 8, 1940, the day before the invasion of Norway, the British fleet had started to establish a minefield in the coastal waters of Norway. The British Admiralty suspected that Hitler might invade Norway, thus obtaining a superior strategic position for their eventual invasion of Great Britain. Those in power in the British government were right in their thinking, but very slow to act. To prevent the Germans from attacking Norway, trained troops, guns, ammunition and ships to transport the British soldiers to Norwegian soil were needed. But Great Britain was sorely lacking in the necessary manpower and equipment. They had the will and the courage to fight, but not the means. It took more than willpower and courage.

During this time the freedom of millions of people hung in the balance. The indecision of both France and Great Britain (who should have been the protectors of freedom, but instead became appeasers to a dictator) opened the way for a war that would engulf the whole world. They both abdicated their responsibilities to their respective nations, and tried to convince themselves, as well as their people, that peace with Hitler was the better part of wisdom.

Contrary to their hopes and desires, troubling events continued to appear on the stage of world affairs. Some of these episodes, like the *Altmark* affair, were kept secret by the Norwegian government, and only released after the invasion had taken place.

---

[5]On the night of April 8, German warships approached Oslo and would shortly land troops and artillery on the dock. The Norwegian defense forces included a minelayer, *Olav Trygvason*, two

---

[5] Winston Churchill "The Second World War" Volume 1, pages 531-532

minesweepers, and shore gun installations. Shortly after dawn on April 9, two German minesweepers entered the Oslofjord to land troops in the neighborhood of the shore gun installations. One of the minesweepers was destroyed and sent to the seabottom by the *Olav Trygvason*, however, the German troops got through, came ashore and silenced the cannons.

The minelayer held off two German destroyers and damaged the cruiser *Emden*. The main German Naval Force, led by the heavy cruiser *Bluecher,* entered the fjord and approached the narrow part near the small town of Drobak, that was defended by the fortress *Oskarsborg*. There, two very old cannons installed in 1905, that went by the names of "Aron" and "Moses", were waiting for the invasion force. Two salvos were launched from the fort and hit the target. The *Bluecher* sank rapidly taking with her the senior officers of the German administrative staff, and detachments of the Gestapo. The other German ships, including the *Luetzow,* escaped. The damaged *Emden* took no further part in the fighting at sea. Oslo was ultimately taken."

Since the sunken *Bluecher* carried German administrative staff officers, as well as Gestapo personnel, it was believed that they had brought with them a long register of names of Norwegians to be immediately arrested. (It was later known that my brother David's name was on that list; and he had reasoned correctly that he must flee from Oslo at the earliest time possible, before the Nazis could find him and have him arrested.)

The German leadership panicked when they heard about the sinking of the heavy cruiser *Bluecher*. It carried [6]top secret documents, including orders from Hitler, and detailed operational analysis, and plans for

---

[6] Samuel Abrahamsen "Norway's Response to the Holocaust" P. 62, Holocaust Library, New York, N.Y.

the conduct of war in Norway, with sketches and maps.

[7]On April 11, 1940, Winston Churchill wrote to the British Prime Minister and the Foreign Secretary requesting them to go through the proper diplomatic channels to urge Sweden to declare war on Germany. Sweden, who didn't want to get trapped into a war with Germany, knew that such action would bring Hitler's wrath on their country, with the result that they would be occupied by the Nazis. If that happened, escape to Sweden for the Norwegian Jews and non-Jews would be impossible. The Swedish government said Thanks, but no thanks.

In order for Sweden to remain neutral, they sold a necessary and strategic raw material to Germany. The German war machine was in dire need of iron ore from the Swedish Gullivare iron ore field, across the border from the Norwegian town of Narvik. The British wanted to stop the Germans from having access to this iron ore field, and on April 12, sent a convoy of troops, operation "Maurice," to seize Narvik. It wasn't an easy task, encountering snow and hostile weather. As late as April 16, the British General Mackesy decided not to try to seize Narvik until the snow melted. Pressure from the British High Command changed his mind. For a short while the British were able to hold on to Narvik, but were overpowered by the superior German invasion force, and came under heavy bombardment from the German Luftwaffe.

(3) These records were stolen in October 1939. A Jewish businessman had the register in his car while parking outside his own business. He ran in and was gone for less than five minutes. When he returned, the roster was gone. He searched everywhere for it, but to no avail. The Norwegian Nazis had targeted him for this

---

[7] Winston Churchill :"The Second World War:" Volume 1, Pages 548 and 549

heist. This was an important register for them, for they used that information to round-up most all the Jews in Trondheim.

(4) The RAF had been successful in bombing the airfield at Stavanger on April 17, 1940.

The British also wanted Trondheim for a base of operation and planned operation "Hammer" to achieve this. The planning for this operation was based on old maps and charts of Norway. There were no recent reconnaissance or aerial photographs available of that area. Therefore, the British discovered it would be too difficult to land troops there, because they lacked trained soldiers and proper equipment.

Of course, there was a great risk involved with such an invasion. Many major ships would be put in harms way, and there was a 30-mile journey from the seacoast in through the fjord before reaching Trondheim. The problem then would be, having arrived in Trondheim, could the fleet get away intact? That was the question that raised its ugly head before the British Admiralty. Upon further planning, and considering what options were open to them, it was decided instead to land troops at Namsos and Aandalsnes (North and Southwest of the objective) in hopes of capturing Trondheim by a pincers movement. The landings were successful, but the attempt to seize Trondheim failed, even though 13,000 troops, consisting of British, French and Canadians, had landed in these two areas.

In an attempt to wrest Trondheim from the Nazi's grip, the contingent from Namsos, under the command of Carton de Wiart, moved south and came within 50 miles of their target. At the village of Verdal they were met with German resistance. The British Intelligence didn't know how badly prepared the Germans were in that area. If they had been able to obtain some knowledge of this it would have enabled de Wiart to easily break through the Nazi defense line and seize Trondheim. Instead, the contingent retreated to Namsos, and returned to England.

The troops at Aandalsnes moved as far East as Lillehammer in an attempt to help the Norwegian resistance movement. But because of bad weather and lack of suitable winter clothing and assault weapons, they retreated to Aandalsnes. At the end of April they returned to England.

The entire British Expeditionary Force, of about 24,000 soldiers at Narvik, retreated and returned to England on June 8, because of their lack of proper winter clothing and lack of better equipment. The French soldiers, who were part of the expeditionary force, left for France to defend their homeland against the German invasion. Also, Great Britain had a crisis on their hands – Dunkirk. The returned British soldiers were used to help evacuate over 300,000 troops. A task that took close to three weeks to accomplish.
(Winston Churchill "The Second World War" Volume 1 Pages 560-581)

(5) "With law the land is built and without law the land is laid waste...." thus it is written in an old Norwegian law from the year 1100. The Roman lawyer Sextus Pomponius who lived in 200 AD said it well,
". . . ut civitas fundaretur legibus." (So that the society shall be built by laws.)
(Kristian Otteson "I Slik en Natt," Page 36, H. Aschehoug & Co., Oslo, Norway.)

Otteson goes on to explain that when the law of the land is changed to such a degree as to favor one specific political party, outlawing all others, and declaring certain people as undesirable and classified as enemies of the state, the cornerstone of a civilized and lawful state is shredded and removed. This then becomes the prologue to the demise of an otherwise cultivated and enlightened State. Unless the law of the land protects all people, guarantees their safety, and provides equal justice for all citizens, dictatorial power becomes the main justification for the existence of such a State.

With a dictatorship comes the necessity to eliminate independent thinkers who, through many years of faithful service, furnished the vitality to the building of the nation. Through the annihilation of those who produced the culture and contributed to its progress and development, a dictatorship thus guarantees its own total destruction.

The next phase of Hitler's reign brought about the demise of a culture that had influenced the world in many fields of endeavor. In March 1933 Hitler was granted dictatorial powers, with the authority to rewrite the constitution. In May and June he broke up all the trade unions, and outlawed all political opposition parties.

Hitler ordered the German Constitution to be rewritten to favor him and his party. He also included in this rewriting a strong and inflammatory text that robbed the Jews of their German citizenship, thus denying them the right to vote in all political elections. In addition the new Constitution declared all Jews to be the enemies of the State. This became the new law that all Germans were compelled to uphold.

The irony of this bizarre constitutional change was that between 1920 and 1930 all the judicial books in Germany were written mostly by Jewish lawyers, constitutional experts and law professors. These books had become standards throughout Europe and were the pillars of jurisprudence in all universities. The only way to prove that the new Constitution was superior to the old one and that it spoke for the Germanic race was for the Nazi government to have these law books destroyed.

With the help from Dr. Juris Hans Frank, who was a member of Hitler's government, it was declared that laws written by Jews didn't reflect the Aryan philosophy, but only the Jewish viewpoint, that these law books were not relevant to the Germanic way of thinking and dealing with justice. Therefore, Dr. Frank declared that these books must be outlawed and destroyed. (Kristian Otteson "I slik en Natt." Pages 36-37, H. Aschehoug & Co. Oslo, Norway.)

The new German Constitution brought panic to the Jewish communities in Norway, and to their horror there was more to come from the dictator in Germany. Events that they couldn't imagine would, in time, visit their families, homes and occupations like a whirlwind of destruction.

In April 1933, the Nazis enforced a ban forbidding all Germans to trade with Jewish merchants. A few years later there was also a prohibition against Jews to enter public parks, restaurants, theaters and public libraries, and to have any contact with non-Jews. In addition they were ordered to have a six-pointed star (Star of David) sewn on their outer garments. That way anyone, especially the police and the Nazi storm troopers, would be able to spot who were Jews and who were not. The noose was tightening around the Jews, slowly choking their lives.

To make a difficult situation even worse, on May 17, 1933, another political party showed its ugly face in Norway. To gather the popular interest it was called "Nasjonal Samling" (National Unity) under the leadership of Vidkun Quisling. It seemed like a patriotic action because of its name alone.

But when the party leader made known its direction, intent and philosophy, many changed their minds. It was nothing more than a Norwegian Nazi party, with the destruction of all Jews as its centerpiece. Yet, there were Norwegians who joined the party to help accomplish its goals.

May 17th is a National Holiday in Norway; the day set aside to celebrate the new Constitution that was adopted in 1814. For Quisling to make the announcement on that particular day seemed like a slap in the face of democracy and freedom.

As early as August 1933, German Jews had been arrested and sent to concentration camps. At that time there were as many as 45,000 Jews who were held in many different camps, the largest being Dachau. Laws were passed to "purify" Germany from foreign and unwanted races. Its true meaning was to exterminate all Jews. After World War II, as we know, six million Jews had been killed in the camps.

In a speech on October 14, 1933, Hitler announced Germany's withdrawal from both the League of Nations and the disarmament conference. This caused great distress and fear among all the European Jews. The newspapers reported his speech in great detail, and the Jews knew that Hitler meant to start a war. For the first time he publicly committed himself to re-arm Germany. It was a clear signal that war was on the horizon.

Unfortunately, the Western leaders were still asleep, not realizing the destructive powers being forged by Hitler. The following years brought out the blitz and ruthlessness of Hitler's intents.

The next year, 1934, the Nazis assassinated the Austrian Chancellor, Engelbret Dollfus, in preparation for the annexation of Austria. It would only be a matter of time before that would be accomplished.

In March 1935, Hitler's troops marched into Saarbruck, France, an area in the Rhineland; and had the territory transferred from French, back to German control. This region in the South-Western part of Germany, near the French border, contained huge deposits of coal. These deposits were essential to the restructuring of the German re-armament program, and for the production of steel and synthetic rubber.

Under the Versailles peace treaty after World War I, this area had been given to France as war reparation. But it was to be under their control for a period of only 15 years, after that the Rhineland area was to be a neutral zone.

Then, in March 1936, the entire Rhineland (the area west of the Rhine River) was annexed by Hitler, who arrogantly violated the treaties of Versailles and Locarno. He explained that Germany was no longer bound by these treaties. This region was not just abundant in coal, but also in many other strategic minerals. To Hitler, treaties were to be kept only as long as they served his purpose. If the French government, with its 100 divisions and a strong Air Force, had mobilized and challenged Hitler's annexation of the Rhineland, the Nazi occupation force would have retreated. Unfortunately, the French government remained paralyzed, and lost the last opportunity to stop Hitler and his ambitions.

The leaders of the Western world were in a state of denial. They had neither the courage, nor the foresight to recognize that they were in the presence of such a potential, enormously hostile force. This force would be of such size that it would develop into gigantic proportions, like a giant octopus; and eventually involve millions of people, with the destruction of millions of lives and much property. Hitler was a formidable threat to world peace, and still the leaders of the West wouldn't believe that he was serious. The free democracies were hanging by a thread, and Hitler, crazed with power, was able and ready to sever that cord.

Chapter 9

David's Escape

David's escape from Norway to America

David was on the Gestapo's hit list!

But he had already escaped from Oslo by the time Heiman called, and was the first of the family to take action after the invasion. For some years David had actively and publicly opposed the Nazis. He had lectured, given radio addresses, as well as written newspaper articles warning the people about Hitler and the threat and terror he represented.

David was recognized throughout Norway for his adamant stand against Hitler. It had been reported that the Gestapo had David's name on their most wanted list. So David knew when the invasion came he would be a target. He was, understandably, quite nervous for the safety of himself and his family. (The following are segments from his published book in Norwegian, which I have translated.)

> [1]Six days prior to Hitler's attack on Norway, I took my automobile out of the garage and parked it in front of my apartment. I checked to make sure that the gas tank was full. The options of escape that I had considered were either to go to Sweden, or the North Sea where I might find a ship going to England. My choice might depend upon last minute events. Early in the morning of April 9th the sound of German planes flying over Oslo awakened me.
>
> There was a blackout throughout the entire city. The radio was silent. I called my loyal journalist friend, Asbjorn Barlaup, who told me that the Nazis had invaded Norway, and advised me to leave the country immediately.

But David was caught between an unplanned desire to stay and fight for his country, and the urgency to leave for his own safety. He discussed this with his wife Lova.

"I don't want to leave my country and flee like a coward. I am a Norwegian, and I am going to fight these Nazis. They have no right to invade my country. Who do they think they are? This is my country, not theirs." His voice expressed his indignation and feelings of betrayal. "However, we can't stay in Oslo.

---

[1] By permission from Tano A/S, Oslo, Norway, 1985 "Jeg er Jøde" (I am a Jew) by Dr. David Abrahamsen. Text from selected pages between 97 to 125 is translated by the author.

We're not safe here. We'll have to get dressed. Pack some things." he told Lova.

> Wake the children and get them ready. It will have to be a quick breakfast. I'll have to tell the maid we'll be leaving for a while; I'll have to pay her. I'm sure she wants to be with her family.

He regretted that he hadn't taken more money out of the bank, but who could have known that an invasion was coming on this day. Panic was rising in his heart, but he tried to remain calm.

"We don't have much time." Lova insisted. "With this blackout we'll have to wait 'til daybreak to drive anywhere." She was anxious, and in a hurry to get started before it was too late.

By early that morning Lova, David and the children were dressed. Though he didn't want to leave, he knew he had to---for his own safety and for that of his family.

The radio silence was broken with the news that German troops had occupied Stavanger, Bergen, Trondheim, and Narvik, and now they were ready to take Oslo. David could see that they had to leave immediately. He assumed that when the Germans had secured the city they would come to arrest him. His first thought was to get to the North Sea. But he had no idea which of the roads would be safe---because of the winter weather, and which ones would have Nazi checkpoints set up along the way. At that moment he didn't know what choice to make, only that he had to get out of the city. Quickly he decided to drive north towards the mountains. He had the presence of mind to pack a few medical instruments, bandages, and a few clothes in a rucksack. Lova was ready with the children.

We drove down Bygdo Alle towards Centrum, parked the car for a moment and I ran to my office. I looked around to see what I could take with me, but left everything there because I couldn't be sure I would be in a place where I could use any of it, and rushed back to the car. Then I drove up Karl Johans Gate (the main street) towards the market place. The streetcars were stopped, which was unusual for that time of day.

Under normal circumstances the streetcars would be packed with people going to work. But as of that morning these were not normal times.

I drove faster down Storgaten and passed Legevakten (a medical center) and was stopped by Norwegian security police wearing green armbands. They searched the car looking for something --- they didn't find what they were searching for. When the security police learned that I was a medical doctor they let me continue.

The security police, who were nervous and agitated over what was happening, gave no explanation for the search. It seemed that everybody was in either a hostile mood, or in a state of shock.
David's car was not the only one that was stopped. Every car was searched, thus delaying the flow of traffic. A few days later, rumors were circulating that this security force was made up of Norwegian Nazis who were searching for weapons of any kind. Whatever they found was confiscated and the people were arrested.

David's Escape

> On our way to the mountains, German planes appeared overhead, and I drove as fast as I could towards the forest. I made it there just in time when a bomb fell not far from us. Our car, a Nash, was just about blown away by the burst of the bomb. Fortunately we were not hurt.

David drove his family higher into the mountains, where, of course, they encountered snow. This was early April, and the snow wouldn't start melting until May. A number of cars, private and military, passed them along the way. Some fleeing from the invasion force, others volunteering for the defense of the country.

> I stopped the car at a wayside café and walked inside with my family in hopes of hearing some news about the invasion. People gathered around the radio, and the news was: 'Oslo and the Royal Norwegian Army Headquarters have been occupied by the German Army. The city has been secured. Evacuation of the city has been cancelled, and all residents of the city are to return.'

David knew better. He didn't trust the Nazis at all. He knew he had escaped just in time. To return to Oslo was unacceptable to him. That was a sure way to be arrested, ending up in a concentration camp or death. Rumors from passers-by indicated that Norwegian traitors now operated and controlled the radio stations. (There was only one radio network, NRK, and that was owned and operated by the government.)

From Hamar, David turned north to Lillehammer. There he heard that the Germans were coming north. So he knew he had to continue on farther north. This meant that he couldn't go back the way he had come. He had to make sure that the Germans didn't catch up with him. Frantically, he continued to drive as fast as he could. It was now starting to get dark, and before nightfall they arrived high in the mountains. It had become very cold, and David and his family needed a place to stay overnight. After some searching, he found a farmhouse where they were taken in for the night.

> On the flight into the mountains Anne-Marie, our youngest daughter, came down with pneumonia. The farmers were very kind, and allowed Lova and the girls to stay with them while I went ahead the next day seeking a place to establish a field hospital.
> I came to the eastern part of the Gausdal valley where I found a big farmhouse. There I set up a field hospital for the wounded Norwegian soldiers that were putting up a gallant resistance. As soon as Lova and the girls were able to join me, she worked as an ambulance driver having an old truck at her disposal.
>
> The first Norwegian soldier brought in had his right hand destroyed. Morphine was the only medicine I had available. After treating the soldier the best I could, the soldier was sent to another hospital out of the reach of the Nazis, who by this time had come closer. There were about 2000 Norwegian soldiers in this area who wanted to know where the Germans were. I volunteered to spy for them, to determine where the closest contingent of the invading force was located. I discovered that the Nazis were

getting too close. I was careful not to allow myself to be caught. By this time several other doctors had come to the field hospital to help with the heavy burden of treating all the wounded soldiers. I knew that as long as there was an adequate staff of medical help, it was time for me to escape across the border to Sweden.

"I have to find a way to escape before it's too late." he kept reminding himself and Lova. The children were too young to understand, and he wouldn't disturb them with those thoughts. The time for escape to Sweden was now. An hour later might be much too late. There was no time to waste. Time was of essence.

My family, in the company of now nearly 4000 soldiers, fled further into the mountain valley until there was no place to go. The Nazis had locked us in. We were all trapped. Mountains surrounded us on three sides, and on the fourth side there was a broken down road that led in the direction of the German Army.

David and Lova decided that their only hope for escape was to take their children and hike by themselves over the mountains. They knew they had to crawl through melting snow and ice packs as they crossed the mountains. He hoped that the Norwegian soldiers could keep themselves out of reach of the German invasion force.

David, Lova and their two children were on their own. It was frightening for them, not knowing what was to happen. Would the Germans overtake them? That night neither of them slept, but kept a vigil over their children, and a watchful eye for any approaching enemy soldiers.

Morning came with brilliant sunshine, until the clouds caught up and blocked the sun for the rest of the day. The roar of German airplanes interrupted the intense quietness that had fallen over the mountains. The four fugitives hid under the cliffs so as not to be discovered. Upon the heels of the departing planes, and the drone of their engines being out of hearing distance, the serene silence settled over the terrain again.

The only reason David hadn't been arrested by the Germans was that they didn't know where he was. But they were searching for him. Their search continued.

The whole family had climbed higher up into the mountains, and the snow became very dangerous. They didn't know how safe their passage would be, because they could fall into a crevice and perish. Therefore they proceeded very carefully, as if they were walking on eggs.

> At one time we crossed a wide brook that had been frozen over. We walked across the ice, not saying a word to each other, and walking as lightly as we could.
> Suddenly our daughter, Anne-Marie, fell through the ice. With a great deal of effort Lova and I were able to rescue her. Then I remembered that I was to lecture for the Nobel Institute on the 11 April on peace. I carried her to a small cabin, which we saw up ahead on the other side.
> Inside, there was a warm room filled with Norwegian and British soldiers.

They all helped to get Anne-Marie dry, and hung up her wet clothes in front of the fireplace. Lova and I took all precautionary measures to make sure that Anne-Marie didn't come down again with pneumonia. The next morning, when Anne-Marie clothes were dry they could travel.

> I was very discouraged, for I knew that it was hopeless to try to carry the children over the snow-packed mountains into Sweden.

We climbed back down to where we had left our car, and put the exhausted children in the back seat, where they soon fell asleep. Outside the car, we discussed our new plan in hushed voices, so as not to disturb the children.

> I was sure that I was on the Gestapo's list. That I hadn't been arrested – it was now three months after the invasion – was because they didn't know were I was.

It was now the month of June. "The snow is still too deep," David said to Lova, "and the ice pack is very dangerous now while it is melting. I want to take all of you with me across the mountain passes, but you can see that I can't do it over this terrain. I am so exhausted, I don't think I have the strength to carry the children across the mountains." After a long pause he continued "I'll have to cross the mountains alone. You and the children must return to Oslo. If I return with you I know that I'll be arrested by the Nazis. You must contact your father in Sweden, and try to get there. Escaping to Sweden from Oslo would be your best option right now. I don't know what route you can take to get out of Norway, but there will be a way. As soon as I can, I'll send for you."

He looked at Lova, whom he loved very much, embraced her, kissed her, and through foggy eyes said "I love you, take care of yourself, and drive safely. Kiss the children good-bye for me. We'll meet again, soon."

He helped Lova turn the car around, and watched as she drove over the mud-covered road out of the mountains. He saw that her face had turned pale. He knew it was from fear of what could await her in Oslo. He turned around and faced the cold and dangerous mountains he knew he had to scale in order to reach Sweden. He suspected that his face was pale also.

> I had to escape – without Lova and the children – a terrifying and bitter farewell, which I shall never forget.

For several hours he climbed over the snow pack, got wet, forded swollen streams, became hungry and very tired. Finally he reached Sweden. He thought of his mother, and the family in Trondheim, and hoped they would escape before it was too late. At the same moment he also thought of Lova and the children. The terror in her dark eyes stood out against her paleness as she drove away. Would they be able to return safely to Oslo without being arrested? Would she be able to obtain an exit visa before it was too late? Their lives would be in grave danger until they reached her father in Gothenburg, Sweden.

> The Swedish border guards told me in a cold uncompassionate voice that I had to leave the country within 24 hours because I had served in the Norwegian Army.

David tried to obtain further information from them, but they gave none, except "those are orders from the higher ups."

Arriving in Stockholm he obtained a student visa for the U.S.A. He was very happy about that, for now he could continue his journey to America. At that time he didn't know the difference between a student visa and a bona fide immigration visa. He evidently believed that they were the same.

He made a quick phone call to Lova's father to explain their situation, and that he had less than 24 hours before he had to leave Sweden.

> From Stockholm I obtained passage on a plane to Helsinki, Finland. From there I was able to secure a seat on a small plane, a Zampa. After a 12 hour uncomfortable and shaky flight, I arrived in Petsamo, Finland.

Petsamo is a small seaport on an inlet that empties out into the Varangerfjord located far above the Arctic Circle.

> It was a city in ruins as a result of being shelled by the Russian army. The people walked around without any goal or purpose. They were in shock. It seemed that everybody wanted to travel to America, but there wasn't any possibility of obtaining passage for such a voyage.

These circumstances weren't encouraging signs for David.

David was exhausted, hungry, scared and freezing, and in that state he inquired about traveling to America.

I had heard that there was a boat that was going to America. I went down to the pier to find the captain who was Swedish. He said that a lot of people would like to go to America. I asked if there was room for me. The Swedish captain answered me very impatiently, 'We're all filled up.'

'I am a medical doctor, and have practiced medicine in Oslo for a number of years. Will you let me go with you if I sign on for this one trip?'

'Do you have any papers that verify that you are a medical doctor?'

I showed him my medical license, which I always carry with me. The captain said that he could take six more passengers and agreed to let me onboard. There would now be a total of 12 passengers. When I located the ship I was shocked at its small size. Only 1,400 tons. I wondered how such a small ship could ever reach America, but that was all there was available.

Since my passage was free, I had to sleep out on the cold deck with a temporary roof over me. Needless to say, the nights were cold, but I was grateful for the passage. The cabins were reserved for paying passengers. (The ship was called the SS Maud Horden, and left Petsamo July 17, 1940.) On the first day out, I climbed up to the bridge and talked with the captain. I thought that the boat was going in the wrong direction.

'No' the captain answered. 'We are going in the right direction.'

'Yes, but you are going North.'

'I have to go north in order to avoid the German submarines. You'd better leave the bridge and get down below and stay there during the day. If a German submarine should spot us the crew may come aboard, and should you be discovered, you will be arrested. So please, leave now and don't return to the bridge any more.'

The ship went far north and they saw icebergs as they traveled between Iceland and Greenland, and then finally turned in a southerly direction.

One night I heard shots coming from another ship. Everybody came on deck, wondering what had happened. From a distance a ship was approaching; everybody believed it was German, and became frightened. I thought that this was my final hour. One of the passengers, a priest, fell to his knees and prayed to God for mercy and help. Everybody on board was in a state of panic. Being captured by the Germans on the high seas meant nothing but disaster.

When the ship came nearer everybody breathed a sigh of relief. I saw that it was a British cruiser. All fear and panic vanished away like smoke on a windy day. It had many, many crates of tea stacked on the top deck. The cruiser tied up next to the ship and started to unload several cases of tea. Then the British officers came onboard and inspected all the passengers. Everybody had to open their suitcases, except for me, who had none. The British, returning to the cruiser, put to sea; and the ship was soon out of sight. Our ship stopped at Reykjavik,

Iceland, after three days the ship was permitted to leave.

After 25 harrowing and tense, nervous days on the high seas, and traveling no faster than 7 knots, the ship finally arrived in New York on August 10, 1940.

When Lova left David in the mountains she had to drive very cautiously over the slippery, wet and muddy roads. Her heart was pounding with fear and apprehension. She wanted to get back to her apartment in Oslo, but was greatly afraid of what she would find both in the city and at her apartment. She was thinking that if her apartment had been confiscated, where could she go? To friends or neighbors? Who could she trust?. All the way back to the city she kept telling herself to stay calm. She also had to look after David's office, determine what to keep, dispose of the rest and then close the facility. The landlord had to be notified that David's office and their apartment would be vacated. She had to notify the electric, gas and telephone companies to shut off the utilities. Then she had to pay all bills, and make sure there were no outstanding debts. Thinking of all the things she'd have to do seemed to steady her. She knew she was a strong person. She would get through this situation. She hoped that there was still money left in the bank account, and that the Nazis hadn't confiscated her financial resources.

With deep-seated anxieties she managed to control her fear and panic when she approached the city limits of Oslo. German and Norwegian soldiers stopped the car and questioned her about where she had been, and to what place she was going.

"We've been in the country for a vacation, and I am going to my apartment in Oslo. The children are sleeping so please don't talk too loud, otherwise they'll wake up. May I go now?" They waved her on.

Fortunately they didn't inquire about her name or about her husband. If they had learned where David was they would have sent the police to arrest him and bring him back to Oslo. There was already a warrant out for his arrest. It was providential that the children didn't wake up, otherwise they might have talked, and innocently told that their father was on his way over the mountains to Sweden.

Entering Oslo was like coming into a foreign country. German soldiers were everywhere. The swastika flag and banners were displayed from all the official buildings. The swastika was even draped over the balcony of the King's palace, showing the arrogance of the Nazis, and their disregard for the Norwegian people. The atmosphere was thick with tension and uneasiness.

As fast as she could, she drove to her apartment, parked on the street; got the children out of the car, and walked up the stairs to her residence. Cautiously she opened the door and, with a sigh of relief, found no one there. The three of them entered. After checking through every room, she was happy to discover that nothing was missing. That was a great relief to her.

"Now we have to find something to eat, and then get some sleep." She looked at the children. They were tired and hungry. She opened the refrigerator and it was empty. The cupboards were equally bare. "You children must stay here while I go and buy food. I don't know what the situation is, if any food is available. I'll be back as soon as I can."

Lova returned after an hour with several bags filled with groceries. They had food for a few days. As soon as she was able she placed a long distance call to her father in Gothenburg, Sweden, and told him that she and the children would be coming there for a "visit." She didn't say anything about David in fear that the Gestapo would be listening in on the conversation.

Now she had to make plans for leaving Norway.

First she had to receive permission to enter Sweden. She went to see the chief of the Swedish Consulate in Oslo. That man hated Jews with a passion, and had great joy in keeping the Jews in Norway from escaping, and hoped to deliver them to the Gestapo when the time was right.

At first there didn't seem to be any hope at all that she would obtain the proper permits. But Lova was persistent and didn't give up at all. She appeared at his office so often that she wore him out. Finally she received the entry permit.

Then she made her way to the Gestapo headquarters, and requested an exit visa to travel to Sweden for a visit to her father. Because she was a Swedish citizen she received the exit visa after only a few weeks of trying. But before her request was approved she had many talks with the leader of the Gestapo, who by that time had become tired and worn out from her daily requests. After several weeks of trying to persuade him he finally told her 'Ja, fahren Sie,' (yes, you can travel) and approved her exit visa. Lova had succeeded in overcoming that obstacle.

Lova was able to rent a railroad freight car to transport some of her furniture to Sweden. She made her freight car available to other Jews who also wanted to ship their furniture to Sweden. So the car was filled with the personal belongings from several Jewish families in Oslo.

Meanwhile, I, who by now was in the U.S.A., had been able to borrow $2,000.00 for airplane tickets for my family. The plan was for them to fly to Portugal and from there to New York. But the Germans wouldn't allow any flights over their territories, so this plan had to be changed. Instead of traveling just by air, she and the children had to journey by land and sea, as well.

In September 1940, she left Oslo with her two children, and traveled to Gothenburg to visit her father. This was the first step before starting on the long and arduous journey to join her husband. Once in Sweden she immediately got busy finding a way to travel to America.

The only way for her to get there was to travel through Russia, over to Japan and then by ship to the U.S.A. She also had to apply for an entry visa to The United States. After much waiting--a time filled with anxieties--she finally received the visas; one for herself and one for each of her two daughters, age seven, and five.

To travel through Russia and Japan she had to have two transit visas, one for each country. She was able to obtain an audience with Madame Alexandra Kollontaj, Soviet Union minister in Sweden. After a long conversation with her, Lova received the coveted permit. Then she had to deal with the Japanese officials, and a transit visa for the three of them was finally issued. With all the legal documents in hand to travel through Russia and Japan, she was now ready to leave Sweden.

Lova and the children flew from Stockholm to Riga, where she obtained passage on another plane to Moscow. In February 1941, they left Moscow on the Trans-Siberian Railway and arrived in Vladivostok 11 days later.

For those 11 days Lova and the girls were stuffed into a smoke-filled, crowded passenger area that closely resembled a delicatessen. The aroma of onions and garlic, all varieties of salami, yeast rolls and tea, filled the air. Lova's canvass bags, full of food for the journey, made its own contribution. Lova remembered that on the first day on the train the dining car had white linen on all the tables. When they arrived in Vladivostok the table linen had turned into a black color.

> They arrived at Vladivostok one evening in February and had heavy suitcases and no one to help them. A Norwegian, who was going to Canada to join the Norwegian Army, helped them with the suitcases. In the dark they walked three miles before they came to the pier where they found a small boat.
>
> From there Lova and the two children sailed on that small ship to Tsuruoka, Japan, a journey that took 24 hours. During the crossing Lova and the children were seasick. From there they boarded a train for Tokyo. A larger ship, the Hamata Maru, took them across the Pacific Ocean to San Francisco, arriving there on February 20, 1941. After entering America, Lova and the

children stayed with a friend they had known from Norway. I called her at our friend and it was good to hear her voice.

Lova and the children traveled to Chicago where we were finally re-united. I cried from joy to see my family again. We had been separated for almost a year.

Lova and the girls made it out of Russia just in time. Only four months after they reached the United States, Russia was invaded by the Nazis. (See Note Page 184.)

They arrived in the new country, and together they were going to make a new start in a much different environment than they had been used to, a very unfamiliar language and a different lifestyle than they could imagine. The changes that challenged them were not much different than what David's parents and relatives had faced many years ago, when they left their native country and immigrated to Norway. But David's thoughts went back to Norway and how his mother and his siblings were surviving.

Note for Chapter 9

On June 22, 1941, at four in the morning, Joachim von Ribbentrop, Germany's foreign minister, delivered a formal declaration of war to the Russian Ambassador in Berlin, Vladimir Dekanozov. On June 30, 1941, the invasion of Russia by Germany, code named "Barbarossa," was put into action. (Winston Churchill "Memoirs of The Second World War" Abridged, Pages 404, 467-469.)

Chapter 10

The Trap

To escape into a world of fantasy in the face of cold, chilly and indisputable evidence of reality is a dangerous journey fraught with peril!

So far the Gestapo hadn't bothered the Jews. That encouraged the Jewish Community in Trondheim to tend to believe that the Nazis had turned into "angels of mercy." Most of the Jews were living in a world of dreams.

Four members of my family were still in Trondheim. On the one hand, they reasoned, it probably wasn't safe to remain there. But on the other hand nothing had happened, and perhaps what had taken place in other countries may never occur in Norway. Some of them vacillated back and forth like a pendulum out of control. It would be so much easier to stay than trying to find a place for safe escape. To flee would terribly disrupt their lives and make it very destructive for them. But if they didn't escape, their lives could still be upset and terrorized should the Nazis arrest them and ship them off to some concentration camp.

But the Gestapo hadn't bothered the Jews - - -so far, except for two Jewish businessmen who were executed by the Nazis in 1941 about a year after the invasion had taken place. This was an incident that many of the Jews refused to believe had taken place, fearing that acknowledging the truth of it and talking about it would bring about their own demise. So, they kept silent about it.

This and much more went through Heiman's mind. He was a deep thinker always trying to know his options. Then he was ready to make the best decision that would produce the most beneficial results. He was a man of five feet six inches, with light brown hair and hazel eyes. He was generous to a fault and was always helping others as best he could. He had a good sense of humor and would often bring home the latest jokes that brought laughter and smiles to everybody. When asked where he got his jokes, he told us that Mr. Gavriloff, who operated a tobacco store next to our building, had a joke book and each joke cost 10 cents. I believed him at first, but after a while I knew he was making that up as well as the jokes.

Heiman was still debating the question whether to stay or leave. There was so much he had in Trondheim. He managed the store that my parents had established, and it became a very prosperous business. Heiman also opened another store across the river. He had many friends among the Jews and non-Jews, and was well liked by everyone. Another important factor that he considered was the familiar surroundings he had grown up in. Here he was born, grew up, went to school and became a good businessman. He was loyal to his profession, very competitive, and carried out his activities with honesty and integrity. He often helped his cousins in their business with advice or contacts to obtain top grade merchandise.

If he escaped to Sweden there would be so many changes to make and he wasn't sure if he could adjust. On the other hand, if he stayed in Trondheim there would be serious consequences for him if the Nazis arrested him. In either case there would be changes in his life. Big changes!

The knot in his stomach was understandable, considering the pressures and challenges facing him.

The Trap

He had so much on his mind, besides the worry of what to do with the stores and properties if he must escape to Sweden. For the time being, he still had to keep the stores open, meet the payroll, have adequate inventory for his customers, and try to take each day at a time. He had never in his life experienced such pressure and tension. But he also knew that these were difficult and trying times. He constantly asked himself "When would the world situation return to normal?"

Heiman was also concerned about whether King Haakon and his government had escaped, and he wondered how the Norwegian Armed Forces were holding up against the overwhelming invasion forces. There were armored vehicles in every city, with thousands of German troops marching in the streets. And to top it off, the Gestapo had already determined who were Jews, what professions they were engaged in and where they lived. At a pre-determined time the Jews would be arrested. The Nazis went about this schedule in a diabolic, systematic and methodical way.

Heiman's concern for the Norwegian Armed Forces and the King and his government was justified.

He learned later that just before the Nazis occupied Oslo on April 9, King Haakon VII, his family and the entire Storting, (Parliament) left Oslo at 9:30 in the morning by a special train for Hamar, 80 miles north of the city. [2]Twenty heavy duty trucks loaded with gold from the Bank of Norway, the country's gold reserves, followed by several trucks packed with the secret papers of the Foreign Office, got away at the same hour. That was just before the roads were closed. They escaped just in time. From there the King and

---

[2] William L. Shirer "The Rise and Fall of The Third Reich" P 703

Parliament went to Elverum, East of Hamar, where the existing government was dissolved. A new government in exile was formed and empowered by the King to carry on the war against Germany until Hitler was defeated and a normal government could be re-established on Norwegian soil. (King Haakon is the only monarch in the 20th century that had been elected to the throne of Norway by popular vote. He is also the first king Norway had had of its own for five hundred years. King Haakon was a brother of Christian X, the king of Denmark. Denmark had been invaded on the same morning.)

The German Army was on the heels of King Haakon, advancing like a bloodhound after its prey. With the Nazis gaining on them, the King and his party now had to decide in what direction to flee; across the border to Sweden, which was not far from Elverum, or flee north into the mountains which were filled with snow?

[3]After a short discussion they chose to move on up the mountains through the rugged Gudbrands Valley, which led past Hamar and Lillehammer and through the mountains to Aandalsnes on the northwest coast, a hundred miles southwest of Trondheim.

This hazardous journey took them 20 days. The King of Norway and the members of his government finally reached Molde where they were taken aboard the British cruiser "Glasgow" and sailed to Tromso, situated way above the Arctic Circle. There, a British cruiser, the "Devonshire," was boarded and it took them to London. It would be five long years, May 1945, before the King could return to his country and his people.

It is believed that it was Mr. Hambro, president of the Storting, who through his actions, saved the Norwegian government from falling into the hands of

---

[3] William L. Shirer "The Rise and Fall of The Third Reich" P.708

the German Army, and was able to transport all the gold reserves out of the country before the Nazis could get their hands on it.

For 63 days the Norwegian Forces stood up against the Germans. With the few resources available to them they fought the Nazis in the mountains, in the valleys, in the streets, in the air and on the water before they surrendered. On Wednesday, June 12, the Norwegian forces laid down their arms. It all ended in Narvik, a small town in the northern part of Norway, where the last battle was fought. The fighting in Norway lasted longer than in Belgium, Holland, Poland and Denmark combined.

The Germans still hadn't deported any Jews from Norway. However, starting in May 1940, by an order issued by the German Occupation Forces, all Jews had to turn in their radios to the police. Of course, the Norwegian and German Nazis were exempted from this order.

Later, radios belonging to all Norwegians were confiscated. This made it impossible for those without radios to listen to BBC (Great Britain) and to keep informed on the progress of the war. This order further stated that anybody caught listening to the Broadcast from England would face death. All appliance stores were ordered not to sell radios to any Norwegian citizens other than those who were Nazis. The stores had to receive permission from the police to sell these devices to any prospective customer. In addition, the names of those whose radios had been confiscated were circulated to all stores. The Jews were locked out from obtaining any listening devices, and so were kept in the dark as to the progress of the war. By that time a number of the Jews had already fled to Sweden, and they kept a watchful eye toward their hometown in case the Nazis should start any violence against those who had remained.

Towards the latter part of May, Mama, after seeing that no harm had come to the Jews in Trondheim, decided to leave Sweden to help Heiman look after her properties and personal belongings. She couldn't be sure, however, how long Norway's Jews would remain safe from Nazi persecutions. She realized the risk she was taking and knew that she might have to flee her home again, but hoped that her fears about that would never come to pass. She didn't want to recognize that the confiscation of the radios belonging to the Jews was the beginning of the persecution.

Heiman believed it was still safe for Abel and the others in the family to return home, so why should they stay in Stockholm? For three months Abel had lived in Stockholm where he had worked in the shipping department of a book publishing company. By that time those of the family who had remained in Norway saw that things were so quiet there that they urged Abel to come back to continue his education. He was in Gymnasium (Jr. College) and in the fall he was going to start his third and last year and then graduate.

Many of the Norwegian Jews from Trondheim, including members of my family, who had fled across the border, returned from Sweden when they believed all was well in Norway. They didn't think that there was any danger for the Jews afterall, and it was true that no vicious action had started against them. The Nazis gave the impression that all was well in Norway, and they were hoping that the Jews would take the bait. It was a trap set by the Nazis, and many of the Jews fell for it.

The Jews had no idea what calamities were waiting for them. In retrospect it would have been much better, and safer for them to remain in Sweden until the war was over. However, they were thinking of all of their personal properties, the stores and the inventories they owned. They had worked for it for many years and when they had finally achieved some independence, it was inconceivable for them to give it up voluntarily. As it turned out, those who were able again to escape were spared annihilation. Those who refused to escape, still believed that their lives were not in danger. Between 1942 and 1943 over half of the Norwegian Jewish population was deported to Poland.

It is very difficult for anybody to voluntarily surrender all they have worked for, and be reduced to helplessness without any means to make a living. This would put them in the category of victims. Under normal circumstances there would be others to help. However, these were not normal conditions. When the Nazis confiscated the properties and personal possessions belonging to the Jews there was no one to intervene. The Jews had nothing with which to sustain themselves, and there was no one to give them aid and comfort except for the underground. If the non-Jewish population tried to help they would be arrested, sent to prison, or executed for aiding the enemy. The Jews, by declaration from Quisling and Adolf Hitler, were enemies of the state.

―――――∽∞∽―――――

On June 22nd 1940, German troops paraded through Paris, and in disgrace, the French government signed an armistice pact with Adolf Hitler. The armistice was signed in the same rail car where, in 1918, Germany was humiliated by signing the armistice after its defeat.

June 23rd witnessed a happier occasion when my sister Asne was married to a Swedish Attorney, Arne Levin. The wedding was performed in a local synagogue, in Stockholm. It was a small wedding, with Julius and Abel from her family, the groom's family and a few friends. Julius gave the bride away.

Dinner followed the ceremony, and to my knowledge the only telegram the bride and groom received came from Samuel and me. It was sent from Berkeley, California with this text: "Fra Kalifornia's solrike land gratulerer vi Asne og Arne som kone og man." (From California's sun drenched land, we congratulate Asne and Arne as wife and man.) This was something to smile and laugh over. In those times people needed to laugh.

Little did we all realize how important a role that marriage would play in helping many of the other family members after they had escaped from Norway. In particular, Asne and Arne played a singularly important role in the years ahead in saving the lives of Beile, Benno and their baby Karin.

On the same day and month, but in Trondheim, Oskar married his childhood sweetheart, Lilly. The wedding took place in the Synagogue and was performed by Kantor Jakobson. 14 months later a girl, Tove, was born. Not long after that, real problems and dangers came crashing down on them.

Abel returned to Trondheim in August. The overnight journey was uneventful, and he arrived without incident. The border was still open, which was a good sign; nevertheless, by the end of August, the borders were completely closed by the Nazis. That same month, Abel entered his third and last year in the Gymnasium, and graduated in the summer of the following year. He was now ready to enter the University if the opportunity was there.

In spite of the potential hostility, my family remained in Trondheim. They were, of course, fearful about what might happen to them in the near future, but all they could do, like so many others, was to live one day at a time. Before the borders had closed, Mama sensed an enormously grave peril approaching, and made preparations to have most of her furniture shipped to Sweden. She was able to put all her belongings on a railroad freight car, and declare that it was a wedding gift to her daughter who was recently married in Stockholm. She made sure that the doors of the railroad car were sealed and would only be opened in Stockholm at the railroad station by the customs officials under the authority of Asne. The authority to open the railroad car was signed by Mama and mailed to Asne. All of Mama's furniture arrived safely. The large crystal chandelier however, was left in the salon because she couldn't find a way to have it shipped safely.

By August 1940 the Germans had arrested all the Jews in northern Norway, in towns like Tromso, Narvik and Bodo where the Fischer family, our cousins, lived. Included in this arrest was also another cousin Dr. Oscar Bernstein. I knew the other Jews who had been arrested because they had lived in Trondheim before moving farther north.

My family was in great despair over these events, but tried not to think much about it, because, in one way, it was so far from Trondheim, and also they didn't think that arrests like those would ever happen in their city. They knew about the German concentration camps, but had not heard about any mass extermination camps. They didn't know, and to some extent didn't want to know, what plans the Germans had for them, and believed that they were fairly safe remaining in Trondheim. For some unexplained reason they believed that they were immune to any persecution from the occupation forces. It is a mystery what made them assume that attitude.

This became a daily dose of turning away from reality in order to cling to the status quo. They were in a state of denial, not wanting to face the intents of the Nazis. The status quo was rapidly changing.

"The Germans really hadn't done anything except to confiscate the radios and the villa from us. So what is there to worry about?" the family continued to say to one another. They were all living in a dream world that soon would turn into a nightmare of the worst kind.

The confiscation of all radios should have been a warning to them. A wake up call! But when the radios belonging to all Norwegians were confiscated, for a little while the Jews thought that the Germans considered these two groups the same --- enemies of the state. There was no difference between Jews and non-Jews, so they convinced themselves.

At that time all the Jews agreed that the Nazis wouldn't dare to do anything to "Us Jews. What for? We haven't done anything to offend them." It was like watching a hungry lion hoping it would never attack.

Unfortunately, they didn't know, nor did they want to know, that just being a Jew was more than enough to offend the Nazis, Hitler and Hitler's "New Order."

Julius disagreed with those who were ready to return home, because he didn't think it was safe to remain in Trondheim. He stayed in Stockholm making plans to leave for America. He applied to the American Consulate in Stockholm, under the Norwegian quota, for an entry visa to The United States. This was granted after waiting many days.

Julius' flight from Norway to Canada.

There were no passenger ships crossing the Atlantic from Stockholm because of the blockade of the seaways by German submarines.

Julius had to find another way to reach America. He was able to obtain a transit visa from the Russian and Japanese Consulates to travel through their countries. On Friday November 1, 1940, he left Stockholm by plane and arrived in Moscow 18 hours later. He found his way to the railroad station and was able to purchase a third class ticket on the Trans-Siberian Railroad all the way to Vladivostok. The train was already booked full and the first available space was Monday, November 4th.

He spent two days in the city using his time to rest, eat and sleep. Between these activities he walked around the city to see what he could find of interest. One sight in particular was a great surprise to him.

Outside the state-operated grocery stores there were long lines of people waiting patiently in the cold, dreary weather to be let in to buy their daily allowance of food. Once inside they waited in another line, and finally bought what they could. Then they had to wait in still another line to pay for their purchases. Having done that they went to a third line to pick up what they had just paid for. A daily "outing" like that would usually take 3-4 hours.

The following Monday, the express-train, the Russiya, pulled out from Yaroslavskiy station and started on its 6000 mile journey. If all went well the train would arrive in Vladivostok seven or eight days later. (See note Page 198.)

Julius didn't have the money to pay for sleeping accommodations, so he slept in his seat. He held on to his heavy overcoat, fur lined gloves and hat lest they be stolen. The train was filled to capacity, and all the 3rd class passengers, including Julius, brought their own food along. Buying meals in the dining car was too expensive. The aroma of meat, cheese and strong tea hung in the train car like delightful clouds.

On Tuesday November 12, the train arrived in Vladivostok. Julius took his small suitcase and went looking for passage to Japan. He was in luck. A Japanese ship was leaving for Kobe in a few days. He bought passage, and was able to sleep on board and eat with the crew. The food was nothing like Norwegian fare, but he made himself like it. It was either that or go hungry. He determined that starving appealed to him considerably less than the Japanese food.

He arrived in Kobe on November 18 and was faced with another challenge. He had to find passage for the last phase of his long journey, with the final destination--America. For many days he searched for a ship that would take him to San Francisco. Though he could have bought a ticket, Julius had so little money by now that he knew he would need to save as much as possible so that he would have some money when he arrived in America. Finally he found a Japanese freighter that was ready to sail for San Francisco. But there was one hitch. The ship needed a cook, and couldn't sail without one.

When Julius heard that, he immediately told the captain that he was a trained cook. He was hired on the spot; and for free passage all he had to do was to cook three meals a day for a crew of 8. Later Julius remarked that if bullets didn't kill the crew, the food he prepared surely would.

He arrived in San Francisco on Thursday, December 19, his birthday, having been en route for almost two months. Neither Sam nor I had any idea that Julius was on his way to the USA, until Sam received a phone call from him stating that he had just arrived in San Francisco. Sam caught the train that traveled across the Bay Bridge, found Julius and brought him to Berkeley. To celebrate his birthday the three of us had dinner at a restaurant in Berkeley called "The Black Angus."

For many years Julius had practiced dentistry in Trondheim and, of course, he wanted to continue in his profession. He thought that Los Angeles might give him a better opportunity. So on Thursday, December 26, he traveled there by bus.

Upon further investigation, however, he learned that he couldn't practice dentistry without a license from the state of California. As Julius searched out the possibilities of obtaining this license he discovered he would have to take more dental courses at the University to meet the licensing requirements. But, he had no money to attend the University. In great frustration he wondered what would become of his future.

Then he had stroke of luck! He heard that the Norwegian government had started a training camp called "Little Norway" in Toronto, Canada, for the

Norwegian Forces. (In 1943 the camp was moved to Muskoka, a two hour train ride north of Toronto.) The camp was in dire need of medical professionals, like doctors and dentists. He applied to join the Norwegian Forces. Immediately he received a telegram that he was accepted, and was ordered to come there right away. Upon his acknowledgement, money would be forwarded to him for his travel and expenses. Early in 1942 he left California for Canada.

In Toronto he met a wonderful Jewish woman, Beckie Ginsberg, and married her. They had one daughter, Sheila. Beckie's two brothers, Morris and Joe were furriers. After the war, when Julius had returned from England where he served in the Norwegian Medical corps, they helped him financially so that he could get his license to practice dentistry in Canada.

Note for Chapter 10

The Trans-Siberian Railroad, the longest rail-line in the world, was started in 1891 by Grand Duke Nicholas, and was completed 13 years later. Between Moscow and its final destination, Vladivostok, it would cross six major rivers, and travel through seven time zones.

Chapter 11

Flight to Safety

Black line shows the escape route
of my mother and two brothers

It was like a deadly game of waiting.
Though all the Jews could escape, most of them thought that the Nazis wouldn't do anything to them. "We are so few Jews here we are sure we will be left alone," they hoped. But the Nazis knew how to play this game of waiting. They were masters at it, and had played it in a number of countries to millions of Jews.
Days had gone into weeks, followed by months of waiting for the inevitable to happen. The Jews in Trondheim tried to hide the strain and the pressures in

their daily lives. What they had read about how the Nazis had treated the Jews was unbelievable. It was first the confiscation of all their properties, then the arrest of all male Jews, followed by all women and children. The final phase was deportation to a concentration camp. But that would never happen to them, they thought. Needless to say, uncertainties and fear pushed out the security they had enjoyed for so many years.

On Tuesday October 21, 1941, Heiman opened the main store, as he had always done. Everything seemed normal, and it looked like another day might pass without any interference from the Nazis. The State Police, an arm of the Gestapo, had never knocked at his door early in the morning (their usual mode of operation) to arrest him. So far, he considered himself very lucky not to have been a target of arrest by the Nazis. The store windows had not been painted with signs like "JEWS! IT IS FORBIDDEN FOR ALL ARYANS TO SHOP HERE." Maybe they would leave him alone, including all the Jews in Norway, he intensely hoped.

He had managed the stores, and carried out his business as if nothing had happened. Yet every moment was spent in fear that any day might be his last one in the store.

He remembered when on the morning of April 21, 1941, without any warning, and operating as swiftly as a lightning strike, the Nazis moved into the synagogue and declared it their property. This was the synagogue where I had my Bar Mitzvah in July 1934, and where some of my brothers went through the same ritual.

News of this blatant takeover leaked out, and the Jews in Trondheim quickly rushed to their place of worship to rescue the Holy Scrolls with their silver ornaments. When they got there two of the three scrolls had been safeguarded, along with several prayer books. They rescued a number of other additional prayer books and prayer shawls. They had to work fast, because the Nazis were already in the building, and what the Jews couldn't carry with them they threw out the windows onto the sidewalk below in hopes that Jews on the outside would pick up the items and carry them to safety.

The Nazis desecrated the entire sanctuary converting it into a barracks for their soldiers, and the gallery where the women sat during the services, was converted into a barbershop. Great damage was done to all of the interior. The Star of David, which was set in the leaded glass windows, was cut out and replaced with the swastika.

Other than that, the Nazis hadn't bothered the Jews at all. That had become like a broken record for the Jews.

It had been 18 months since the invasion, and from what Heiman knew, the Nazis would usually arrest and deport all the Jews within a few weeks after having occupied a country. This baffled him because he now couldn't anticipate correctly what the Nazis would do and when. After all he had the safety of the family to think of. Of course, he still didn't trust the Nazis to leave the Jews alone; and he was aware that they really wouldn't be safe until the German Army was out of Norway. He knew that if the Nazis didn't leave, the family would eventually have to escape; which was an option he didn't even like to think about. Not just then.

Being realistic about the situation, he tried to show an outward cheerfulness. This became increasingly difficult for him as the days and months wore on. He lived daily fighting the feelings of anxiety and fear. He didn't sleep too well, and there were many nights when he stayed awake into the early hours of the morning. That he was greatly worried was an understatement.

Mrs. Paulson, a long-time clerk in the store, interrupted his troubled thoughts; "Ingebjorg called from the apartment. It's almost time for your coffee break, and there aren't any hard rolls. She thought you might want to go over to baker Hoff and buy some. There's plenty of cheese."

"Both kinds?"

"Of course. Both Swiss and the Gjetost. We'll take care of things while you're gone."

Heiman looked forward to his coffee break, and was ready to go to the baker when he was stopped in his tracks. It was less than two hours since he had opened the store. His illusion of safety and security was about to be crushed.

Then it happened suddenly!

The door flew open, and into our store stormed a Norwegian Nazi, Reidar Johan Duner Landgraff, accompanied by two State Police officers, all in civilian clothing. Heiman recognized Landgraff from pictures he had seen in the local papers. (The Norwegian State Police worked under the direction of the Gestapo. By orders of the Gestapo, they carried out all the arrests of Jews and the confiscation of their properties. The Norwegian police deliver all arrested Jews to the Gestapo.) [4]Reidar Landgraff, who worked under Gerhard Flesch, Commandant for the Security Police in Trondheim, was the bureau chief in charge of confiscation of all Jewish properties in Trondheim.

Heiman knew what it meant, and in fear, trembled like cold jello. He knew that one inappropriate word would lead to his arrest, and then he couldn't help the family escape.

---

[4] Bjarte Bruland, "Forsoket paa aa tilintetgjore de Norske Jodene" (The attempt to liquidate the Norwegian Jews) Masters Thesis at the University of Bergen, Spring 1995

That day brought all his fears to culmination; and he knew the Nazis were serious about carrying out their program of extermination of the Jews in Norway.

Mr. Landgraff called out in a loud and arrogant voice:

"This store and all your properties in town are confiscated by the authority of Vidkun Quisling. Hand over the keys to the store." He held out his hand. "This includes," he continued, "all the inventories, the bank accounts, all insurance policies and the cash monies in the upstairs safe. I will be in charge of this store; somebody else will take care of the store across the river, and the gift shop in mid-town." He looked at Heiman with a disgusting frown that had the charm of a running chain saw. "The keys!--Now! Don't forget the keys to that large cash register." and he pointed to it. "Leave all the cash there."

Heiman had no choice. He handed him the keys to the store.

"Every morning at precisely nine, you will report to me right here in the store and then leave. You will not be allowed to work here anymore. Don't forget, tomorrow morning at nine you will report to me. You live in an apartment on the third floor, don't you? Who else lives there?" He spoke as fast as a machine gun, and it was obvious that he had memorized his orders from a directive that the police department had received a few days earlier from the Gestapo Headquarters in Oslo.

"Yes, I do live there. My mother, my brothers Leopold, Jacob and Abel, and our maid lives there."

With that Reidar Landgraff, a long time member of the Norwegian Nazi party, and a dedicated Nazi, ordered Heiman out of the store.

While this was taking place all the store clerks watched with frightful expressions. None of them dared say anything on Heiman's behalf, for fear of being arrested and sent to prison themselves.

Defending a Jew was a capital offense punishable by a jail sentence, or in some cases execution.

For the first time in his life Heiman was out of work. In less than five minutes he had lost the family stores, the inventories, including what was in the free zone warehouse, all the bank accounts and all the buildings; and everything the family had worked for all their lives. There was nothing else he could do but to follow the orders from Mr. Landgraff. If that wasn't all, 15 months earlier the Nazis had also confiscated the family summer villa at Vikhammer. Somehow Heiman hadn't computed that as the prelude of what was coming next. (See Note 1, Page 221.)

There was no other option! To survive was to escape. If he and the others in his family didn't escape soon, they would all be arrested, sent to a concentration camp, and be faced with a high probability of certain death. It would be certain death for Mama, as old as she was.

Slowly, and in shock, he walked up the two flights to the apartment. Upon entering he found Ingebjorg, Leopold and Mama in the kitchen. They saw that he was disturbed, and very angry. His face had become ashen, and for a short while he was speechless.

"The Nazis have confiscated all our properties!" Heiman stammered between gasps of breath. "They have taken all the inventories, bank accounts and all cash. They know where our safe is! One of our clerks must be a Nazi. I am not allowed to enter our store except to report every morning at nine o'clock. The Nazis took all the keys and the only one I have left is the key to the apartment. It just happened a few minutes ago." Then, after a pause in a staccato voice he continued. "It - won't be - long - before we're arrested." And then very rapidly "Where are Jacob and Abel?" (See Note 2, Page 221.)

He was so upset it was difficult for him to talk. He got a cup of coffee, and tried to calm himself. He was now without any means to make a living. Fortunately Mama and Heiman had a great deal of cash in the apartment, which only he and Mama knew about. That should last them for a while.

"Jacob will be here for dinner as usual." Ingebjorg offered. "He has a heavy load of patients today, you know. Abel is attending a special student course, and will be home by 2:00 o'clock." She had been our faithful maid for many years, and had long become a member of the family. She made it her duty to know the whereabouts of every family member.

"They can't do this!" Mama declared. "This is our store. We have worked for over 40 years for this store and our properties. Nobody is going to take that away from us. I'm going down to the store and tell that Nazi to return the keys, and then I'll throw him out! He can't steal from us!" Mama was adamant. Her strong will showed through her words, and she was determined that nobody was going to take away her properties. Though her intentions were noble, she didn't realize at that moment how futile they were, and how really helpless they were, and what great danger she and the entire family were facing.

She was ready to make good her words; got up from her chair, and had her hand on the kitchen door-handle leading out to the hallway.

"Don't do it!" Heiman warned her. "There are two State Police officers with him. They will arrest you, and that may be the last we'll see of you. Let's go into the living room and discuss this, and try to make some plans. Remember to speak softly, sometimes walls have ears."

They had by now become suspicious of everything, and finally were convinced that their lives were truly in danger. The cruel and unexpected events of that morning had made it clear that they faced an imminent peril.

What they had feared had now come upon them. In hushed voices they discussed what they could and must do in order to save their lives. Who could help them? How and when would they be able to escape, and by what means? The borders had been closed for some time.

With tears running down her cheeks, Mama looked around the living room and was thankful that most of her good furnishings, except for the large crystal chandelier, were safe with Asne in Stockholm. Nevertheless, by no means was she willing to give up what she had kept in her apartment. It all belonged to her, and nobody else had any right to it.

Finally, she resigned herself to the loss of the stores and everything that went with them. She also knew that the only thing she could do to save her life was to escape. But even that she hesitated to do. Afterall, she was getting old, she reasoned to herself. Trying to escape just seemed more than she could handle! Either way she might die – so why not just stay where she was?

At 12:30 Jacob came up to the apartment. While eating dinner he heard about the confiscation of the properties. He was very angry, but knew there wasn't anything any of them could do about it.

Abel walked in at about 2:30 and was equally disturbed.

"What happened?" he asked. "I walked into the store and was told by some Nazi to get out. He knew who I was, and he also knew about the rest of the family. He arrogantly asked me where they were. I told him I didn't know."

"The stores and everything we own have been confiscated." Heiman explained. "The situation is grave. Any day now we stand a good chance of being arrested. We'll have to make plans to escape. Make sure nobody speaks to anybody about this."

"Where do we go Heiman?" Mama asked. "We'll need transportation. There isn't anybody we can trust now. Or is there?" Mama looked to Heiman for an answer.

Heiman told them that he knew of a cab driver who owned his own taxi. He could be trusted. "I'll contact him. I'll inquire of him this afternoon if he can take us to someplace near the Swedish border. Wherever he lets us off we'll be able to walk across the border. I'll find out and let you know."

"But why can't we take the train to Sweden?" Mama continued. "That will be so much easier. I'll pack a few suitcases, you do the same Heiman, Abel, and the rest of you, and tonight we will be on the train for Stockholm. But what about Ingebjorg?"

"I can't leave just now." Jacob broke in. "I have a lot of patients waiting for their dental work. It's impossible for me to go now." He was thinking of Julius, the other dentist in the family, who had left the year before.

"I'm so glad that some of the family are already out of Norway." Jacob continued. "I'm very concerned," Mama picked up the thought, "about Beile, Benno and little Karin. Who knows where they are, and if they are well." There was a long pause. They were all thinking about the other family members, Aron, Samuel, Julius, and David and his family and their safety. But now they also had to make sure that their own safety was secured.

"The Nazis check the trains regularly. We could never escape that way. The borders, as you know, have been closed for some time. If we are caught at the border, and for sure that is a possibility, that will be the end of us. But we have to find some way. We should each pack some clothes, and keep them ready for the time when our escape plans are finalized." Heiman had given the orders. Everybody was to wait until he returned from his visit to the cab driver.

Through some acquaintances Heiman discovered that one of the members of the Norwegian underground lived in our building. His name and that of his wife were given, and by all means, he was admonished, do not even breathe that name to anybody. "Anybody" was greatly emphasized. (See Notes 3, Page 221 and Note 4, Page 222.)

The young married couple, who were members of the underground, lived on the top floor of our building. Heiman walked up to the fifth floor, rang the doorbell, and the young man opened the door. "Mr. Holmgren, may I come in? I need to talk to you before it is too late." He talked in a whisper.

Egil Holmgren, (not the real name) an engraver by profession, understood and waved him in. The front door was closed very quietly.

"Our stores and all properties have just been confiscated by Reidar Landgraff. We need help to escape. I know of a taxi driver who will take us anywhere we tell him, but we don't know where. Can you help?"

"Reidar Landgraff, that traitor!" the young man said in an angry, but controlled voice. "I hope the underground gets him before long. Of course we'll help. I'll contact the underground leader today, and we'll find the best place for you and your family members to cross the border. The mountains in this region are filled with snow, deep snow, by now. So you'll have to travel South, where the weather is milder and, hopefully little or no snow, and no mountains to climb. I'll let you know as soon as I know. Don't panic. Be ready to escape the moment it is possible. Tell your mother and the others not to panic. That's a dead give-away to the Nazis." At that moment his wife Astrid entered the living room. She was a beautiful, young woman, and like her husband despised the Nazis with a passion. She listened as Egil continued his conversation with Heiman.

"I'm so sorry to hear about the confiscation of your properties." Holmgren sympathized. "At least you are still alive, and under these circumstances that's a big plus." He walked Heiman to the door and before opening it said in a whisper, "Don't worry Mr. Abrahamsen, we'll get you out of Norway. Go about your day in a normal way, lest the Nazis suspect you of planning to escape. You should know Mr. Abrahamsen that your family is among the few to seek help from our underground here in Trondheim. At least so far. I wonder why the other Jewish families haven't contacted the underground for assistance to escape. Are they afraid?"

"They have convinced themselves that the Nazis will leave them alone," Heiman explained, "that they'll never be arrested, or at least that their properties won't be confiscated. They need to observe what has happened to our properties and learn to read these ominous signs. Perhaps they are hoping against hope. I have talked to some of them about escaping, but so far they haven't shown too much interest in such a drastic endeavor."

Heiman thought for a moment and concluded with "I just don't understand them. Their lives are at risk and they are denying that such catastrophic events, outright tragedies, could ever take place here in Trondheim, Norway. Goodbye, and thank you so much for your help." Astrid smiled at him, "Try not to worry, we'll get you across the border in a few days. If there is anything more we can do, please let us know."

Heiman thanked them again, and felt encouraged. He had found somebody who would help him and the family to escape. It was comforting for him to know that there was somebody on the side of the Jews.

Upon confiscation of the properties, reality descended upon Heiman like a boat suddenly sailing out of a fog bank. No longer was there doubt in his mind that they must escape as soon as possible. The extremely hostile situation my family found themselves in caused them to be filled with terror. But in spite of this, they all tried to go about their daily lives calmly.

Two days after meeting with Mr. Holmgren, on Saturday October 24th Heiman, coming from the grocery store, met one of the clerks who still worked in the family store.

"Heiman, you and everybody in your family must escape from here as soon as possible." Mrs. Paulson whispered. "Something terrible is about to happen."

"Is that a rumor, or do you know for sure?"

"It's both. Rumors have been circulating that the Abrahamsen family will be arrested soon. But I also overheard Mr. Landgraff talking to the other Nazis who work in the store; he said that an arrest order for your family is being issued in Oslo. What I heard was that the documents for your arrest should arrive in the Trondheim police station by Wednesday or Thursday. The next day, no later than Friday, early in the morning, as early as five a.m., the police will be at your front door to arrest you, your mother, Leopold and Abel. They intend to surprise and frighten you. All of you will have to escape within a few days.

"You should consider yourself lucky," she said, "if that is the right word, that your stores and properties are the first ones to be confiscated. Perhaps that'll make it easier for you to escape. The Nazis are very methodical. Confiscation of all Jewish properties will take place in alphabetical order. The Buchman family is next, and so on down the line. I can't talk any longer. Good luck." She smiled at him, with tears rolling down her cheeks, while she hurriedly went on her way.

Mrs. Paulson had been employed by my father for many years, and after his death she continued working in the store. She was a loyal and trustworthy woman. Heiman had a good rapport with her, and knew she could be trusted.

As soon as he got home he took the groceries into the kitchen for Ingebjorg to put away. Then he slipped away quietly and scaled the two flights of stairs to the top floor. He rang the doorbell with a frantic touch. The door opened, and without a word he was invited in.

"There are arrest orders being issued in Oslo for all of us. They might be here Wednesday or Thursday. We have to leave very soon. Have you heard anything from the underground regarding our situation?"

"I have already made contact with them, and will immediately get in touch with them again. I'll request a reply without delay. I should hear within a day or so. We have to be careful, you know. I'll be leaving here a few minutes after you leave. You'll hear from me within 24 to 36 hours."

At six Monday morning October 26, the doorbell rang. Heiman feared that it was the State Police with arrest orders for all of them. Very carefully he started to open the door, then called out "Who is it?"

"This is Egil - - -"

That's all Heiman needed to know. Quickly he opened the door and saw Egil Holmgren waiting to be let in. Heiman just about pulled him inside.

"You will have to travel down the Eastern Valley, there is much less traffic on that road, and therefore much safer. Be sure to tell this to the cab driver. Travel from here to Kongsvinger, then go to Skotterud. Go to this address. Knock rapidly three times, and wait. This is the underground headquarters for that region. They will take you to the border, and show you where it is safe to cross. There is very little snow to walk through, and there are no mountains in that area.

"Memorize this address, and tell no one else in the family. Let the cab driver know your destination only. Then get out of the cab, take all your luggage with you, and send the cab driver back to Trondheim. He must not know to what address you are going. Be very careful when you get out of the cab that no German soldiers see you. Be sure to look around first, then go quickly to this address. Again, tell no one. Good luck. It would be best if you could arrange to arrive there after dark; it'll be safer that way. As soon as you can, burn this slip of paper with the address on it." He opened the door, and quickly ran up the two flights to his apartment.

At nine in the morning October 27, Heiman, as he was required since the store had been confiscated, reported to Reidar Landgraff on the first floor of the store.

"I see you; I know you are here. Good-bye." was the usual statement from Landgraff.

Late that afternoon Heiman contacted the cab driver who would drive them south. He was instructed to come to the apartment at eight in the evening the next day. "Park on the side street, and wait. Don't get out of the car, we'll be there. If we are delayed I'll send the maid down to inform you. See you tomorrow night."

At nine in the morning, October 28, Heiman reported again to Mr. Landgraff. He didn't suspect that my family was planning to escape that night.

The escape was set for eight that evening. (This was Samuel's birthday. Fortunately he was already in Berkeley, California.)

(My family wasn't the only ones who were dealing with life threatening disasters. The residents of Moscow, Russia, were in a state of panic as the German invasion force approached the city. According to Hitler, the Russians were surrounded, and the war was almost over. Instead, the war continued, resulting in a disastrous defeat for the Nazis, who finally retreated.)

Heiman, Abel and Mama had packed clothes in a few suitcases and had been ready all day Tuesday. Leopold decided not to leave because he was engaged to Bilka, and didn't want to leave her. Oskar and Lilly were married in June 1940, and they had a little baby girl, Tove, so they decided to wait. Traveling with a small child would be difficult, as well as dangerous. They were hoping for a better time to leave.

The resistance movement had decided that eight in the evening would be a safe time to leave. By that time the streets would be almost deserted. Chances of any Gestapo patrols being out in the city were slim. They had checked on the evening schedule for the patrols over a period of several days, and Heiman was assured that this would be the safest time. But there was no telling how long it would remain safe. The window of escape was very narrow, this Heiman knew quite well.

By seven p.m., Heiman and Abel were ready to leave. Mama wasn't dressed yet for the escape. At that point it was obvious that she had no intention of escaping. Ingebjorg had made lots of sandwiches for them to take along, together with four thermos bottles filled with hot coffee, cream and sugar. The resistance movement had warned Heiman not to stop at any restaurants along the way, for fear that they might be discovered by the German soldiers. If they did, all would be arrested for attempting to escape, including the cab driver.

The instructions for Ingebjorg were that she should remain in the apartment after they had left. When Heiman hadn't reported to Mr. Landgraff by nine the next morning, Mr. Landgraff was sure to come up to the apartment and ask where Heiman was. She was to tell him that he was still asleep. Ingebjorg had to play a convincing role, otherwise she would be arrested for helping Jews to escape. That was aiding the enemy, a major offense punishable by death.

" It's eight o'clock. The taxi is here. I just saw it from the window. It's waiting for us. We have to go down the back stairs. Be very quiet so no one knows that we're leaving." Heiman motioned to Mama to get dressed in a hurry, and Abel to put on his overcoat. Heiman and Abel were dressed in knickers, warm sweaters, woolen caps, heavy wool mittens, heavy socks and ski boots. Mama just sat in her chair looking at her two sons, ready to say goodbye to them, and hoping that she would see them again.

"It's time to go, Mama. You must get dressed right now." Heiman implored her.

"I'm not going. All my sisters are still here. I want to stay with them. This is my home. The Nazis are not going to chase me away from here. I will not let them treat me like a criminal, having to escape just because I am a Jew. Why should I have to leave my home? Besides, I'm scared. What if we're caught? They'll shoot us. No! I am staying. You two go ahead."

She looked at Heiman and Abel, and with tears running down her checks, told them to leave immediately, before it was too late. She tried to convince them that with Ingebjorg at her side she would survive. There wouldn't be anything to worry about.

"I'll see you after the war. I'll be here waiting for you. Hurry now, otherwise it will be much too late to- - - " she ended her sentence in sobs.

"If you stay you'll surely face certain death. Escaping will at least give you a chance to live. We're all scared, Mama. But we're more terrified of being caught by just sitting here than escaping to save our lives. Either way it's risky. But to do nothing, and wait to be caught in the web of the Nazis, is even more risky. We'll go. Ingebjorg, help Mama to get dressed in a hurry." Heiman tried to rescue the situation but it didn't look hopeful.

In a troubled and distressed voice Mama pressed on "but what if we get caught? It would be too great a risk. I think it will be better to stay here because there is no assurance that we would reach the Swedish border alive."

"You're right, Mama, there is no assurance that we will reach the border. That is a risk we'll have to take, but it is a far greater risk to stay and do nothing. At least we are trying." Heiman again tried to explain to Mama.

Ingebjorg moved towards Mama.

"Stay away, Ingebjorg, I am not going. That's that."

Mama showed her stubborn streak. She was afraid to leave and terrified to stay. It would be at least a 12-hour drive by taxi ahead of them, in cramped quarters, and in a very tense situation. Mama knew all that. She had been through similar circumstances many years earlier. She reminded herself of her flight from her native country almost 45 years earlier. How difficult and painful it had been then, and now it looked like a repeat of that traumatic event. She shuddered to think that she would have to go through the same experience again. Then she reminisced about her life in Norway. It seemed to have been such a short time since she arrived here, she was thinking.

By eight-thirty Heiman sent Ingebjorg down the backstairs to tell the cab driver to wait. Some complications had set in.

Time rushed on.

The old clock struck eleven.

It was getting late. Perhaps too late.

The safety time zone that the underground had told them about was long past. By now it was a good chance that the streets would again be patrolled by the Gestapo and the State Police. Escape might be impossible. Nevertheless, they tried to persuade Mama to leave with them as soon as possible. She was shaking with fear, and her voice trembled when she responded with "No – please don't ask me to leave my home. This is all I have, besides my children. Why should the Germans arrest me? I haven't done anything wrong, and I'm a 63-year-old woman. What are they going to do with an old woman?" She looked at the two of her 11 children with deep sorrow and great fear in her eyes.

The silence in the living room was cold and disturbing. All that could be said in trying to convince Mama had been said and repeated many times over, with the same result. Mama wouldn't think of leaving her home. At eleven-thirty Abel, turning to Mama finally said, "If you don't go, I won't go. I'll stay here with you. Heiman, you take the cab, and leave Mama and me here."

"No, you must go Abel, mien kind," Mama said. "You will be arrested otherwise."

"Sorry Mama, I won't leave without you." The air was tense.

They all looked at Mama. Several minutes, that seemed like hours, went by in silence. It looked as if she wouldn't change her mind, and Heiman had resigned himself to travel alone to reach the Swedish border.

Then all of a sudden: "I'll go. Ingebjorg help me get dressed. Get my coat and hat. Good-bye and God take care of you." Mama had put on a heavy dress, heavy shoes, a warm hat and a heavy overcoat. With tear-filled eyes and a tired voice, she said good-bye to her faithful and loyal maid. Leaving Ingebjorg would be like leaving a member of the family.

It was so hard for Mama, Heiman and Abel to say good-bye to Ingebjorg, and to leave their home. Would they ever see her again? Mama took one last look at her apartment. She saw the large crystal chandelier still suspended from the ceiling in the salon. She remembered when they had purchased that light fixture. It was on a business trip to Germany when she and Papa saw this fixture through the window of a fine store. For some time they stood there and admired it. Then the owner of the store came out and invited them in so that they could have a closer look. Mama and Papa walked around the crystal chandelier. It was much larger than they thought, and it was magnificent. It had a gold-filled rim, 12 inches high, four inches thick with a diameter of four feet. There were 36 strands of crystal balls forming an elegant sway. They bought it, and had it shipped to our home in Trondheim. For many years it hung in the salon, and all of us enjoyed it very much. She regretted that she hadn't been able to ship it to Sweden. It was impossible to take it along now.

A million thoughts flooded their minds. They had been secure for so many years, and in just a very short time the family status had been drastically changed from property owners to literally homeless. There was, of course, no assurance that they would be able to reach the Swedish border. Nevertheless, there was always hope that the escape would be successful. It was fortunate that none of them knew what lay ahead.

Abel, by his insistence of not leaving unless Mama came along, had saved her life.

They descended by the back way, down a steep flight of stairs, and carefully opened the big door that led out to the side street where the taxi was waiting. There was no traffic, so it should be safe to travel out of the city and then south, down the Eastern Valley. Quickly they whispered goodbye to Ingebjorg, and told her to be sure to lock the big door before she went upstairs to the apartment. Hurriedly they put their suitcases in the car and crawled over them to find a seat. Heiman sat up front with all the sandwiches and the thermos bottles filled to the brim with coffee. He had their destination memorized.

Fortunately this taxi, as so many others at that time, didn't use gasoline. The engine had been converted to use alcohol. This gave the taxi a much larger range of travel, so it was unnecessary to stop at any gas stations on the way. The entire roof of the cab was taken up with the tank containing alcohol, and there was also alcohol in the regular gas tank. Driving through town they found to their relief that there weren't any Gestapo soldiers patrolling the streets.

They entered Roros, a small town southeast of Trondheim, at a slower speed, and found the village fast asleep. As soon as they had passed that hamlet they resumed speed. The underground was right, there was hardly any traffic at all along the route.

Around one p.m., the next afternoon, they arrived in Skotterud. This place is about 75 miles East of Oslo. Heiman made contact with the underground and there they spent the rest of the day. During that time, those in the resistance movement told the cab driver to wait for further orders. Later they gave him instructions about his next destination, and where to let off Mama, Heiman and Abel. After dark, on October 29, the taxi driver, following the directions from the underground, managed to get them close to the border. At this point they left the car, took their luggage and walked towards the Swedish border. The taxi returned immediately to Trondheim.

They didn't dare use a flashlight for fear the Nazi soldiers would discover them. However, their eyes had by now adjusted to the dark, and they were able to see a little ahead on their path.

The underground leader had told them that on their way to the border they would have to cross a small lake. They would find a rowboat there for their use. They found the boat; and all three, with their luggage, got in. Mama sat in the back with a few pieces of luggage, the rest was placed up front. Heiman and Abel did the rowing. To their horror and dismay they discovered that there was only 3 to 4 inches of freeboard. (Distance from the water surface to the railing of the boat.) If there had been any wind, or any other disturbance, the boat would have capsized and they would have drowned in the ice-cold water.

On the other side of the lake it was only a few hundred yards to the border. They crossed over to Sweden at nine in the evening of October 29, 1941.

While Mama, Heiman and Abel were waiting in Skotterud for nightfall, to cross the border into Sweden, events in Trondheim took the expected course. When Heiman hadn't reported by nine thirty on the morning of October 29, Reidar Landgraff came up to the apartment and asked where Heiman was.

"He must still be sleeping." Ingebjorg told him.

"As soon as he wakes up and is dressed tell him to report to me immediately. I don't tolerate tardiness. If this continues we'll just arrest him. Be sure to tell him that. Understood?"

He didn't wait for an answer, turned around and slammed the door on his way out.

By noon he stormed up the stairs, rang the doorbell with a violent gesture, and let it ring. Ingebjorg knew who it was, but took her time. She walked very leisurely down the hallway, and then opened the door very slowly. Landgraff pushed her aside, and shot into the apartment. Ingebjorg followed him, saying that Heiman's bedroom was another flight up. She would take him there. They both walked up to the next floor with Ingebjorg leading the way, one step at a time. She was thinking to herself "Why be in a hurry? He'll discover soon enough that Heiman isn't here."

Very carefully and ever so slowly she unlocked the door to the bedroom. Again Landgraff pushed her aside and stormed in. There, in one of the rooms, he saw the likeness of a body asleep on a bed under a down comforter. He ran over to the bed and pulled back the covers. There was nothing there but a few pillows that had been placed there to give the impression that there was a real person in bed.

Landgraff looked at Ingebjorg, who had followed him into the room, and screamed at her:

"Where is he? Where is he? I have to find him. Do you know where he is?" He kept looking at her with a violent expression that could peel the paint off the wall.

"I don't know where he is. They didn't tell me anything. Who knows what those Jews have planned? Maybe he went to the country and is on his way back now."

"I'll find him if it's the last thing I do. You can't fool me. He has escaped. That's it! And so have his brother and mother. Who else of the family has escaped?" he yelled at her and stormed out of the room. He made a loud, angry clamor as he ran down the three flights of stairs. (At that time he didn't know that three brothers were still in Trondheim.)

Ingebjorg, relieved, dropped into the nearest chair, lest her shaky knees gave out. Rehearsing in her mind what had just transpired, Ingebjorg was confident that she had played her role convincingly. She could only hope that Landgraff had believed her. If he hadn't, she knew she'd be arrested.

She was proud of the part she had played in protecting my family. Happily, she thought to herself, "I hope they make it safely to Sweden."

Notes to Chapter 11

1. The villa was confiscated in August 1940 and the Nazis named it "Haus Marianna." Our stores were the first of 29 Jewish businesses in Trondheim to be confiscated by the Nazis. The Nazis, with alarming regularity and stern discipline, confiscated the Jewish stores in alphabetical order.

2. It was frightening to know how many Norwegians supported the Nazis. With over 40% of the police force joining the Norwegian Nazi party, it became increasingly difficult for the Jews to stay out of their reach. Many people from other civil and professional organizations supported the invaders. Heiman understood that some had to, out of fear and the necessity for their own safety.

3. The Norwegian Resistance Movement, also known as the underground, (in Norwegian "Hjemmefronten") started as soon as the Nazis occupied Norway. It had a slow beginning. Ordinary people like laborers, truck drivers, bank clerks, and professionals like engineers and medical doctors, both men and women, took part in this operation. After April 9, 1940 over 3000 Norwegians escaped to England, but that escape route was just about closed in the spring of 1942 because of the German blockade of the sea passage. From then on the only escape routes open were over the border to Sweden. Between 900 to 1000 Jews used that route to reach Sweden.

   By 1942 the underground was well organized, and even dared to rescue from prison the underground

members who had been arrested by the Gestapo. When the underground leaders learned that the Gestapo knew who they were, they escaped to Sweden. They were replaced by new leaders whose names weren't in the Gestapo records.
(Ragnar Ulstein "Svensketrafikken" (Traffic to Sweden) Det Norske Samlaget, Oslo, Norway 1974)

4. Another group called "Theta-Theta," operating from Bergen, was organized shortly after the invasion. Their mission was to obtain information about the position of German war ships, and radio that information to their contact in London. Then the London officials would send ships out to sink the German marauders. This group was instrumental in locating the Battle Ship *Admiral von Tirpitz*, which was eventually destroyed by the British. It took from the beginning of 1942 to the fall of 1944 before *Admiral von Tirpitz* was caught near Tromso, and finally sent to the bottom of the sea.
(Kristian Ottosen "Theta Theta" H. Aschehoug & Co., Oslo, Norway 2000)

Chapter 12

Crossing the Border

As soon as Mama, Heiman and Able had crossed into Sweden the border guard told them to report to the sheriff. By nine in the morning the three of them, tired, hungry but enthused that they had escaped from the Nazis, appeared before the sheriff. His office was bare except for his desk and chair. An atmosphere of animosity had already filled the room like a cauldron of venom. Heiman, with the other two, were exhausted after the ordeal they had just come through. In great detail he explained to the sheriff everything that had happened to them. He was sure that the sheriff would understand and would give them permission to remain in Sweden. To do otherwise would be brutal and barbaric.

Though Heiman was nervous and filled with anxiety concerning the outcome of the situation, he was nevertheless confident that all of them were safe and wouldn't have to face the storm of the Nazi terror anymore. What he didn't know at that moment was that in a short time, and to his horror, the events would take a turn for the worse.

"Do you have any identification papers?"

They handed over to him their papers and he recorded the following:

"This day, October 30, 1941, arrived from Norway across the border three Norwegian citizens who were apprehended by the military border guard who turned them over to me, namely:

"1. Heiman Abrahamsen, merchant, born December 19, 1904 in Trondheim, Norway. His last address was Bakklandet 70, Trondheim. His identification card number 18887, issued February 22, 1941 by the chief of police in Trondheim. He carried Norwegian money in the amount of 607.00 Kroner, and Swedish money in the amount of 99.00 Kroner, together with miscellaneous papers.

"2. Abel Abrahamsen, student, born September 7, 1923 in Trondheim, Norway. His last address was Bakklandet 70, Trondheim. His passport number 290/1940, issued April 9, 1940 by the chief of police in Trondheim and valid until April 9, 1942. His identification card number 39645, was issued March 31, 1941 by the same authority. He carried Norwegian money in the amount of 629.00 Kroner, and Swedish money in the amount of 99.00 Kroner, together with miscellaneous papers.

"3. Mrs. Miriam Abrahamsen, born September 14, 1878 in Lithuania. Her last address was Bakklandet 70, Trondheim. Her passport number 87/1940, issued January 30, 1940 by the chief of police in Trondheim and valid until April 9, 1942. Her identification card number 39644, was issued March 31, 1941 by the same authority. She carried Norwegian money in the amount of 629.00 Kroner, and Swedish money in the amount of 99.00 Kroner, together with miscellaneous papers."

The sheriff took his time in reading and studying these papers. Ever so often he would utter "hmm," and "aha," while drinking coffee and munching on a sandwich. He nonchalantly leaned back in his office chair, putting his feet on the desk, took off his glasses, cleaned them, and put them back on again. All this was done in a deliberate and calculated slow pace. He peered at them scornfully over his small pair of glasses that revealed a pair of beady eyes. With a hostile and arrogant voice he questioned them:

"Are you Jews?"

"We are." Heiman answered. "This is my mother and youngest brother" as he pointed to them and repeated, "Our properties, our stores and inventories were confiscated on the 21st of October. I was thrown out of my business and knew that the next phase would be my arrest. We were left without any means to make a living."

"Were you arrested?"

"No, we weren't. But from what I heard, arrest orders were on their way from Oslo. The plans were that we would be arrested within a few days."

"You can't rely on rumors! Up to this time the Germans hadn't done anything to you then? Except for confiscating your properties, had they threatened your lives or imprisoned you?"

"No, we hadn't been threatened or imprisoned. Knowing the past record of how the Nazis have dealt with the Jews in countries like Poland and Germany, we had reason to believe that they would treat us in like manner.

"Therefore, our lives were potentially in danger. The confiscation of our properties was only the beginning of the program of annihilation the Nazis had planned for us Jews." Heiman knew that there was trouble ahead and went on the offensive.

"You must allow us to stay in Sweden! We have no other place to go. Returning to Norway will mean death for us, especially when the Nazis know that we have tried to escape. You must understand that our situation is desperate and critical, sir, and you must give us permission to remain in Sweden. There is no other place for us to go for safety."

"I don't believe that the Germans are as bad as that. Many Norwegians have come across the border, and we have sent them all back. The Germans never knew that they had escaped, so no harm ever came to them." The sheriff spoke up with a cold and heartless voice and a facial expression to go with it. It was obvious that the sheriff wasn't convinced, and he didn't want to be convinced, that they were in mortal danger.

Heiman was flabbergasted that the sheriff could be so arrogantly prejudiced, ignorant and blind, but refrained from discussing their dangerous situation with him any further. Heiman had by now become agitated, and exhausted from frustration. The color on his face had turned to an ashen gray, and he noticed that mother had started to cry for fear of returning to Norway. Tension and apprehension had filled the room, and the environment was like a Siberian blast. Heiman had to play his cards, the few he had, very carefully. The sheriff was in charge, and Heiman didn't want to antagonize him, hoping there was a chance for them to remain in Sweden.

"I am gong to send you back to Norway. However, your mother who is 62 years old, can stay here. Be ready to leave right now." His tone of voice was as cold as ice. They found out later from the Norwegian resistance movement that this sheriff was a devoted and loyal Nazi.

"If you do that you are sending us back to a certain death. You must understand that we are in grave danger. There is no other place for us to go and remain in safety."

The three of them protested, but there was no use. On October 31st the sheriff ordered them to return to Norway. The only way to return that they knew of was to retrace their steps, find the rowboat and take it across the lake and hopefully get in touch with those who had helped them across the border. There was no assurance they would be able to contact them, as there was a strong possibility they could run into a German patrol that would arrest them.

They said good-bye to Mama and while they walked away she called after them "My sons, my sons, take care of yourselves. Shalom!"

Mama didn't know what to think or do. She was left all by herself in a foreign country and without any relatives or friends to look after her. She had no idea of what was going to happen to her. Would she have to stay at the border station for the rest of the war? Where would she live and how would she be able to pay for her expenses for the time she would stay there? She spent a restless night without much sleep, worrying most of the time about her family and herself.

The next day she was able to make a phone call to her daughter in Stockholm. With the help from the border guards she was put on a train that would take her to Asne and her husband Arne. At least her daughter and son-in-law would provide a family for her for the time being.

Once on the Norwegian side, Heiman and Abel met Leopold who was going to cross the border into Sweden at the same place they had just come from. Leopold had tried previously to cross the border at another place but was refused entry. Heiman and Abel told him that they had tried to cross at this area but the sheriff had sent them back. Now they were going to try another place. Leopold became so discouraged when he heard this that he turned around and went back to Trondheim. They tried to persuade him to stay with them, but his mind was made up.

Heiman and Abel found their way to the resistance movement and told them what had happened. The resistance forces were perplexed and astonished on hearing their story. They couldn't imagine something like that could ever take place, and that the Swedish sheriff had sent them back to Norway.

"Don't worry, we will go a little farther south, along Charlottenberg, and you can cross the border there. Come with us and we'll find a place where you can stay. You must be tired and worried about your mother."

There was no doubt that they were extremely concerned about Mama. Could the sheriff have sent her back across the border in spite of having told them that she could stay in Sweden? They were greatly worried about her welfare. They were also very tired, to the point of exhaustion.

After dark the next day, Saturday November 1, they crossed into Sweden for the second time. The border guard told them to report to the Sheriff. When they did he called the sheriff they had encountered the first time they crossed the border. They were told to wait in the room next to his office while he made the phone call. Through the thin wall they could hear him talk to the first sheriff. Then they heard:

"I am not going to help them at all. I'm just going to send them back to Norway, like you did."

The sheriff told his orderly to send for them. They were informed in the same "charming" and "compassionate" tone of voice as the first sheriff, that they would be sent back to Norway the next day.

Heiman and Abel protested. But to no avail. Then Heiman requested to make a phone call to Stockholm, to his sister and brother-in-law. After a few anxious moments of waiting, the phone at the other end answered, and it was the maid. She said that Asne and Arne were out shopping. Heiman left an urgent message with her that he and Abel were at Charlottenberg and Arne had to intercede immediately to help them, otherwise they would be sent back to Norway the next day.

They were hoping that the maid would give the message to Asne and Arne. They obtained a room at the nearby Park Hotel for 50 Kroner per night including all meals. That evening was spent in suspense and uncertainty and fear. Returning to

Norway was a frightening prospect to look forward to. Their future didn't look promising at all. They could see nothing but disaster ahead of them. Though they were very tired they slept very little that night.

The next morning, Sunday November 2, by orders from the sheriff, Heiman and Abel were ready to go back to Norway the same way that they had arrived. They had their rucksacks on their backs, just waiting for the sheriff to tell them when to start on their trip. Just then, a train from Stockholm pulled up at the nearby station and Heiman and Abel hoped that Arne might be on board. They were ready to leave on their trek back to Norway when suddenly the door to the sheriff's office flew open and in rushed Arne.

He had received the phone message, caught the first train early that morning and arrived at Charlottenberg just before Heiman and Abel were to leave. Arne, being an attorney, convinced the sheriff in legal terms, "that he (the sheriff) would be held accountable to the Swedish civil law authorities if he sent them back, and no doubt, could forfeit his position, pension and serve a prison term plus a fine." Arne emphasized his sharp words and dire warning by pounding his fist on the sheriff's desk.

The sheriff called the State Department in Stockholm and told them what the situation was. Fortunately, this was Sunday and the State Department had only a skeleton staff on duty. Whomever he talked with gave him permission to let Heiman and Abel remain in Sweden. Very grudgingly and very slowly the sheriff signed the entry permits. But he took his time filling out all the necessary papers and inspected each page with scrutiny. Arne watched him with a suspicious eye to make sure the right forms were filled out correctly. At that point he didn't trust that sheriff, and the sheriff knew it.

On Tuesday, November 4th after three nights at the Park Hotel, instead of returning to Norway,

Heiman and Abel found themselves on a train headed for Oreryd, a camp for Norwegian refugees. They stayed there for five days, and then they were free to travel to Stockholm on Sunday November 9.

On November 12, Leopold arrived in Stockholm. But it was a miracle that he was able to escape. It was unthinkable that he would return to Trondheim risking arrest, and if that happened, imprisonment and possible deportation to a concentration camp in Germany.

After Leopold had returned to Trondheim, several of his friends told him, in strong language, to get out of Norway. It was much too dangerous for him to stay there. If the police caught him, and they surely would, he'd be arrested. Another long time friend spotted Leopold as he was walking down Nordre Gate. He approached Leopold, pulled him aside and whispered to him asking what in the world was he doing here? Didn't he know that the Nazis were arresting all the Jews and sending them to labor camps?

Then he told Leopold about a party of nine Jewish men who had been arrested, and had been placed under guard in Buchman's apartment. At twelve noon the two guards left them to go to lunch. The Jews were alone in the apartment unguarded. That was a clear sign for them to escape. The guards gave them an opportunity to flee to the border but none of the Jews took advantage of it. When the guards returned three hours later they were astonished to see that all nine Jews were still there.

The Jews were in a state of denial and didn't believe that anything destructive would ever come to them. They hadn't done anything wrong or committed any crimes. Norway was their country now, and there was no reason why they should be treated like criminals. This was the mentality that colored the reasoning power of the majority of the Jews, not only in Norway but also throughout Europe wherever the Nazis had occupied foreign countries.

The guards, who had been hoping the nine Jewish men would have escaped, had no choice but to hand them over to the Gestapo. All were sent to labor camps where they were treated like slaves, working 16 hours a day. Many Jews died from this harsh treatment.

Leopold wasted no time to inform his fiancée, Bilka, that he had to leave immediately, and urged her to get out as soon as she could. With the help of the resistance movement, he was transported as close as possible to the border. From there he traveled on skis through deep snow over the mountains until he crossed the border into Sweden and reported to the sheriff who noted:

"This day, October 31, 1941, arrived over the border a member of the Abrahamsen family, namely:

"Dekorator Leopold Abrahamsen, born January 28, 1908 in Trondheim, residing at Bakklandet 70, Trondheim. He had two birth certificates issued by the Mosaiske Trossamfund in Trondheim. Cash in Norwegian Kroner 357.00, in Swedish money 00.00."

Leopold had crossed the border at a point farther north than Heiman and Abel, therefore they never met. The sheriff at the border station allowed Leopold to stay, and issued a pass so that he could remain in Sweden for the duration of the war. He went to the refugee camp at Oreryd, stayed there for eleven days arriving in Stockholm on Wednesday November 12th 1941.

A short while later Jacob, who had been in hiding, was helped by the resistance movement to cross the border south of Storlien, the border station to Sweden. He went on skis, came to the Swedish border station and received a permit to remain in Sweden until the war was over. Jacob arrived in Stockholm on Sunday November 16th 1941.

Oskar waited too long to escape. He had a wife, Lilly, and a three-month old baby. He knew he was in danger of being arrested, but didn't know what else to do. To leave his wife and daughter behind while he escaped was out of the question. These were days filled with anxiety and fear for all three as they lived from day to day.

Then, just before Hanukkah everything changed.

On Tuesday December 2, 1941, at eight in the evening the state police came to his home and knocked angrily and very loudly on the front door. Oskar suspected that it might be them. With fear and trembling he opened the door. Outside in the cold dark night stood three Norwegian policemen. They looked at Oskar with disdain and hatred. If looks could kill, this would do it. The leader was the tallest and yelled the loudest:

"Are you Oskar Abrahamsen?"

"Yes, I am. What do you want?"

"By order of the state police you are under arrest. Pack a few clothes and be ready to go in 15 minutes. We'll come in to make sure that you don't escape." With that, all three marched right in. Oskar had to get out of the way or be pushed aside.

This was the time when one didn't dare oppose or question the state police. Under these circumstances they never asked to come into a home, they just did! They carried the cold night on their uniforms right into the living room. The situation was like a quiet ice storm ready to let go of its fury.

"Can't you come back tomorrow morning? It is already 8 in the evening. My baby is asleep and my wife is tired."

"You will come with us now. Pack what you can. You have 15 minutes." The leader looked at his watch, and then at Oskar with the same "captivating" expression he displayed when he arrived at the front door, similar to that of a lightning storm.

Oskar walked quickly into the bedroom and told Lilly, who was watching over Tove, what had happened. She became almost hysterical but calmed down when she thought about her child asleep in the crib.

"We'll have to keep calm. I'll escape, and then I will come for you. If I can't reach you, I'll try to let you know where I am. If you don't hear from me, meet me in Stockholm at Asne and Arne's." They spoke in a whisper while he was putting a few things in a rucksack. "Do you have enough money, Lilly, to last for a while? Here, take this. I'll keep a little money in case I need it. I won't need much money in captivity. Remember when you have a chance to leave, take only the bare necessities with you. The main thing is that you and Tove are safe. The furniture and pictures can be replaced. You and Tove can't." They looked at each other, hugged and kissed. There was so little time, and so much they wanted to tell each other.

"I love you, Lilly. Tell Tove I had to go away on business."

"I love you too. Take care and stay well."

The door opened abruptly. Oskar knew he had to leave. One more quick kiss and a last glance at Tove still sound asleep.

The police transported him to Vollan prison where he spent that night. There he met several of his relatives and friends, "Most of the men were crying and complaining. It was dreadful and a very discouraging experience, to say the least." Oskar shared with me after the war.

One day Oskar was assigned to carry large chunks of raw meat from the huge cold storage facilities to the trucks that would take them to a state owned retail outlet. He was working with another Jewish man by the name of Josef Klein. The entire morning was spent with that work. By noontime, Josef had to go to the restroom. He was allowed to go with a guard. When they returned, Oskar needed to do the same. He started to walk towards the rest room, and the guard remained with Josef Klein.

"Aren't you going to follow him, like you did with me?"

"No," the guard replied, "he knows the way to the restroom and also knows how to get back here."

Oskar walked towards the restroom, but instead of going there, he walked down the stairs and into the street below. He then started to run, faster and faster in hopes of reaching home, get Lilly and Tove, and then escape to Sweden. On his way he came to the main railroad station and saw a large company of German soldiers lined up outside the station. He stopped running and walked slowly past them.

He jumped on a streetcar, paid for his fare and got off where he could catch a bus that would take him to his home. On the way, two German soldiers came on board the bus. Panic set in. Oskar thought that they might be after him, got off the bus at the next stop, and in heavy snow walked the rest of the way to his home.

Upon approaching his home he saw that his house was surrounded by German soldiers. News of his escape had been reported to the headquarters, and the soldiers were guarding his home in case he tried to return there. The only thing Oskar could do was to hide in some bushes across the street. He could see Lilly through the front window in the house, but didn't dare make any motion to her that would attract the attention of those watching his house. At one time Lilly came out on the front porch and shook out a small rug. Knowing that Oskar had escaped, she looked around in hopes to see her husband. There was no sign of him as best as she could determine, so she went back inside.

By two in the afternoon it was already dark, and Oskar saw his chance to get away. That night he spent with a trusted friend who was employed in the bank. The next morning, while it was still dark, Oskar knew that he had to find someone to help him escape. His friend gave him money for the travel, Oskar had only a few coins; and then the resistance movement was alerted. They arranged transportation for Oskar to the border. He was given a pair of skis, and told in what direction to go and what to look out for. The same night, he managed to ski across the border where he met a friendly sheriff who gave him a permit to stay in Sweden. He arrived in Stockholm on Thursday December 11th, 1941.

The war was going full speed ahead. On that same day Germany and Italy declared war on the USA, and Hitler's army was losing battles at the Russian front.

On Tuesday, January 20th 1942, a directive was published by the Chief of the Norwegian Police in Oslo, and in conjunction with the Gestapo, giving orders that passports and identification cards belonging to the Norwegian Jews had to be stamped with a big red "J." The Jews were to report to the local police department for this stamping. Refusal to obey this order was punishable by fine, imprisonment or, in some cases, execution.

About two months after Oskar's arrival in Stockholm, on Monday February 2, 1942, Lilly and Tove, Bilka and her sisters, with the help from the resistance movement, were placed in a covered truck and transported to the border. There the women were outfitted. with skis. This way they were able to cross the border into Sweden, Lilly carrying Tove in a rucksack on her back. They reported to the Swedish sheriff, who then questioned them as to why they had fled from Norway. They were given assurance that they could remain in Sweden, but papers had to be filled out and a report made before they could proceed to Stockholm. Four days later, on Friday Feb 6, they came to Stockholm. Lilly located Asne and Arne, and was soon re-united with Oskar. Bilka and Leopold found each other in Stockholm and were married on March 8, 1942.

Most of the family was now together, and they were all in good health.

Leopold obtained a position in a retail store, and Heiman and Oskar also found work. Abel graduated as an Electrical Engineer from Stockholm Technical Institute. For the moment it looked as if everything had turned out very well and would remain that way.

In March 1942 Samuel joined the Norwegian Army in Lunenberg, Canada and was transferred in May to London. He crossed the Atlantic on a troop transport. In London he was assigned to the Norwegian Brigade at Braham Castle, near Dingwell, Scotland.

But a great personal tragedy was on its way, and it would hit Oskar like a bombshell.

In the summer of 1942 Oskar and Lilly, with Leopold and Bilka had rented a summer cottage for a vacation. The cottage had no kitchen so they bought a camp stove that operated on alcohol. They received instructions from the salesman on how it functioned, and were told to use extra caution when starting the stove. If they weren't careful it could explode and cause a great deal of damage. All of them believed they could use it without any trouble.

One morning Lilly was going to light the stove so she could make some coffee and cook breakfast. She read the instructions very carefully, lit a match, and then it happened.

The portable stove exploded with a piercing deafening burst. It sounded like a bomb had detonated. The whole cabin vibrated. Lilly cried out and screamed for help. Hot burning alcohol had doused her and within seconds all her clothes were set on fire. Oskar came running, grabbed a blanket in hopes of putting out the flames. Though it took only 10-15 seconds before he was able to help her, it was too late. By that time 99 per cent of Lilly's body had been burned. There was only a small spot on her forehead that was intact. In the struggle to help Lilly both of Oskar's hands were severely burned.

They sent for the ambulance, and got her to the hospital. The only thing the medical doctors knew to do was to put her in a bathtub with cold water. At that time the medical profession knew very little about burn victims and how to care for them.

The next day, August 2, 1943, Lilly died. She was 26 years old. She was buried in the Jewish cemetery in Stockholm.

Mama and the rest of the family were in shock. First their properties were confiscated by the Nazis, then Oskar had been imprisoned; the family had escaped from their home in Norway, had arrived safely in Sweden and all had gone seemingly well. Nobody was lost during that ordeal. Now this tragedy with Lilly had taken place.

Oskar cried and cried all day and all night. He had lost his childhood sweetheart, his wife and Tove's mother. His hands were so badly burned that for some time he wasn't able to feed himself. Somebody else had to do it for him. The family members were at a loss as to how to comfort and console him. They also mourned Lilly, but not in the same way and to the depth of caring and loving as Oskar did. But they tried to console him as best as they could. Mama didn't know what to say to Oskar. Every time when she began to say a few words to him she started to cry, and it ended up with Oskar, or the others, having to comfort her.

Mama had been able to obtain an apartment for Heiman, Jacob, Abel and herself, a block away from where Asne and Arne lived. Oskar and Tove moved in with Mama and the others. It was close quarters but they made do with what they had. By then Leopold and Bilka had their own living quarters.

After a while, when Oskar's hands were healed, he, Abel and Jacob, were seeking to go to England to join the Norwegian Armed Forces. Jacob was already serving as a dentist in the Norwegian refugee camp at Oreryd.

The situation for the Jews in Norway continued to deteriorate and towards the end of 1942, mass arrests of all Jews were ordered by the Gestapo. However there were those, among them, two of my mother's sisters, who had gone into hiding late that summer.

[5]One of them, Rosa Kahn with seven other Jews, had been in hiding at a farm across the fjord from Trondheim. The place was about 90 minutes by boat from the town. They understood early that year that

---

[5] Ragnar Ulstein "Svensketrafikken" (Traffic to Sweden) Vol 1 &3, Det Norske Samlaget, Oslo 1977

there was peril ahead, but didn't really believe that their lives were in imminent danger. So after they had gone into hiding they would from time to time return to Trondheim to do some shopping and as quickly as possible take the ferry back to Leksvik where the farm was.

One day Rosa Kahn decided to travel to Trondheim by herself. While in town she was approached by two Nazi policemen who asked:

"Do you have your identification card?"

"Yes I have one. What do you want with it?" she spoke in broken Norwegian with a thick Yiddish accent.

"We want to see it – Now!"

Rosa fumbled around in her purse and finally found it. As soon as she showed it to them the big red "J" gave her away. She was immediately arrested and kept in prison until she was deported. On November 26, she, with many other Jews from Trondheim, were sent by train to Oslo. From there, she joined hundreds of Norwegian Jews who were deported to Stettin, Poland on the ship "SS Donau." From there, a two days journey in cattle cars, took them to Auschwitz, where she was murdered in the gas chambers. During the trip from Stettin to Auschwitz, the Jews received no food or water.

In November 1942, Berta Buchman, the other sister, came to Selbu, outside of Trondheim. She looked up a man who the previous summer had helped her family to escape to Sweden, and now she needed help to get across the border. But it was difficult to travel to the border now, there was three feet of snow in the mountains and Berta couldn't use skis. The farmer, who was hiding her, told her to stay there until spring when the snow would be gone. Then he could help her get across the mountains and into Sweden. But she wouldn't wait till springtime when other arrangements could be made.

Instead, she returned to Trondheim to check on her store. It was difficult for her to leave everything behind. Besides, her store, along with those of all Jewish businesses, had already been confiscated by the Nazis. Why she felt she had to check on her store is still a mystery. It would seem that saving her life would be more important than checking on a confiscated store. As it turned out, she was arrested in the same manner as her sister Rosa, and the two, with many others were deported and perished in the gas chambers.

Another of my mother's sisters, Mina Micle Levinsohn, who lived in Oslo, was also deported and perished in Auschwitz.

The other sister had already escaped to Sweden.

Among those murdered in the gas chambers at Auschwitz were over 75 of our relatives. Whole families were wiped out, old and young, male and female.

In November 1942, the Allied forces landed in North Africa, routed Field Marshal Rommel, and took Egypt. Winston Churchill considered this victory as historical. This conquest, however, was not enough to save the Jews from the gas chambers. The defeat of Hitler did not come until several years later.

On March 12, 1942, a directive signed by Vidkun Quisling, Ministerpresident, was made official, stating that Paragraph 2 in its original format of the Norwegian Constitution, and signed on May 17, 1814, was reinstated, thereby again banning all Jews from entering Norway. This was the paragraph that Henrik Wergeland had fought so hard to have abolished and caused to be amended in 1851, permitting Jews to enter and live in Norway. Now, because of Quisling, Norway had taken a step backward.

Around Christmas, 1942, one month after over 700 Jews had been deported to Germany, an article appeared in all major Norwegian newspapers making it known that the Norwegian citizenships of 70 people had been revoked. Among those named were my mother and four brothers. See below for further details. I have included only the names of my family.

Revoking of Norwegian Citizenship

The article on the page appeared in Norway's leading newspapers around December 1942. A total of 70 persons were named, of which six were Jewish. The first five on this list, shown on page 242, were my mother and four brothers. David's profession was printed in error. It should have been "Physician" and not "Dentist" (tannlege.) The birth date of my mother should have been "14th September, 1878," not "15th of January" as printed. After each Jewish name, except my brother David, the word "Jode" (Jew) is printed. The article below declares that all their possessions were confiscated for the benefit of the State. The citizenships of those named in this article were terminated by the state.

Frakjenning av norsk statsborgerrett.

Nedenfevnte personer som oppholder seg i utlandet og viser en atferd som vitner om fiendtlig sinnelag mot den norske stat og er egnet til å skade dens interesser, fratas, med virkning fra kunngjøringen i Offentlige kunngjøringer, norsk statsborgerrett i medhold av forordning av 15. november 1941 om frakjenning av norsk statsborgerrett:

1) Abrahamsen, Abel, f. 7/9 1923, jøde, Nedre Baklandet 68/70, Trondheim.
2) Abrahamsen, David, f. 23/6 1903, tannlæge, Fr. Stangsgt. 42, Oslo.
3) Abrahamsen, Heinmann, f. 19/12 1904, jøde, Nedre Baklandet 68/70, Trondheim.
4) Abrahamsen, Mirjam, f. 15/1 1878, jøde, Nedre Baklandet, Trondheim.
5) Abrahamsen, Oskar, f. 20/8 1913, jøde, Paul Fjermstadvn. 22 A, Trondheim.

I medhold til samme forordnings paragraf 2 blir samtlige ovennevntes formue i innland og utland å inndra til fordel for statskassen. Lever vedkommende i formuesfellesskap med i Norge gjenværende hustru, deles felleseiet etter de vanlige delingsregler ved oppløsning av formuesfellesskap.

De av forannevnte som var embetsmenn er avskjediget fra sitt embede med tap av titel og verdighet. De som innehadde offentlig stilling, er likeledes avskjediget ,og de som innehadde offentlige verv er entlediget fra diss.

Chapter 13

Scattered Abroad

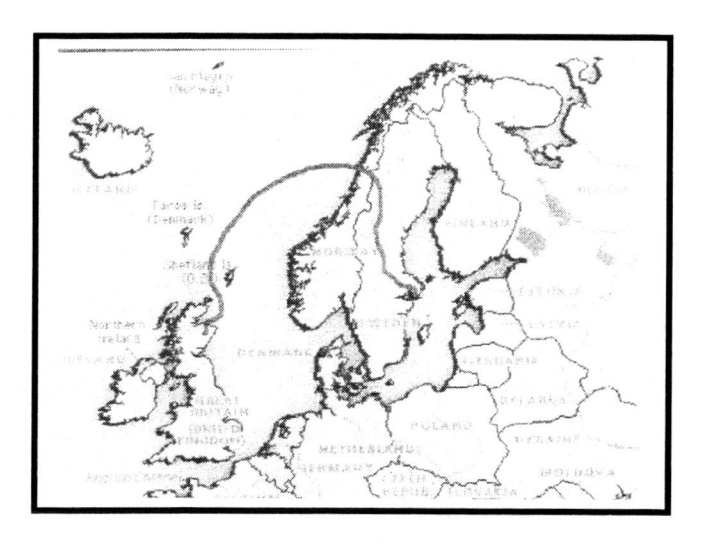

Airplane route from Stockholm to
Scotland that my brothers used

The war, as it tore through Europe, had taken its toll. Like a typical tornado it destroyed everything in its path except for a few buildings and cathedrals.

Personal possessions had been confiscated.
Families had been uprooted, separated and many Jews perished.
Millions of people had been exterminated.
Better than 50% of the Norwegian Jews were among those murdered.

By 1943 there weren't any Jews living in Norway except for the few who were married to non-Jews. They were spared the terror of deportation to the gas chambers.

By 1944 the greater Jewish population in Poland had been exterminated.

Germany had retreated from Stalingrad.

The Third Reich had lost the battle at El Alamein.

1944 was not a good year for Nazi Germany, but it was the turning point for the Allies. D-Day (Operation "Overlord") on June 6th brought encouragement to all nations who had been victimized by Hitler's terror. Hope for Allied victory emerged in the hearts of many, and in the words of Winston Churchill, "Without victory there is no survival."
(Statement in the House of Commons, May 13, 1940.)

Those of my brothers who were still in Sweden had been searching for a way to get to England where they could join the Norwegian Forces. They thought that they had to get there before they could enlist, but to their delight they discovered there was another way. The Norwegian legation in Stockholm accepted applications for the Norwegian Army, Navy, Air Force and the Medical Corps.

Oskar was very concerned for his daughter Tove. He could have left her in Stockholm with Mama, but he wanted Tove near him wherever he would be. He had enlisted in the Royal Norwegian Navy, and was waiting for his travel orders. Tove was his only child. He was constantly thinking of Lilly and how wonderful everything might have been if she hadn't died. If the stove hadn't exploded - - - . But before he left for England he had to make sure that Tove would be able to leave Sweden. He had no idea how that could take place, but he discovered that our cousin, Olga Buchman, was leaving for England.

"Olga, I have just heard that you are going to England, and I have a favor to ask of you. How will you travel, by the way?"

"The only way out is by airplane, and it's difficult to get a seat on the weekly flight. Fortunately I have a position with the Norwegian Government in exile and will be stationed in London. That position entitles me to a priority rating guaranteeing me a seat on the flight leaving in two weeks. What favor do you want?"

"I want Tove to get to England because I expect to be stationed either there or in Scotland." Then after an awkward pause, "Do you think that you would be able to take Tove along and find a home for her to stay until I can make other arrangements?"

"I don't know if I can, but I will certainly find out and let you know. I'm very busy right now with packing and deciding what I can take along and what to put in storage. Get in touch with me in three or four days, and maybe I'll have an answer for you."

Oskar was encouraged, and went home and started to pack all of Tove's belongings, making her ready for the journey to England. A few days later he contacted Olga and was told that she could take Tove with her. The plane would leave on Nov 12, and the first stop would be Scotland and from there to London.

Three months later Oskar left for London, where he was re-united with his daughter, and from there he went to his duty station in Dumbarton, Scotland. He was able to find a family, the Ritchie's, where Tove could stay for as long as necessary. Oskar's responsibilities in the Navy were to keep the accounting books, pay the bills and purchase office supplies. This was nothing new to him in as much as he had a great deal of experience in that area from running his store in Trondheim.

A few days later Jacob, who was a dentist, was flown over to England. He had signed up with the

Norwegian Army. The Medical Corp was in dire need of dentists and they wasted no time in putting him to work.

Abel and Heiman, who were still in Stockholm, were scheduled to fly to England. But there were no planes available. At that time there was only one plane a week leaving Stockholm for England, with only a limited number of passenger seats, reserved for VIP's.

The situation was critical!

More planes were needed to ferry enlisted personnel to England for training. Fortunately help was on its way.

The Norwegian government requested from the U.S. two large airplanes for use by the Norwegian government in exile. The planes were ferried over to Stockholm, and then an exodus started for England.

One night in April 1944, Abel and Heiman were called and ordered to stand by. They could expect to be flown out any night, depending on the weather conditions. A few evenings later they received a phone call and were told that arrangements had been made for them to leave immediately.

"Mama, we're leaving for England tonight and will have to get to the airport right away."

"What's the hurry? You have to pack, rest a little, have a glass of tea, and then we'll see if you can leave. Remember how many times they have called before and told you to stand by and nothing happened? How do you know that this is for sure?" It was obvious that Mama didn't want them to leave, but her stall tactics didn't work.

"Mama, we have to leave now. Our suitcases are packed and we have been ready for several weeks." Heiman looked at Mama, kissed her goodbye and left. Abel followed him.

"Shalom, mein kind; take care of yourselves. I'll be here when you return." Mama cried a great deal at their departure. She wanted to go with them to the airport. When she was told that visitors were not allowed, she cried even more.

Mama would be alone in her apartment. Fortunately Asne lived around the corner and another son, Leopold, who remained in Stockholm, also lived close by.

Heiman and Abel took a taxi to Bromma Airport where many other Norwegians were waiting for a place on the same plane. When they finally boarded their flight, the only place for them to sit was on the floor with their luggage. It would be a long and uncomfortable journey.

To avoid any anti-aircraft fire from the German occupation force, they first flew North, then West across the township of Bodo, a narrow part of Norway, and finally South-West over the North Sea to Scotland. From there they boarded a train that took them to England, where they were housed in a school with many other nationalities.

A period of intense interrogation started for them that lasted for three weeks. The British Army had to treat all these men coming from Norway as spies, and interrogated them twice each day. The fact was that 40% of all the Norwegian police force had joined the Nazi party. There were many Norwegian Nazis who had infiltrated into the Norwegian Resistance Movement, giving grounds for the British to be very cautious and suspicious. The British had to make sure that none of those Nazis got into England.

It was shocking to learn that the British knew everything about our family, where each family member was, and what they were doing. They knew that I was in the U.S. Navy and was being trained as a Radar Technician, which was top secret at that time.

Abel and Heiman knew that the interrogators had the answers before they were asked and, of course, there was no reason for not telling the truth when questioned. Finally the Norwegian Embassy in London vouched for all those who had come from Norway, and they were set free.

Heiman, still a civilian, was then employed by the Norwegian government to purchase uniforms for the Armed Services.

Two months before D-Day, Abel received orders to sail for Canada. He had already met Julius, Jacob and Oskar in London, and for a few short days he had a reunion with his brothers. Julius had flown from Toronto, Canada in 1943, for assignment in the Norwegian Air Force Medical Corps in London. Abel said good-bye to them wondering when they would meet again and boarded the IL De France that had been converted into a troop ship. This was a very fast ocean liner that outran the German submarines.

Four days later the ship tied up in Halifax and from there, he and 30 other Norwegians, went by train to Camp Little Norway, in Muskoka, Canada. They arrived there toward the end of May 1944. By that time the Russians had recaptured the Kerch peninsula on the Black Sea, Hitler had given permission for full German withdrawal from the USSR, the Allies had linked up in Italy, and had broken the stalemate at Anzio and were marching towards Rome. The German army was on the run, and it appeared that it was only a matter of time before Nazi Germany would be defeated. There were strong signs that the war was winding down.

One month after Abel's arrival in Canada, the invasion of Europe, Operation "Overlord," began. All of the new arrivals to Camp Little Norway were quite upset because they wanted to be in on the action in that theater of the war. They all knew that first they had to have basic training, which would take more than a year for them to complete. Abel received training in astrophysics, celestial navigation, instructions in the identification of airplanes, be they friend or foe, and other basic disciplines.

He then went to bombardier school for about eight weeks and from there he was assigned to Prince Edward Island for a course in navigation. When Abel received his "wings" he was allowed to wear an officer's uniform even though he was only a sergeant. This was permissible for all the graduates. It was protection so that in case they were shot down over enemy territory they would be treated as officers and not as enlisted men.

The first time I saw Abel after having left Norway, was in Toronto, Canada, in August 1944. We were the guests in the home of the Ginsberg's, Julius's in-laws. We stayed up till the early morning hours talking about what had taken place over the last four years. We had a lot of territory to cover, and I had so many questions about the family - - - how everybody was doing and where they were, about Norway, and of course Vikhammer. It was strange; here the two of us were sitting in Toronto, both of us in military uniforms, far away from our large family, and far away from Trondheim, Norway. For the time being we had each other and memories from former days. During the course of our long conversation Abel asked me how I got in the U.S. Navy, and why I hadn't joined the Army instead?

"A few days after Pearl Harbor I went to every recruiting station and wanted to enlist. But for some reason, because I wasn't a citizen I suppose, I couldn't enlist. However, I could be drafted. I registered with the draft board and was classified 1A. In June 1943, I received a letter advising me to report to the recruiting station in Los Angeles. I was given a physical exam and many other tests. Then I was asked what branch of service I wanted to enter. I told them I'd like the Navy.

When I came to the officer who was to sign my papers, he looked at me and said:

'You aren't a citizen, are you?'

'No, I am not. Is there a problem?'

'Not really. You can consider yourself lucky. Two weeks ago the U.S. Congress passed a law that would allow non-citizens to enter the Navy.'

I reported for duty two weeks later and was sent to Farragut, Idaho, for basic training. I made good enough grades on all the tests they gave me to allow me to go to the Top Secret Radar school. I just graduated from the school on Treasure Island, in San Francisco Bay. That's why I'm on leave. When I return I'll be given a new assignment. After the war, when I am separated from the Navy, I plan to go to college and get a degree in Electrical Engineering."

Abel had to be back at Camp Little Norway on Monday morning, so we didn't have much time together. He planned to return for another visit the next weekend and we would have a little more time.

After the war I learned that my other brothers had also met in 1944, in London, and they were together for a few days. They were all eagerly following the news reports hoping that the war soon would be over.

Two weeks later I left for Treasure Island, where I requested duty in the European Theater. I was shipped to Noroton Heights, a former retirement home for veterans of the Spanish-American war, near Stamford, Connecticut, and was assigned to a communications unit. The objective of this unit was to be in the first wave of an invasion assault, secure a beachhead and set up communications with the flagship. There were a total of 11 men: two officers, one cook, one motor mechanic, six Morse code operators and one radio technician. That was me.

Every morning we went to our assigned position, which in our case was the beach. There we set up communications with headquarters and received and sent traffic all day. After two months I was sent back to California, and a few months later I was on my way in a convoy to the Philippines. May 30, 1945, after 38 days on the seas, we landed on the island of Samar. (I later learned that Norway was liberated on May 8, 1945.)

The war in the Pacific Theater was still going on. A battle for Okinawa was in progress, and it would continue another three weeks before the island was secured. My assignment was to update the Radar equipment onboard the PT boats in preparation for the invasion of Japan. I heard that the Navy was in the process of building a hospital with 5,000 beds with all the supporting medical staff and equipment on the island of Samar. The plan, from what I heard, was to fly the wounded service men from Japan all the way to Samar. Everybody on the island anticipated a fierce and brutal battle, should Japan be invaded. There were even rumors that casualties could reach several millions. We were all psyched up over the seemingly inevitable future events. I also heard that the invasion of Japan was set for early November. There was fear because of such a dangerous mission, and yet the eagerness to attack Japan and end the war.

On August 8 the U.S. dropped the Atom bomb on Hiroshima; and four days later another bomb fell on Nagasaki. A few days later, on August 15, Japan surrendered unconditionally. Though great damage was done and thousands of lives lost, it was much less than had the invasion of Japan taken place.

In early November of 1945, I was sent back to the mainland on a hospital ship, because of a severe skin disorder caused by the extreme heat and humidity in that area. In April of 1946, I received an honorable discharge from the Navy at Lido Beach, Long Island.

Most of my brothers, including Abel, were in London when the war in Europe ended.

On this and the next page are pictures of the seven brothers in military uniforms.

David, 1929, Oslo, in the Norwegian Medical Corp. In 1940 he establed a field hospital for the wounded Norwegian soldiers.

Left to right: Julius and Jacob
Standing left to right: Samuel and Oskar
London, England, 1944.

Left to right Aron and Abel
Toronto, Canada, 1944.

Chapter 14

Life in Jeopardy

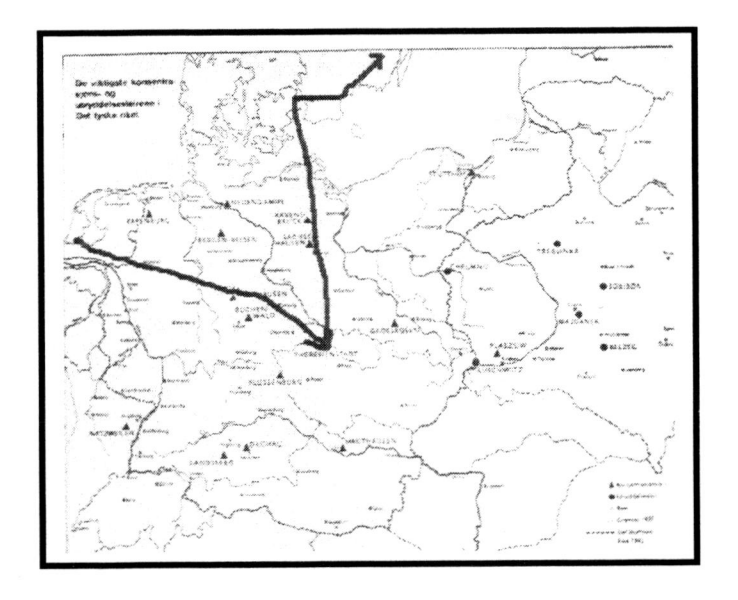

The route of Beile, Benno and Karin from Amsterdam to Theresienstadt concentration camp. After the Liberation she flew to Copenhagen Denmark, from there by train to Stockholm, Sweden.
(Map courtesy of Oskar Mendelsohn "Jodenes Historie I Norge.")

"Just a moment there. Where do you think you are going?"
"Is this train going to Stockholm?"
"It is, and it is leaving in fifteen minutes. Why are you asking?"

Life in Jeopardy

"I *must* take this train. My sister will be waiting for me at the station in Stockholm. I *must*, -- *must* be on this train. I can't wait."

"Do you have a ticket? If you don't, you can purchase one from me."

"I have no money. But, please, you *must* let me on the train. My sister will pay you when we get to Stockholm. I *must* take this train. Do you hear me? I can't wait any longer." The conductor heard very clearly. These were desperate words that were carried in a pleading voice.

But he responded in a stern and unrelenting manner, "I have no authority to let you ride for free."

The train conductor looked askance at the one who had been pleading with him. She was very thin, painfully skinny. So skinny that it was a good chance her bones rattled when she walked. Her clothes didn't fit her at all. The dress was much too large for her, the hemline hung far below her oversized overcoat. She had neither hat nor gloves. Her shoes were a pair of hiking boots, also several sizes too large. She didn't look like the kind of person you'd invite into your home for a cup of coffee.

The conductor looked her over very carefully, wondering where she had come from. He couldn't remember when he had ever seen such a pitiful sight. How could anyone get into a situation like this woman? She even had a child with her.

"Is this your daughter?" pointing to the little girl beside her. Then, "Where is your husband?"

[6]"We have been in a concentration camp, in Thereseinstadt near Prague, and we have been just released. I was separated from my husband in Pilzen, but was able to catch a plane ride to Copenhagen, and here I am. But I *have* to get on this train, *now*!" At this

---
[6] Taped information from my sister Beile Hess recorded by Abel Abrahamsen, August 26, 1990, Amsterdam, Holland.

point, with the little strength she had, she was talking as loud as she could. "I am not leaving this train until you let me on." and she placed one foot on the first step of the short stairway leading up to the train car.

"Look madam, as you know, this is a Swedish train. Sweden had nothing to do with the war, because Sweden was neutral. I wasn't responsible for your being sent to a concentration camp. I don't make the rules. I can't help you." These words came out like steel-heeled boots and he looked at her with penetrating, cold eyes.

Then suddenly a well-dressed gentleman approached. He stopped and asked what was the problem.

"This woman insists that she has to be on this train that is leaving for Stockholm in a few minutes. She told me that she just came from a concentration camp near Pilzen. But she has no money to buy a ticket for herself and her daughter, and I can't let her on unless she has a ticket. That is the problem."

"I'll pay for the tickets. Do you have a first class section available?"

"The only available seats are in the second class section." With that the conductor told him how much the fare would be.

"Here is the money for their tickets and one for myself also."

The gentleman looked to be in his mid fifties, very well dressed, his shoes were polished to a mirror finish. His overcoat was of excellent cut and quality, with a velvet collar. Everything about him was elegant, including his well-kept fingernails and his fashionable hat.

He got them on board; found the stateroom he had paid for and ordered some food, arranging for a cup of hot chocolate for the little girl. As soon as she finished it she fell asleep on her mother's lap.

That's how my sister Beile and her daughter Karin were able to travel by train from Copenhagen to Stockholm.

"You must have some story to tell. I'd like to hear It." the gentleman turned to her.

Beile was quiet for a long while. So much had happened to her, she hardly knew where to start. When she had collected her thoughts she began.

"On February 10, 1940 I thought it was still safe to travel from my home town of Trondheim, Norway. I was eager to see my husband, Benno, who had gone ahead to tend to his business in Amsterdam, Holland. With my newborn daughter, Karin, I was looking forward to establishing my new home there. This was a new experience for me. There was a new language to learn, a new culture to become adjusted to, and new friends to meet.

"We had a beautiful apartment in a well to-do neighborhood.

"Life among the Jews in Amsterdam was pleasant and quiet. Everybody seemed to get along very well with one another. For me life had taken on a different perspective. I was away from Trondheim; Asne, my sister, was no longer close by; there was no one to talk with as I had in Trondheim. Changes had knocked at my door, and there were many more to come. However, the weather in Amsterdam was much like Trondheim - - - damp, cold, windy and lots of rain.

"The Netherlands declared its neutrality in 1939. We had all assumed that this would keep the country safe. How could we have known Hitler would ignore this neutrality? He ordered an aerial bombardment the very next year that, by the way, destroyed the greater part of Rotterdam. The German Army immediately overran the country. Much destruction came also to other parts of the country, not only by the Germans, but also by the Dutch, themselves, who opened many dikes as desperate defense measures, and later by the

Allies in aerial assaults on German-held positions. The country was occupied, as you may know, until the war ended."

"Yes." the kind gentleman nodded his head. "I was aware of those events."

"After the Germans invaded Holland they entered Amsterdam in May of 1940. My greatest fears had become a reality. Naturally we were very nervous, not knowing what they would do. Not long after the occupation, the Nazis requisitioned our apartment. It had been our lovely home for only a few months. We were ordered to vacate it within 24 hours, and pack just enough clothes for several days. They ordered us not to remove any furniture but to leave everything for the new occupants. We were then to wait for the Germans to transport us to the place they had designated for us to live. As it turned out we were taken to the worst residential area in town. It was so terrible I can't even describe it to you.

"The Gestapo showed us no mercy. They confiscated whatever they wanted. It was very difficult for us, being forced to give up what we owned and cherished. Family pictures were destroyed, and our heirlooms and wedding gifts became somebody else's property. We left most of our personal clothing, furniture, linen, dishes, silver and gold - - - almost everything we had. My husband and I ended up with practically nothing. We felt we had been raped by the Nazis."

Beile started to weep quietly, remembering what had happened to her a few years back. Her "Angel" bent over to her and put his hand on her head in an effort to comfort her. He understood her anguish and pain. After a short silence she continued.

"The apartment buildings we were taken to were ready to fall apart. The whole area had a nauseous odor, the furniture was dirty and so were the few dishes and knives and forks. Fortunately, we had packed some dishes, glassware and cutlery without the knowledge of the Germans. The toilet facilities had to be shared with many others on the same floor, and the electric service was almost non-existent. Many of the windows were broken and we had to cover the open spaces with cardboard to keep the cold air out, and there was no heat in the apartment.

"Every day became more and more difficult. The only comfort to us was our daughter Karin. She was only four months old. That was all we had, besides each other.

To shop for food was the most difficult of all the daily tasks. It was exhausting to have to shop at only the designated places that the Gestapo directives ordered. Stores that we used to frequent before the invasion, and whose sales personnel we considered friends, had now become very hostile and off limits to us. Especially after the SS troops had posted signs "Jews forbidden to shop here." These stores had a better selection of goods but we could only shop in stores with a very limited selection, and high prices. We had become enemies of the State, by the declaration of Hitler."

Her "Angel" was listening attentively. He was shocked to hear about the restrictions to which they had been subjected. He couldn't, and wouldn't understand (and made it known to Beile) how such a monstrous prejudice and hatred for the Jews could exist in this modern century. He was dismayed at the appalling behavior of humanity.

Then Beile continued: "I told my husband that I didn't know for how long I could stand this. The Nazis were watching every move we made. There was no privacy. We were subject to interrogation and arrest at any moment. We couldn't go to the restaurants like before, movie houses and theaters were closed to us; even the parks and park benches were off limits to us. How much longer would this go on? I was very nervous, and worn out by the stress and prohibitions we all were subjected to, and the fear and dreariness of our daily life.

"Maybe it will be over soon Beile," Benno, would tell me, "and then we can claim our own apartment back. Everything will be the same again, as before. We have to have hope, don't ever give up hope. That's all we have, for now. Let's go for a walk. Perhaps we'll hear some good news and be liberated soon." That was all my husband could find to say. He too was discouraged, but had to keep up his hope that someday, even tomorrow, the Germans would be defeated. We had no radio, and the only news we received came from the Nazi controlled and censored newspapers.

"We could congregate only with other Jews. To contact Gentiles was strictly forbidden and a major offense. We met some of our Jewish friends as we walked, and they asked if we had heard anything about the war. Everyone was in the dark about it, and all were nervous, frustrated and apprehensive about what would happen to us.

"We heard from other Jews that as soon as we had vacated our apartment our Dutch neighbors descended upon it like vultures, and carried away anything and everything they cast their eyes on. That hurt us very deeply, for we had thought that we could trust our neighbors. The same happened to all the apartments belonging to Jews. The Jews had become a commodity at the disposal of the Germans.

"For some strange, and unexplainable reason, and for some time thereafter we weren't troubled any further by the Gestapo. There had been no arrests and this made us feel a little secure. However deep down in our consciousness we 'knew' that one of these days - - - it would happen."

"How were you able to sustain yourselves in the midst of all that danger?" the gentleman asked. "It must have been terrifying for you, and you must have been worn out every day from the uncertainty and instability?"

"You're right. It was very difficult." Beile agreed. "Then in May 1941, we were able to contact the underground. We knew we might be arrested any day, and we needed to have a place where we could hide our daughter. After talking to the underground members about it, they took Karin and placed her with a family who would take good care of her. I had no idea who the family was, nor where she was kept.

"In November of the same year I was notified that Swedish passports (because of the help from Asne and Arne, my sister and brother-in-law) were available to us from the Swedish State Department. We were now Swedish citizens, and Sweden was a neutral country. We believed that we were now safe. There were three passports, one for each of the family members. My husband and I were together, but where was Karin? In order to claim the passports, all three of us had to appear at the Gestapo headquarters together.

"We had to find Karin. We had no idea where she was hidden. Through the underground a message was sent to the family where Karin was and she was returned to us. She had been gone about six months. The three of us went to The Hague and claimed our Swedish passports. We were so happy to be Swedish citizens, since Sweden was recognized as a neutral country. We believed that we were protected from any further mistreatment.

"Then in May of 1943, we were arrested and taken to a Jewish prison. The unfortunate part was that the Germans didn't honor the Swedish passports. We believed that our fate was sealed.

"At one time my husband approached the Gestapo prison clerk and told him that we were Swedish citizens, and demanded that we be treated as such. He insisted that we be released from this prison, and that the Gestapo should deal with us as citizens of a neutral country. My husband by now had become very angry. But the clerk paid no attention to Benno. The harsh, uncompromising and callous facial expression of the clerk should have told my husband it was useless to protest.

'Let me see your passports first before I can make a determination in your case.' He lied to Benno because the Gestapo clerk knew that he had no authority to make any decision regarding the Jewish prisoners.

"Benno got the passports from his coat pocket, opened one and showed it to the clerk. He reached out for it, but Benno held on to the other end, not willing to let it fall into the hands of this Gestapo clerk. He gave it a quick glance, looked at Benno and again at the passport. After a short silence he said in a harsh voice to my husband:

'This passport, and any others you may have in your possession for your wife and child, is not recognized here. Leave your passports here, that's an order. You have to realize that you are not the only Jew in this prison. There are many hundreds of Jewish people here, and many of them have been here for many weeks. Go back to your cell, and we'll call you when it's time for you to be sent to the concentration camp.' With that he turned away from Benno and busied himself with other "official" business. Benno went back to his prison cell, but he kept the passports in his possession."

"It was a good thing that your husband kept the passports, otherwise you would have been sent to the extermination camp. Isn't that so?" Beile's "Angel" broke in.

"You are so right. However, another problem surfaced. During our stay in the prison, many Jews came down with diphtheria, and Karin was among them. The German doctors examined the prisoners to determine where the source of this disease was. It turned out that I was the source.

"I was sent to the hospital, and while I was there, Karin and Benno were sent by train to Westerbork. That was a staging area where the Gestapo shipped prisoners to a number of different concentration camps. I had heard that this was the first stop for those being sent to Auschwitz, or to other extermination camps. You can imagine how distressed and worried I became when I heard that. But there was nothing I could do. I had to be in the hospital until released, and then hope to be reunited with Benno and Karin.

"An SS soldier was stationed outside the hospital room watching me day and night so that I wouldn't escape. As weak and frightened as I was, how could I possibly escape? I knew that if I were successful in trying to escape, the Nazis would execute Benno and Karin. As it turned out I was kept in the hospital for several days, and then released.

"Shortly after I was dismissed from the hospital I was put on the train headed for Westerbork. There I saw Benno and Karin the next day. From Westerbork there were ten different transport trains leaving every day that took prisoners to Auschwitz, Bergen-Belsen and all the other concentration camps. Karin, Benno and I were sent to Theresienstadt, which is an hour from Prague, Czechoslovakia. Though it was depressing I was glad that we were together. If we were sent to an extermination camp we would at least die together.

"We arrived there on January 1st, 1944. There were already 165,000 people in that camp. All 'enemies' of the German Reich.

Beile had slumped to the back of her seat and closed her eyes. For a moment fear and dread overcame her. The thump-a thump-a thump of the railroad wheels traveling over the track took her back to the time when she, Benno and Karin were on the train for Theresienstadt. Suddenly she opened her eyes, looked out the window to the darkness outside. She saw the gentleman seated across from her and with fear and panic in her voice asked where she was.

"You are on your way to Stockholm to see your sister. You told me that you just came out of a concentration camp. Your daughter is sleeping on your lap. Just look." he assured her.

She smiled with nervous tension, looked down on her lap, and saw Karin sound asleep. "I feel a little better now."

After a long silence he spoke consolingly: "You have been through so much, and I still haven't heard your full story." Then with deep concern, "It will probably take some time before you can begin to adjust to a normal life. But that too will come." he assured her.

Beile continued. "During our internment the Germans, on three occasions, tried to send us to an extermination camp. On one of these times I was already on the steps of the train car. The rucksacks we had brought along had been confiscated as soon as we approached the train. There we were. We had no belongings, except for the clothes on our backs. No identification papers. Our passports had been confiscated. We were people without any identity--persona non grata. We knew for certain that if no one intervened, the extermination camp would be the next and final stop for us.

"Then the camp Commandant, a Nazi officer by the name of Karl Rahm, with swift steps approached the train-car where we were. I remember that he had only one eye. He was a cruel man, and his face expressed every detail of cruelty. He was also short and fat. Having one eye made him look like a pirate, and he looked like he enjoyed playing that part. There were several soldiers following him, and I spotted a civilian man, in a black overcoat and black hat, in the company. I had seen men dressed like that on many occasions both in Amsterdam and during our stay in the concentration camp, and I knew they were part of the Gestapo.

"My heart sank to the bottom of my feet when I saw him, because I believed that the Commandant had brought along a Gestapo officer to make sure that we were sent to the extermination camp. Commandant Rahm didn't want any difficulties in sending three citizens of Sweden, a neutral country, to the extermination camp. To insure that all would go well he had brought along this man whom we thought to be from the Gestapo.

"You can't imagine how I felt at that moment. Shear panic raced through my body. My mind was spinning out of control. I was completely paralyzed, and looking at Benno I could see he didn't take the situation any better. Karin was just three years old and didn't understand anything, and I was relieved for that. At least she didn't have to be scared and frightened like we were. But I was surprised, almost shocked, at what I heard next."

"Are you the family Hess?"

"We answered 'Yes – we are.' We feared the worst. He told us to get off the train because we were Swedish citizens, and return to our barracks. We then realized that the one in the black overcoat and black hat was the Swedish Consul, and not the Gestapo. We were greatly relieved that we had been rescued in the nick of time." (When Nazi Germany invaded Holland in 1940 there were around 140,000 Jews living there, some 120,000 lived in Amsterdam. After the war there were only 20,000 Jews left in all of Holland.)

"All the time that I was at Theresienstadt I was assigned to washing stairways. It was very difficult because I was tired all the time. My body was weak from lack of food. I was always hungry. The overseer, a woman, told me that she liked the way the stairways were washed, and wanted me to continue with that. I was so angry at her that I wanted to throw the whole bucket of water at the woman. But of course I didn't dare do that."

"You can be glad you didn't do that," the gentleman "Angel" remarked. "Otherwise you would have been put to death. I've heard of the cruelty of these prison overseers. What a horrible experience you've had. It sounds like a nightmare. Such an affront to human dignity. What a human tragedy. All this because righteous people had refused to take courage and stop Hitler when there was still time. Millions of innocent people paid the price - - - a very high price. How did you live, and where did you sleep? Under your circumstances wasn't it difficult to take care of your little daughter?" He nodded to Beile for her to continue.

"Yes it was. Other women took care of her while I did my work. Our living quarters were very spartan. We were housed in a small barracks, consisting of one room with ten people in it, six women and four children. (The only boy who was there is now a famous Rabbi in Holland.) It was so crowded that we just about slept on top of each other in three high bunk beds with loose straw as mattresses. There was no linen. I don't remember how many times I changed places with others so that I could try to sleep a little more comfortably. A very small stove burned most of the time but it never warmed up the room.

"Every morning we were awakened at five. We washed our hands and face in ice cold water. The Germans furnished us with a bar of very hard soap, and we dried ourselves with the hard towels they supplied us.

"At one time a woman was brought into our barracks from a train that had just arrived. She had 10 pairs of silk stockings sewn into the lining of her overcoat. I asked her if I could have two pairs in return for food. But the woman said 'no.' Then I walked over to her and just took two pairs. With these stockings I was able to barter for food with the other prisoners. Through this type of exchange my daughter and I were able to survive. I'm sad to say that the woman was transferred to Auschswitz and I never saw her again.

"On the other hand, the Danish Jews had it quite well, receiving every luxury you could imagine. King Christian X, the Danish Monarch, had made sure they were well cared for. When they received something special, like food, they gave me some of it. The Germans told them that they didn't have permission to give anything away. Nevertheless, that didn't stop the Danish Jews. Whenever they could, they smuggled food to me. The children from Holland were starved and starving. They were given sugar cubes to help their hunger pains and hopefully stop their crying from hunger. I received 1/4 loaf of bread, about 1/4 pound of margarine and 1/2 cup of marmalade. That was to last Karin and me for one week. We all had to stand in long lines to receive each week's starvation ration. I despised having to do that.

"Three times I received packages from Asne. Every time a package came for me I had to appear before Commandant Rahm to claim it. I had to sign a receipt for the package so the Swedish consulate in Prague would know that I was still alive. In those packages there was just about everything: Warm shoes, warm slippers, and warm overcoats. There was also food, and that was the most important of all things. I had become seriously undernourished.

"Towards the end of the war when the Germans knew that the British were coming, they held back some of my food, especially sardines. One time when I went to the Commandant's office to claim my food package the Commandant told me to step on the scale."

"I want to see how much you weigh," he told me. If you weigh too much you don't need your sardines. Oh, you weigh 32 Kg (about 70 lbs.) You don't need the sardines. Someone else will get them. That was the Commandant's final determination. Then I asked one of the German soldiers if I could have at least one can of sardines for my daughter, but he said that she was so heavy that she didn't need it, and neither did my husband. That's the way it was. And there was no appeal. But my daughter and husband were both starving, as I was.

"On several occasions the Red Cross, on their scheduled inspection trips, came to survey the camp. Before they arrived, and the commandant had been notified ahead of time, vegetables and tulips and many other flowers were planted to show the inspection team that this was a model camp. Each of the prisoners received a carrot to chew on for the whole day to show how well we were treated. As soon as the Red Cross personnel left, everything was confiscated. All the vegetables and flowers were removed. It was obvious that this was no model camp. It was all a cover up for their cruelty to innocent people.

"In June of 1945, at the end of the war, the Russian Army came and took over the camp. Nobody was allowed to leave because there was an epidemic in the camp.

"But we paid no attention to that order, and left anyway, and went to Prague. However, in leaving the camp I had an experience that gave me great concern, because it was so unusual and frightening, something I hadn't expected.

"Though the camp was very large and housed thousands of prisoners, yet we kept to those in our own barracks. Coming out of the camp I was very frightened, so much so that I almost panicked when I saw other people who were strangers to me. For example, I was too scared to take the streetcar. When I saw the conductor I believed him to be a Nazi, for he wore a black uniform - - - like the SS troops. I couldn't line up with other people waiting to buy food, because it reminded me of the many times I had to stand in line for the little food dished out to me. It frightened me to see myself responding to my freedom this way.

"From Prague we were able to obtain transportation to Pilzen. There we found ourselves among many thousands of other refugees who had come from the concentration camp in Thereseinstadt. They were mostly young people, the old Jews had been sent to the gas chambers as soon as they had arrived. There was complete bedlam. Men looking for their wives and children. Women looking for their families in hopes to find them intact. My heart went out to them. At least Benno, Karin and I were together. There were so many different languages being spoken, it appeared that you were in many different countries at the same time. Some people found each other and cried for joy.

"While watching all this taking place and wondering what to do, my husband told me that he was going to look for an airplane that would take us to Amsterdam. After he had gone out of sight, an announcement came over the loudspeaker system making it known that women and children of Norwegian and Danish nationalities should report to a particular place if they wanted to go to Copenhagen. There was an airplane leaving in 20 minutes.

"I told Karin, who was now five years old, to come with me. I went to the one who had made the announcement and told him I wanted to go with him to Copenhagen. But he told me that he was neither Norwegian nor Danish so he couldn't go.

"I told him that I was Jewish. 'Jewish? he exclaimed. Where have you been during the war? I am also Jewish.' In the rush of things he didn't take the time to tell me what country he was from.

"Then I told him that I had been held in Theresienstadt for almost two years.

"He looked at me and Karin, and told us to come with him.

"Then he asked me where my husband was. I told him I didn't know, but that he had gone to look for an airplane to take us to Amsterdam. But I didn't have any idea where he was. I was hoping that Benno had found transportation and was now looking for us.

"If you don't come with me now, you'll have to wait at least six weeks before any transportation will be available. If you choose to stay, where will you and your daughter live? And how will you feed yourself? Food is almost non-existent in Pilzen he continued."

"To make a long story short, Karin and I took the plane to Copenhagen."

"You didn't have much time to decide, did you?" her travel companion said. "What happened after that?"

"When Benno returned to where he had left us, he asked those who were still waiting there if any of them knew where we were. The one who had taken us to the airplane explained that Karin and I were on our way to Copenhagen; and he pointed to a plane taking off. Benno was very happy that his family was on its way out of Pilzen. He knew that we would be going to Stockholm to be with my sister there. We had discussed together what to do when we were released from the camp if we were ever separated. We promised each other to meet in Stockholm.

"As soon as I arrived in Copenhagen I found my way to the Red Cross. I tried to find Asne's phone number, but wasn't able to. I knew a Rabbi Friediger in Copenhagen, and called him. He came to the Red Cross headquarters to see if he could help. Fortunately he had Asne's phone number. I called her and explained that as soon as I received an exit visa from Denmark I would come to Stockholm. Two days later I received the exit visa. It was now about three days after the war was over.

"I hurried to the train station to catch the train to Helsingor in Denmark and on to Sweden.

"Then you came along and paid my train fare. I'm very grateful to you. That is my story. There were millions of others who didn't survive. We're among the fortunate ones who did."

Daybreak had come, and the train was approaching Stockholm. Beile became excited. She woke up Karin, and took her to the restroom. They washed up as best they could and returned to their seats.

The "Angel" asked if there was anything else he could do for them. Beile thanked him for all he had already done, which she greatly appreciated, and said there wasn't anything else he could do.

"When my sister meets me at the station she will pay you for our fare." Beile promised him.

She would soon be with her family. At last she and Karin were safe. Her thoughts went to Benno and hoped for his soon arrival.

At the station Mama, Asne, and her husband Arne were waiting for Beile and Karin. Leopold was working, and the rest of the family members were spread throughout the world. Beile looked at herself. I'm so thin, she thought to herself. So poorly dressed to be meeting the family this way. Karin was dressed as "elegantly" as her mother.

At first nobody in the waiting party recognized them. Suddenly Asne spotted Beile a few train cars away and as loud as she could, called out "Beile, Beile" and ran as fast as she could towards her sister. Mama and Arne followed on her heels. There were hugs and tears in large amounts. They leaned on each other and cried and cried for joy. The concentration camp nightmare was over. Beile and Karin were safe. And so was Benno.

After they had dried their tears and were able to talk, Beile wanted them to meet the gentleman who had helped her with her train fare and had showed such kindness and generosity to her and Karin. Believing that he was behind her, she turned to introduce them to her "Angel." But to her surprise he was nowhere to be seen. He had disappeared among the people in the train station in Stockholm, just as suddenly as he had appeared in the train station in Helsingor. She never saw him again. She didn't even know his name!

With Beile and Karin safe in the tender care of the family in Stockholm, Benno was scurrying about in the bedlam and confusion in Pilzen, searching for transportation to Amsterdam. That was hard to come by, like a taxi on a rainy night in a big city. As luck would have it, he came across two happy soldiers in a big truck headed for Paris. After some "negotiation" he joined them hoping that his business associate there would be able to help him get to Amsterdam.

Arriving in Paris, the truck was stopped and searched by the M.P.'s. What they found was grounds for the arrest of the soldiers. Transporting stolen goods in a government vehicle was an invitation to calamity. Benno, who was an innocent passenger on the truck, was let go, and he wasted no time in contacting his friend. Money was made available for Benno to travel to Belgium and from there he made it to Amsterdam.

Benno arrived in Amsterdam on a bicycle and went to Beethoven Stradt. Before Benno and Beile were arrested by the Nazis they had established a password for communication with their underground friends. Actually the password was part of a melody. As Benno traveled on the bicycle he whistled the few notes from that tune in hopes that his friends would hear it and render aid to him. Their friends, who still lived there, heard the tune. They looked out the window from their apartment and saw Benno. They called out to him and were able to help him with money so he could travel to his wife and child – wherever they were.

He didn't know for sure where Beile and Karin were, but he hoped they were with Asne in Stockholm. So he called her, and Arne answered the phone, assuring him that Beile and Karin were there. He took the first train to Stockholm, where the family was reunited on July 26, 1945.

Upon returning to Amsterdam, Benno opened his business in the import-export trade.

The three had been spared death, for, as we later discovered, survival was in the family.

Chapter 15

Worlds Apart

My family, Mama and her 11 children, though it had experienced many traumatic encounters with the Nazis, and had been greatly impacted through fear and anxiety, had come through the war intact. For this I am forever thankful.

Many of my family members returned to Norway and picked up their lives again from where, at one time, it had been so crudely and shockingly interrupted. Other family members decided to remain where the events of World War II had taken them.

Samuel was stationed in Scotland, until May of 1945, when he was flown to Oslo. From there he was immediately sent by car to Trondheim to report to the local Norwegian commander. Samuel was the first one of the family to return to Trondheim.

As soon as he arrived he went directly to Mama's apartment, and to the stores to see what the conditions were.

To his horror he found the apartment in ruins. It was completely empty. The furniture was gone. The linoleum had been ripped off the floors and the wallpaper had been torn off the walls. The Germans had made sure that they left it in complete devastation. The large crystal chandelier that had been in the salon was gone. Stolen by the Nazis. It was never recovered.

The apartment wasn't only empty of furniture but silent, very silent. Samuel walked slowly through the empty rooms. Memories of the former times with the family flooded his thoughts. Now - - -

Gone was the laughter.

Gone were the jokes.

Gone were the music and the family who at one time had filled every room.

Gone were the discussions about world affairs.

Gone was the gossip that interested so many members of the family.

Gone were the plans for the summer vacations at Vikhammer.

Gone were the carefree and happy times at our summer villa.

Gone were all the people who used to gather with us there.

Gone were most of our relatives, in some cases entire families had perished. They had been murdered in the gas chambers of the Nazi "master race."

Samuel knew that everything had changed and it would never return to what it used to be. To him it was frightening how fast the whole world around him had changed. The only things that were left were the memories of a former peaceful, happy and secure period.

Samuel called Mama in Stockholm. He told her about the condition of her apartment, and promised to have linoleum installed and wall paper hung. He would have it ready for her when she returned home.

Shortly after my family had escaped to Sweden, Ingebjorg went back to her home in Mo i Rana. She returned to Trondheim after my mother arrived and continued working for her as she had before.

Every time Samuel went into the store, it was like entering a cave. It used to be well lit, stocked with a large variety of inventories. All the shelves, on both floors, that before had been filled with rolls of silk, cotton and brocade, were now completely empty. It was a stern reminder of the Nazi's atrocities and their thoroughness in causing disaster and destruction.

Wherever he went in the apartment, in the stores, and out to the villa at Vikhammer – it was so depressingly quiet – a chilling quiet.

Samuel inquired of the officials at the Police Department where mother's furniture could be.

"You'll have to go to this big warehouse and search for it yourself. Here is the address of the warehouse. You will find there a great deal of furniture that at one time belonged to the Jews in this town. After they were deported all of their furniture was moved from their apartments and stored. Nobody knew what to do with it all, and it has stayed there all these years.

"I hope you find what you're looking for. You can hire a moving van to transport whatever you find to your mother's apartment."

Samuel searched through all of it and found several pieces belonging to Mama and had them transported to her apartment. At least Mama had something to work with until she was able to have all her other furniture shipped back from Sweden.

Before Mama returned home, she was able to borrow 50,000 kroner so that she could buy a little inventory for her store.

With the apartment cleaned, new wallpaper on the walls and new linoleum on the floor, Mama had a decent place to live. She came home after being away for almost four years.

It wasn't easy for her to return and face what was not there. Would her sisters be there? Had her relatives returned to Trondheim already? She was anxious to see them again, and believed that everything would return to what it had been before the war. Sadly, for Mama, everything had changed.

She had no idea what had happened to her relatives, and wouldn't believe it when it was told to her. "How could that be? Last time I saw them they were in good health. There wasn't anything wrong with them. It's too hard to believe that the Nazis were as cruel as you say. I believe all my relatives are still alive, and one day they'll come home."

She couldn't and wouldn't bring herself to accept the truth.

Mama kept herself busy in the store and went about her daily chores as she had done before the war. She was happy to be back. But every day she did something that created a mystery for Samuel.

At the same hour every day, Samuel noticed that she disappeared for a few hours, and then came back to the store. Nobody knew where she had been. She didn't tell anybody where she was going or where she had been.

Finally, one day Samuel decided to follow her to try to discover what she was doing.

She went first to the pier where the ship from the South arrived on its daily schedule. She would stand and watch the passengers disembark. When the last one had come off the ship, she walked to the railroad station and observed those who came off the train. For several months she did this, and then one day she decided to stop her routine.

She was looking for her three sisters, Mina Micle, Rosa and Berta, hoping they would return.

They never did.

These three sisters perished in the gas chambers of Auschwitz. From a total of six sisters there were now only Mama and her last sister Cecille, alive, both had returned to Trondheim. The Nazis had executed Cecille's husband, Abel Bernstein, on trumped-up charges. Another sister living in Sweden died there.

Mama was happy to be home in Trondheim, but had mixed feelings. Gone were scores of relatives. Nothing was the same, but she recovered all her properties, except for the crystal chandelier. Mama died in 1974.

Heiman took over the management of the store like he had done before the war. In 1952 he married Sonja Jakobowitz. Heiman died in 1994.

Leopold, with his wife and son Herman, returned from Stockholm and took over the gift shop that Oskar had managed before the war. During the War, while he was in Sweden, Leopold married Bilka who was his fiancée before they fled Trondheim. They had two sons and one daughter. Leopold died in 1964.

Jacob re-established his dental practice in Trondheim. For many years he had been in love with Sonja Meyer, and she with him. She was a beautiful and very talented local Jewish girl. But he never had the courage to tell her of his love and that he wanted to marry her. Finally she married someone else. For years, after that, he was very melancholy, thinking about what he had missed. He never married. Jacob died in 1982.

When Oskar returned with Tove, he took over the store that I had managed before leaving for the U.S.A in 1940. He married Golde Isaksen. With his new wife they had two children. Oskar died in 1991.

Beile returned to Amsterdam with her husband Benno and their two children. A son had been born to them in Stockholm after the war. Beile died in 2005

Asne remained in Stockholm with her husband Arne and their two daughters. Asne died in 1958.

Julius returned by ship to Toronto, Canada, to his wife Beckie and their little daughter. After he received his license to practice dentistry he opened his own dental office. Julius died in 1999.

David settled in New York City, with his wife Lova Katz, and their two daughters. He established his medical practice, specializing in forensic psychiatry and wrote a number of books on psychiatry and mental health. David died in 2002.

Samuel returned to New York in the spring of 1946. He obtained his Ph.D. in Political Science and taught in the Brooklyn College until he retired. While there he established the Department for Judaic Studies. He wrote several books, such as "Sweden's Foreign Policy" and "Norway's Response to the Holocaust," plus several articles on political science and the Holocaust. He married Minerva in 1947 and they had two daughters. Samuel died in 2001.

After Abel returned to Trondheim, he obtained a scholarship from U.S.C. Los Angeles, California, to study cinematography. From there he went to New York and obtained a position as a TV cameraman for CBS. Then he opened a gift shop featuring Norwegian jewelry, china, silver and crystal, and later added Norwegian leather furniture. He also promoted Norway in a significant way, and for that effort the King of Norway knighted him. He married Tulla Gaaso in 1954 and they have two daughters.

I returned to California, and in 1950 I received a Bachelor of Science degree in Electrical Engineering from California State Polytechnic University, San Luis Obispo, California. I married Doris Ballengee in September of the same year.

During my career as an engineer I was at one time a member of a scientific study team to determine the feasibility of sending a manned expedition to the moon and bringing the crew and the vehicle back safely. This became known as the Apollo project. I wrote several technical articles and presented them at scientific symposiums, and I often lectured on the Apollo Program.

Those of us settling in Sweden, Holland, Canada and the U.S. have taken with us into these countries a little bit of our Norway; the memories of our family gatherings in the living room, and our summers at the villa will always be a part of us wherever we are.

We look back with unspeakable gratitude that we all persevered, and cherish all the more our gift of life. While the destruction of the war threatened our lives, and scattered us worlds apart, we still found the courage to survive.

References

Abrahamsen, Abel "Jewish Life and Culture in Norway – Wergenland's Legacy" 165 East 65 Street, Suite 14C, New York, NY 10021 USA 2003

Abrahamsen, David "Jeg er Jode" (I am a Jew) Tano A/S, Oslo, Norway, 1985

Abrahamsen, Samuel "Norway's Response to the Holocaust," Holocaust Library, New York, NY USA 1991

Bruland, Bjarte "Forsoket paa aa tilintetgjore de Norske Joder," (The Attempt to Liquidate the Norwegian Jews) Master Thesis at the University of Bergen, Norway 1995

Churchill, Winston S. "The Second World War" volume 1, Houghton Mifflin Company, Boston, MA 1948

Churchill, Winston S. "Memoirs of the Second World War" Houghton Mifflin Company, Boston

Chronicles of the 20th Century; Chronicle Publication, Mt. Kisco, NY 1987

Fischer, Klaus P. "Nazi Germany, A New History"

Lukacs, John "Five Days in London" Yale University Press

Mendelsohn, Oskar "Jodenes Historie I Norge gjennom 300 aar" (History of the Jews in Norway through 300 years) Vol. 1 and 2, Universitetsforlaget, Oslo, Bergen, Stavanger, Tromso 1969

Ottosen, Kristian "I Slik en Natt" (In Such a Night) H. Aschehoug & Co. (W. Nygaard) Oslo, Norway, 1994

Ottosen, Kristian "Theta, Theta" H. Aschehoug & Co. (W. Nygaard) Oslo, Norway, 2000

Shirer, William L. "The rise and Fall of the Third Reich" Simon and Schuster, New York 1960

Trondjems Historical Institute, "300 aar med Cicignon" (300 years with Cicignon) 1981

Ulstein, Ragnar "Svensketrafikken" (Traffic to Sweden) Vol 1 & 3, Det Norske Samlaget, Oslo, Norway 1977

ISBN 142513403-3